For prof Götz v. Rohr

With the Compliments of
Tor Fr. Rasmussen,
Schultz gt 6
0365 Oslo

URBANIZATION AND COMMUNITY BUILDING
IN MODERN NORWAY

By

Joel S. Torstenson
Michael F. Metcalf
Tor Fr. Rasmussen

To be ordered from:
URBANA PRESS
Rasmussen, Schultzgt. 6, N-0365 Oslo 3
or J. S. Torstenson, 4800 – 12th Ave South,
Minneapolis, 55417 Minnesota.

Printed by:
S. Bern. Hegland A.s
Flekkefjord, Norway

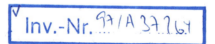

URBANIZATION AND COMMUNITY BUILDING IN MODERN NORWAY

By
Joel S. Torstenson
Michael F. Metcalf
Tor Fr. Rasmussen

URBANA PRESS
Oslo 1985

Abouth the Authors:

Joel S. Torstenson, Ph.d. in Sociology 1958, University of Minnesota.
Professor of Sociology and Department Chairman, Augsburg College 1958–1976.
Director of Metro-Urban Studies Program, 1971–1978.
Founder and first Director of the Scandinavian Urban Studies Term (SUST) 1973.
Director and Author of several major Twin-City Community Studies.

Michael F. Metcalf, Fil.dr. In History 1977, Stockholm University.
Acting Lecturer in History, Stockholm University, 1975–1977.
Associate Professor of Scandinavian History, University of Minnesota, 1980 -present.
Acting Director, Office of International Programs, University of Minnesota, 1983–
Director, Center for Northwest European Language and Area Studies, University of Minnesota, 1981–

Tor Fr. Rasmussen, Fil.dr., Docent, in Geography, 1967, The Royal University of Lund, Lecturer, Oslo University, Department of Geography, 1960–1964
Senior Research Officer, Norwegian Institute for Urban and Regional Planning Studies (NIBR) 1965–1970.
Professor of Geography with Urban and Regional Planning, Nordic Institute for Studies in Urban and Regional Planning (NORDPLAN) Stockholm 1968–1975.
Director of Research, City Planning Office, Oslo Municipality, 1975–1981.
Professor of Geography, University of Oslo, 1981 – present. Department Chairman.

CONTENTS

LIST OF FIGURES

XII

LIST OF TABLES

PREFACE

In the early summer of 1969, the University of Minnesota's Program of Continuing Education in Urban Affairs presented a conference on "The Scandinavian City: A Model for Urban America?" The conference featured such Scandinavian keynote speakers as Sune Lindstrom, Architect and Professor of Town Planning from Gothenburg, Sweden; Architect Erik Rolfson, Director of Urban Planning for Oslo, Norway; and Jesper Harvest from the Institute for Center Planning at Lyngby, Denmark. It was this conference that precipitated a series of events that ultimately led to the writing of this book.

As Professor of Sociology and director of Metro-Urban Studies at Augsburg College, I had become intensely interested in the exploding literature regarding urbanization and its socioeconomic, political and cultural concomitants. During the 1960s, I had participated in establishing one of the "semester in the city" programs which had brought students and faculty from several uppermidwest colleges into a Minneapolis neighborhood where the fruits of America's "urban crisis" had been made manifest in racial confrontation, street violence and burning.

The Conference on the Scandinavian City raised the question whether America's "urban crisis" was a necessary consequence of urbanization per se or whether it was more understandable as a consequence of America's particular perspectives and policies concerning the city and urbanization. My growing interest in comparative urban studies was sharpened by this conference and prompted my initiative in establishing a "semester in the city" program in Scandinavia called the Scandinavian Urban Studies Term (SUST). The program was jointly sponsored by the International Summer School of the University of Oslo and the Higher Education Consortium For Urban Affairs, of which I had become the first president.

The rationale and intellectual assumptions guiding the launching of this program have in many ways provided the contexts out of which this book has emerged. It was assumed that urbanization had become one of the most pervasive forces of world-wide change in the twentieth century; that community-building and environmental planning had become universally compelling challenges for a world whose habitat was being dramatically altered by the dynamics of urbanization. It was also assumed that each part of the world would respond to these challenges out of its distinctive history and socio-cultural ethos. It was further assumed that since urbanization and community-building involve vir-tually every aspect of life, their proper study would necessarily reflect insights and perspectives of a wide variety of academic disciplines.

Those of us involved in the SUST program soon learned that scholarly sources in English that could inform our study of urbanization and community-building in Scandinavia were sparse. This was par-ticularly true of sources for the study of Norway. It was a desire to solve this problem that has motivated my research and the writing of this book.

Out of my concern for an interdisciplinary approach, I am especially grateful to the historian Michael F. Metcalf of the University of Minnesota for writing the second chapter of this book on the "Norwegian Urban Development in Historical Perspective." I am similarly grateful to Tor Fr. Rasmussen, Chairman of the Department of Geography at the University of Oslo, for writing the two concluding chapters of the book on the economic and political setting of contemporary Norway and on Norway's urban future.

Although this book is primarily a case study of urbanization and community building in only one of the Scandinavian countries, it is presented as being illustrative, even if not scientifically representative, of similar developments in the other countries of the Scandinavian cultural region.

Besides meeting some of the special needs of English speaking students in Norway, it is our hope that this might be counted on as another instructive source in the growing literature on world urbani-zation. It is also hoped that it might be perceived as a valuable addition to the growing literature available for the Scandinavian Studies Programs in the U.S.A. and other parts of the world.

For urban and regional planners in the U.S.A. and for the shapers of its local and national policies for building a more humane urban habitat, it is also hoped that this book might stimulate a continuation of the kind of dialogue that was precipitated by the Conference on the Scandinavian City that provided the initial impetus for the writing of this book.

It is impossible to acknowledge here all who have been helpful in the writing of this book. But I cannot fail to mention several, without whom the book would not have been written. I am indebted, in the first place, to the International Summer School at the University of Oslo for providing the academic setting for beginning my research. I am especially grateful to Dr. Philip Boardman, its director, who responded favorably to my proposal for establishing the Scandinavian Urban Studies Term at this University. His helpfulness in launching the SUST program was critically important.

He secured Professor Gullik Kollandsrud from Oslo's School of Architecture as the principal Norwegian academic resource person and leader for the first term in the fall of 1973. Professor Kollandsrud introduced me to the overall socio-political system that was guiding Norway's response to urbanization. He led me to important Norwegian scholarly works and opened up channels to institutions and organizations from which I secured a wealth of both primary and secondary sources. His constant encouragement for my getting this book written was always helpful.

The friendly and generous helpfulness that I received from staff people at libraries, such as the library at Oslo's school of architecture and from research institutes such as the Norwegian Institute for Urban and Regional Research, made my research work both pleasant and rewarding. The same can be said for the leaders and staff people from the planning bodies in the Oslo region as well as other regional city centers of Norway.

Professor Tor Fr. Rasmussen has been especially helpful in getting this book written. His continuous encouragement has had much to do with my completing this work. Besides writing the two last chapters for the book, he took on the responsibility of getting the book printed in Norway. Together with his wife Kari he secured and prepared for printing the illustrations in the book. He also helped bring the manuscript as up to date as possible.

Here in the U.S.A., I have been especially helped and encouraged by Professor Michael F. Metcalf, historian and Director of Scandinavian Studies at the University of Minnesota. His agreeing to write the chapter on the "Norwegian City in Historical Perspective" has added both depth and perspective to the study.

I also wish to acknowledge with gratitude the services of Shirley J. Dahlen for her editorial assistance and for preparation of the manuscript.

Throughout my studies in Norway and my years of preparing this document, I have had the good companionship and sympathetic understanding of my wife Frances, to whom I lovingly dedicate this book.

Minneapolis   Joel S. Torstenson
April, 1985

CHAPTER ONE: PATHS IN THE URBAN EXPERIENCE

INTRODUCTION

Urbanization has become one of the most pervasive forces of world-wide change in the twentieth century. At the close of the nineteenth century only about 15% of the world's population was urban. By 1960 that percentage had approximately doubled. Out of a total world population of three billion, one billion were urbanites. By the end of the twentieth century more than half of the world's population will be urban (Ward 1976, p. 3).

As was dramatically demonstrated at the United Nations' Habitat Conference at Vancouver in the summer of 1976, every part of the world is grappling with issues related to the changing habitat associated with urbanization. Virtually all aspects of life and culture are being transformed by these urbanizing forces of change. The challenge everywhere, is how to direct the forces of change toward positive social and cultural conditions conducive to a sound humane habitat.

I. Divergent Paths in the Urban Experience

But even though the processes of urbanization have become universal, they are not everywhere the same. Each part of the world responds to them out of its distinctive history and socio-cultural situation. As Professor Berry has observed, world urbanization involves "fundamentally different processes that have arisen out of differences in culture and time" (Berry 1973, pp. XI-XX).

A proper understanding of world urbanization, therefore, requires intellectual frameworks that are applicable to different historic and socio-political circumstances. As Professor Berry intimates, neither the conventional wisdom about urbanization, nor the theoretical orientations emanating out a particular setting and time--such as those developed at the Chicago School of Urban Sociology for example--will adequately explain the varied paths of urbanization. They will not adequately interpret the urban experience of European nations which have

1

developed various means of regulating urban change in the public interest, and instituted public counterpoints to speculative private interests. The consequences of these public interventions are markedly at variance with the outcomes of the American experience with the industrial city (Berry 1973).

II. Norway and the Scandinavian Urban Experience

Since it is becoming increasingly evident that efforts must be "aimed at substituting urban design and redesign for the accidental city" (Owen 1979, p. 12), case studies of such European urban experiences provide special insights relative to ways of controlling and directing urban growth. This book constitutes a case study of one such European nation belonging to a distinct regional sub-culture of Europe. It analyses urbanization and community-building in modern Norway, one of the members of the Scandinavian cultural region. Living on the "roof-top of Europe," the Scandinavian countries have long been bracketed together by important geographical and climatic considerations as well as by their common cultural traditions. As one writer has observed, a kind of "northern fellowship" has developed that has "proved itself in every aspect of life from the earliest of times—in language, in culture, in legal concepts, in way of life—and that has endured despite mutual wars and many other complications in which our history abounds" (Sletten 1967, p.7).

While any adequate account of the fundamental elements binding these countries into a common cultural region would require a full-length book by itself, an identification of some the salient ones are useful for the purposes of this book. In the first place, even if they have not established a unitary political nation-state, the Scandinavian countries all share a long historic commitment to the importance of law in the ordering of human affairs. The thousand-year-old motto that has inspired legislation in these countries since the days of the "Sagas" has been translated as follows: "Land shall by law be built; not by unlawfulness shall it be laid waste." The significance of this commitment for Scandinavia's developing policies for controlling urban growth and community building will be made evident in this book.

The strong sense of justice, also traceable to the days of the "Sagas," according to a Danish scholar, has inspired "that respect for human rights and human dignity which underlies the modern social legislation" that has become characteristic of the social democracies of Scandinavia (Sletten 1967, p. 32). This ancient legacy has been strained through a religious history that is common to the nordic nations. Christianity was spread throughout Scandinavia during the late Viking period and in the twelfth century constituted an ecclesiastical province of the Catholic Church. During the era of the Protestant Reformation, Lutheranism replaced Catholicism as the official state religion in all of Scandinavia.

These and other shared cultural legacies led to a great variety of formal and informal cooperative activities among the peoples and governments of Scandinavia. Even in relatively remote Iceland, with less than a quarter million inhabitants, there are nearly 150 societies and organizations actively concerned with Scandinavian cooperation (Sletten 1967, p. 36). These and other historic events led eventually to the establishment of the Nordic Council in the 1950s. This Council is a consultative body whereby the prime ministers and representatives from the parliaments of the member-nations regularly consult with each other and share ideas and information concerning political, social, and cultural affairs (Anderson 1967).

Since its first annual session in 1953, the Nordic Council has been instrumental in developing a variety of policies and programs for promoting a sense of community and a spirit of cooperation in Scandinavia. To facilitate travel and labor mobility within the region, a single passport zone and a common labor market were created in 1957. In 1955 a social security convention was negotiated aimed at making every national of any member country equal in this respect. Steps have also been taken to coordinate the public health services of the

3

member nations, including a formal agreement to a northern "medical market" in 1965. A Nordic Cultural Commission has been created to promote cooperation in the fields of science, education, and the arts. Several scientific institutes have been established to promote cooperation in research. In 1962 the Nordic countries entered into a formal Treaty of Cooperation, committing each member nation to maintain and further develop cooperation between the member nations in juridical, cultural, social and economic affairs (Sletten 1967, pp. 81-87).

Of special relevance for this study was the establishment in 1968 of "Nordplan," the Nordic Institute for Studies in Urban and Regional Planning. This institute, located on the island of Skeppsholmen in Stockholm, has as its goal advanced post-graduate teaching and research. Its aim is to give the participants better multi-disciplinary background for their planning profession as well as a deeper insight into their own field of specialization. Its students and faculty are principally drawn from the four participating countries of Denmark, Finland, Norway, and Sweden; but Icelandic students are also accepted upon application.

In the context of these realities of Scandinavian cooperation, the similarities among the Nordic countries in their perceptions of and responses to urbanization and community building become readily understandable. They share a common historic identity with the typical European perception of the cultural and socio-political role of city centers. Like other European cities, the historical, momumental, and symbolic values of most Scandinavian cities impose "constraints upon commercial, administrative, and industrial cities" (Sacco 1972, pp. 172-173). In an age of increased travel and leisure, entertainment and cultural functions are added to the other historic city-center legacies. These legacies help explain the relative absence of the kind of disinterest in the old city centers that has been typical in many

4

American cities. They also help explain the resistance to the kind of suburbanization most dramatically illustrated by the sprawling metropolis of Los Angeles.

These and other characteristic Scandianavian responses to urbanization have attracted increasing world interest in recent years. As one writer has observed, "Scandinavia has become in effect the world's laboratory for advanced thought and action in environmental and social matters (Koening 1975, p. 9). Annual workshops and special university programs on Scandinavian approaches to urban and regional development, to land-use planning and community building, architecture and environmental design have transformed some of the former "sight-seeing" tours of Scandinavia to "life-seeing" tours for studying how the nordic countries are dealing with the many problems facing all advanced industrial societies. One U.S. writer, after participating in such a tour, observed that Scandinavia had seen "the future long before the rest of us" (Koening 1975, p. 10).

In 1976, the Scandinavian Review devoted a special issue to the care of the environment in Scandinavia (Scandinavian Review 1976, No. 4). It accented Scandinavia's positive attitude toward national planning and its widespread acceptance of public social welfare programs. It noted that even though they are among the most democratic nations of the world, they do not rely on the sovereignty of private market place for producing environmentally sound decisions. It called attention to Scandinavia's long and pervasive love of nature and how this helps explain its policies and programs for environmental protection. It described the gradual transformation from a traditional conservation policy focused on the landscape preservation, to a more contemporary and comprehensive ecological approach. It contrasted Scandinavia's public land use planning and administrative arrangements for environmental protection with America's environmental assessments and regulatory action.

III. How the Issues Are Presented

These and other aspects of Scandinavia's urban experience will be documented in this case study of modern Norway. It will make clear that even though its scale of urbanization is relatively small, Norway has become predominantly urban, challenging the conventional romantic perceptions of this country as a nation of farming, fishing, and forestry that has been shielded from the complex realities of an urban world.

As Chapter Two documents, that perception of Norway has never been altogether accurate. An examination of Norway's urban past reveals a long history of city-centered commerce reaching back beyond the Middle Ages. Due to its distinctive geography, most of its cities began as ocean outlets for extensive trade and fishing activities along the country's long western and southern coast. Both the shape and the culture of these historic cities have for centuries been influenced by this ocean-orientated environment. The various socio-cultural epochs of their history, have left their imprints on both the architecture and the culture of Norway's cities. Unlike so many American urban centers that emerged as industrial cities, the cities of Norway bear the marks of both the medieval and renaissance city, as well as the imprints of the pre-industrial modern, the industrial, and post-industrial influences. All these historic legacies have formed Norway's perceptions of urbanization and community building.

Like other European cities, Norwegian cities are perceived as having played an important role in the building of a national culture and civilization. As the historian Frank J. Coppa has noted, such historic cities are regarded as the appropriate containers of "theaters, opera houses, music halls, libraries, universities, museums, sports stadiums, zoos, and churches." They are perceived as communities for sharing the basic conditions of a common life and history (Coppa 1976, pp. 167-171).

The downtowns of Norwegian cities are typically referred to as "sentrums" rather than as "C B D's" (Central Business Districts) so typically done in the U.S.A. Their cities are perceived as centers of culture and community as well as of commerce, industry, and communication. Informed by such perspectives, city-building becomes a public trust and responsibility rather than the more privatistic "accidental" citybuilding associated with the market-oriented culture of the U.S.A. Urbanization and urban planning become publicly intertwined with community building, nurtured by a sense of community rooted in Norwegian social structure and culture that has persisted since the days of Vikings (Papa 1981, pp. 135-36). It is not unthinkable that this historic interplay between a sense of history and a community-oriented consciousness may have contributed to the Norwegian receptivity to the ideas and writings of the well-known urban philosopher and planner, Lewis Mumford (Mumford 1938).

Chapter Three describes Norway's twentieth century urbanization, and examines the demographic and settlement changes associated with it. As in other modern nations of the western world, Norway's population is shown to have become predominantly urban, establishing their homes in the context of expanding city regions. The dramatic occupational shift from the primary industries of farming, fishing and forestry to the tertiary industries of a post-industrial age is described. It documents how Norway's phenomenal development of hydro-electric energy transformed the nation's economy and made possible a decentralized urbanization unique in modern times. It identifies some of the most compelling challenges associated with that urbanization such as the problems of population concentration, the diminishing opportunities in the remote areas, the problems of housing shortages and community-building pressures in the growing cities, and other problems of managing urban and regional growth.

Chapter Four examines Norway's responses to these problems and challenges. It describes how these responses have been informed by the cultural value-orientations Norway shares with the other social democracies of Scandinavia, as well as by some of the cultural attributes that appear to be

7

more distinctly Norwegian. Norway's regional policies, for example, reflect Norway's strong commitment to the ideologies of equality and equal opportunity, a commitment that contributed much to Norway's settlement system of several larger city regions throughout the country rather than in a few metropolitan centers. Norway's planning system is similarly shown to reflect the nation's social democratic values as well as other historic socio-cultural and political orientations. The paradoxical combination of a strong central government with a highly durable tradition of municipal autonomy provides an intriguing illustration of socio-cultural ecology. Norway's developing national policies on energy conservation and environmental protection provide similar illustrations.

Chapters Five and Six describe how these developing national policies and programs are reflected in the planning and development of Norway's major metropolis--its capital city of Oslo. A description of its growth and development into a modern polycentric metropolis yields much information about urbanization and community-building in modern Norway. The dramatic expansion of Oslo's municipal boundaries through its merger with the vast area of the largely undeveloped rural municipality of Aker in 1948 provided the city a unique urban laboratory for translating some of the political and cultural value-orientations of social democracy into the fashioning of a modern multi-cellular metropolis. Rejecting the unlimited sovereignty of the market-oriented determination of urban development, the city sought to control and direct its development by municipal acquisition and ownership of lands needed for urban expansion and of the extensive Oslo forests for the preservation of vast public parks and recreational resources.

Publically planned and developed satellite towns became the new community containers for much of Oslo's expanding population. This is one of the most striking contrasts between Norwegian city-building and that characteristic of much of the U.S.A. Oslo's first garden city experiment of "Ullevål Hageby" built around 1920, Lambertseter--

8

the first post-war satellite town and Romsås--one of
the newest--are described in sufficient detail to
illustrate their developing rationale and strategies
for urban development and community building. They
constitute Norwegian counterparts for such other
well-known satellite towns as Vällingby in
Stockholm, Tapiola in Helsinki, and similar developments in Copenhagen. The coordination of these
developments with the building of a public transit
system and other aspects of metropolitan planning
provides an important illustration of comprehensive
urban planning and development in modern Norway.

Chapter Seven describes the planning and
development of some of the leading regional urban
centers of Norway, such as Tromsø, Trondheim,
Bergen, Stavanger, and Kristiansand. The experiences of these leading regional capitals provide
important clues to understanding Norway's emerging
urban and regional policies.

The two concluding chapters serve as both a
postscript and a general summary to the book.
Chapter Eight provides an account of the political
and economic contexts out of which Norway's urban
and regional policies have been fashioned. It is
emphasized that, in a democratic society, efficient
planning (i.e., planning that is implemented) can
only take place within a context of harmony and
consensus within a given cultural and social
framework, where the majority share similar values
and pursue the same goals. This has, until now,
been the case in postwar Norway. Signs are now
showing up that there will be less harmony in the
future because newer active and smaller pressure
groups argue strongly for their own group interests.
The challenge for the coming years will be that of
coordination and moderation in order to keep the
socioeconomic forces in balance within a holistic
framework together with its limitations.

The final chapter examines some likely
prospects for parts of Norway's urban future. After
forty years of economic expansion, Norway has
reached the post-industrial stage of development.
No major changes are expected with regard to
location and size of the city regions. In newly
urbanized Norway, the vital question will be: how

will the urban community adjust and change in order
to meet new needs and conditions produced by
demographic changes in a population of low fertility
and an increasing number of old people? The
municipal economy and the local public resources are
crucial for both the urban future and the welfare
state which have accompanied urbanization.

REFERENCES

Anderson, Stanley R. 1967. The Nordic Council:
A Study of Scandinavian Regionalism. Seattle:
University of Washington Press.

Berry, Brian J. L. 1973. The Human Consequences of
Urbanization. New York: St. Martin's Press.

Coppa, Frank J. 1976. "Cities and Suburbs in Europe
and the United States," in Suburbia: The
American Dream and Dilemma, Philip C. Dolce
(ed.) Garden City, New York: Anchor Books.

Daedalus, The Nordic Enigma and Nordic Voices.
Winter and Spring. 1984

Dolce, Philip C. (ed.) 1976. Suburbia: The
American Dream and Dilemma. Garden City, New
York: Anchor Books.

Koenig, Helmet 1975. "Scandinavia's New Tourism,"
in Scandinavian Review, Vol. 63, No. 1. March
1975, pp. 4-11.

Mumford, Lewis 1938. The Culture of Cities. New
York: Harcourt, Brace & World, Inc.

Mumford, Lewis 1961. The City in History. New York: Harcourt, Brace & World, Inc.

Owen, Wilfred 1979. "Transition to an Urban Plane" in The Bulletin of the Atomic Scientists, Vol. 35, No. 9 (November) pp. 12-81.

Papa, Mary Bader 1981. "Vikings to Invade Minneapolis" in Twin Cities, Vol. 4, No. 2 (February).

Sacco, Giuseppi 1972. "Morphology and Culture of European Cities" in Europe 2000 Vol. 1. pp. 162-187. Amsterdam: European Cultural Foundation.

Sletten, Vegard 1967. Five Northern Countries Pull Together. Copenhagen: Nordic Council.

Ward, Barbara 1976. The Home of Man. New York: W. W. Norton & Company, Inc.

Weber, Max 1958. The City. (Translated and edited by Donald Martindale and Gertrud Neuwirth). New York: The Free Press.

Westergaard, John H. 1966. "Scandinavian Urbanism: A Survey of Trends and Themes." Urban Social Research in Sweden, Norway, and Denmark. London: University College.

CHAPTER TWO: NORWEGIAN URBAN DEVELOPMENT IN HISTORICAL PERSPECTIVE

I. Definition of Towns and Locations in the Viking Age

Living in our late twentieth century industrial and postindustrial societies, we take the city for granted and seldom stop to consider just what it is that defines the city in terms of its surrounding environment. When we search for the roots of urban development in historical times, however, the need for such a definition becomes immediately apparent, for the city did not assume its present characteristics until well after the onset of the industrial revolution. The definition of "city" or, more correctly, of "town" used here includes four criteria: greater density of population than the surrounding area, fulfillment of central functions for the surrounding area, year-round habitation by people engaged in economic and other pursuits that distinguish them from those living in rural areas, and a legal status that distinguishes town dwellers from those living in the surrounding area.

In Norway, as elsewhere in Scandinavia, the beginning of urban development dates back to the Viking Age (roughly 780-1000). Then, as now, Norway's mountains, fjords, and inland valleys severely limited the land resources available to the Norwegians while at the same time obliging most of the population to live close to the sea. There were many sites in Viking-Age Norway that served the trading needs of the population, and all of them had a central geographic location between a valley and a fjord or at the mouth of a river (Gunnes, p. 320). Yet, only one of them--Kaupang--appears to have approached the status of a town (as we have defined it here) during the Viking Age. We now know of nine Viking-Age sites bearing names based on the word kaupang (marketplace), seven sites with names related to the word bjarkøy (linked with the legal practices of Viking traders), and five or six sites bearing names related to the term lahell (an unloading site) (Helle & Nedkvitne, pp. 199-202). Of these sites it is only Kaupang, located in the southern coastal area of Vestfold, that appears to have surpassed the status of a simple marketplace in Viking times.

Archaeologists excavating the Kaupang site argue that it served as a center for trade and the crafts from the late eighth century until the late ninth century, and that Kaupang's clearest foreign trade connection seems to have been with the Danish town of Hedeby, located in present-day Schleswig/Holstein. Evidence of year-round habitation at Kaupang is, however, inconclusive, and the archaeological finds remain less impressive than those for Hedeby and for the Swedish town of Birka, located just west of present-day Stockholm (Helle & Nedkvitne, pp. 196-97). In sum, as a recent authoritative study put it, "population was too thin in relation to the available area; the volume of trade and crafts was too modest; and the culture, legal, and political administrative central functions were too little developed and were not sufficiently permanent for towns to develop in Norway already during the Viking Age" (Helle & Nedkvitne, p. 206).

By the 1070s, however, Adam of Bremen was referring to Trondheim as a large town (civitas magna), and by the 1130s the Anglo-Norman historian Ordericus Vitalis was referring in his Historia Ecclesiastica to six Norwegian coastal towns, namely Bergen, Konghelle, Trondheim, Sarpsborg, Oslo and Tønsberg (Helle & Nedkvitne, pp. 209, 206). In fact, historians and archaeologists believe that five other towns not listed by Ordericus Vitalis existed alongside of these six. The fascinating question that arises from this rapid rise of towns between the end of the Viking Age and the 1130s is what had happened in Norway's economic, social and political life to bring it about. Most scholars now agree that that which was new was that the eleventh-century kings of Norway encouraged, and themselves became involved in, the development of towns, and that the Church began to make itself felt as a more or less independent stimulus to urban development in the years following 1100.

II. The Legal Status of Towns and the Role of Kings

Theory tells us that, since they face legal situations unanticipated in rural society and unaddressed by the legal traditions developed to serve agricultural society, early town dwellers sought special legal status for their towns and for themselves within the context of the broader society in which they lived. In Norway, this legal status was first formulated in a special commercial and maritime law known as bjarkøyretten during the Early Middle Ages (Helle & Nedkvitne, p. 317). In return for granting this status, and in return for providing security for the towns and for merchants travelling to and from the towns, the secular authority--i.e., the king--demanded and received payment of special customs duties and taxes. Then, too, as kings came to recognize the advantages offered by the central location and the status of the towns, they came to utilize them as administrative centers and often attempted to establish new towns in districts where none existed. What we know from historical documents and archaeological evidence suggests that this is what happened in Norway in the eleventh century.

Both the Icelandic saga literature of the twelfth and thirteenth centuries and the most recent archaeological evidence from Oslo and Trondheim support the idea that town development was actively promoted by the kings of the eleventh century, although there is inconclusive evidence that the kings did more than lend their support to developments already underway and strengthen their influence by building strongholds in these towns (Helle & Nedkvitne, pp. 218-19). Be that as it may, the presence of a special royal officer--a bailiff known as a gjaldker--in Trondheim, Oslo, Bergen and Tønsberg by the first decade of the twelfth century indicates that the Norwegian kings contributed to the administration of these new towns (Helle & Nedkvitne, p. 220). The influence of the Church on the development of Norway's towns stemmed, on the other hand, from the sheer number of priests, monks and nuns who settled in the diocesan and

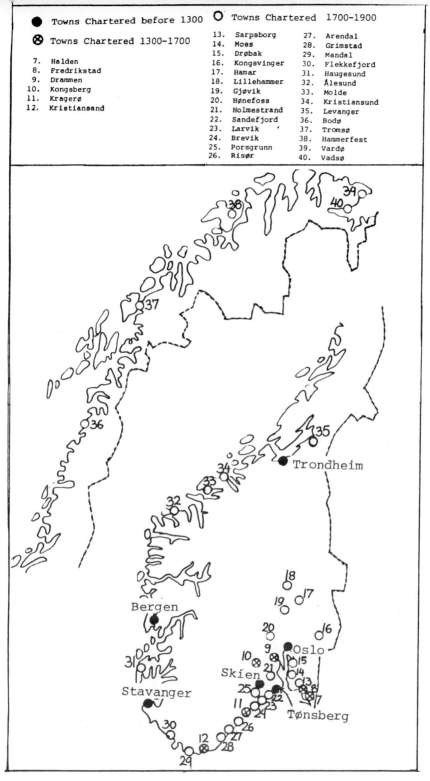

Legend:

● Towns Chartered before 1300   ○ Towns Chartered 1700-1900

⊗ Towns Chartered 1300-1700

7. Halden
8. Fredrikstad
9. Drammen
10. Kongsberg
11. Kragerø
12. Kristiansand

13. Sarpsborg
14. Moss
15. Drøbak
16. Kongsvinger
17. Hamar
18. Lillehammer
19. Gjøvik
20. Hønefoss
21. Holmestrand
22. Sandefjord
23. Larvik
24. Brevik
25. Porsgrunn
26. Risør

27. Arendal
28. Grimstad
29. Mandal
30. Flekkefjord
31. Haugesund
32. Ålesund
33. Molde
34. Kristiansund
35. Levanger
36. Bodø
37. Tromsø
38. Hammerfest
39. Vardø
40. Vadsø

FIGURE 2A   Cities and Towns up to the Nineteenth Century

monastical centers once Norwegian kings allowed--and
encouraged--the Church to establish itself. In
addition, the Church, as the first institution to
construct monumental stone structures such as
cathedrals and palaces, stimulated and supported
urban craftsmen and builders for decades at a time
(Helle & Nedkvitne, p. 222).

Thus, urban development in medieval Norway
benefited from the consolidation of royal power and
from the introduction and expansion of Christianity,
as well as from growth in population and in
agricultural production in the years after 1000. In
some towns, such as Stavanger, these administrative
and ecclesiastical functions served as the principal
justification for town status, but the towns that
became the most important Norwegian population
centers in the later Middle Ages were the ones that
united these functions with extensive domestic and
foreign trade, as well as with the successful
production and distribution of handicraft products
such as shoes and ironware. These were the towns
that were in a position to take advantage of the
general expansion of European trade that took place
in the eleventh century and that reached Norway
toward the end of that century.

III.   The Role of Merchants and the Church

Positioned between the important fishing
grounds off the northwestern coast of Norway and the
urban centers of consumption in Western Europe,
whose demand for imported fish had been stimulated
by the expansion of trade, Bergen was the town best
able to capitalize on the new international
circumstances after 1100 (Helle & Nedkvitne, pp.
223-24). Whereas Trondheim (then known as Nidaros)
and Oslo had hitherto attracted the most royal
attention, the kings of Norway began in the middle
of the twelfth century to build royal residences and
a series of churches in Bergen in response to
Bergen's growing importance as a center of international trade (Helle & Nedkvitne, p. 241). During
the High Middle Ages and the early modern period--
and indeed right up to the middle of the nineteenth
century--Bergen was to dominate Trondheim and Oslo

17

in terms of trade and population, if not (after the High Middle Ages) in terms of political and religious affairs.

The High Middle Ages (1130-1350) witnessed a significant development of Norway's towns, as their population grew, the density of settlement increased, and the productivity of Norwegian agriculture and overall population of the country expanded. International and domestic trade, the crafts, royal authority and the Church apparatus all continued to grow and to fuel urban development until the Black Death and other epidemics ravished the Norwegian population in 1349 and subsequent years. Characteristic of these still rather modest Norwegian towns was the fact that, unlike their more important counterparts in Scandinavia and on the Continent, they were never walled and never provided with moats (Helle & Nedkvitne, p. 236; cf. Lunden, pp. 324-26). On the other hand, they did increasingly assume the function of local and regional administrative centers, with Bergen and Oslo assuming certain aspects of national political and administrative centers during the thirteenth and the early fourteenth centuries, respectively.

It is very important not to underestimate--as it is so easy to do in the twentieth century--the overwhelming presence of the Church in Norway's urban centers during the High Middle Ages. The Church is estimated to have acquired ownership of some 40% of the arable land in Norway by the early fourteenth century, and about one-third of that land was controlled directly by the bishops and cathedral chapters at Trondheim, Bergen, Oslo, Hamar and Stavanger. In the latter two episcopal seats, the cathedral, the bishop's palace, the buildings of the cathedral chapter, and the cathedral school completely dominated the town. While this was not entirely true in the other towns, where both trade and the royal presence were in evidence, one can well imagine the impression made on the pilgrim arriving in Trondheim to visit Saint Olav's grave and finding fourteen churches, one or two hospitals, and four or five monasteries in addition to the cathedral, the archbishop's place, the palace of the cathedral chapter and the school. Visitors to

Bergen and Oslo must have been similarly impressed, whether by Bergen's twenty churches,' by the fortified bishop's castle in Oslo, or by some other manifestation of the Church's presence (Helle & Nedkvitne, pp. 246-47).

Thanks partly to the fact that our written sources for the High Middle Ages are much richer than they are for earlier periods, we are able to follow the tremendous expansion of foreign trade during this period with a high degree of accuracy. We are also able to follow the active measures taken by the Norwegian monarchs to promote the growth of towns by limiting the privilege of trading to their inhabitants. In 1299, for example, all trade in rural districts was forbidden, and the sale of all goods was limited to the towns. Likewise, in the early 1300s, King Håkon V issued an edict requiring foreigners to buy timber for export in the towns, rather than in the countryside (Helle & Nedkvitne, p. 250). Such practices were to continue right down to the mid-nineteenth century, but the fact that it was difficult to enforce such laws is belied by the fact that such edicts were issued repeatedly over the years.

Another factor contributing to the growth of the towns in the High Middle Ages was the fact that foreign merchants--primarily Germans--settled in Bergen, Oslo and Tønsberg beginning in the mid-thirteenth century. These foreigners, whether they settled permanently and became Norwegian subjects or whether they served as part of the growing expatriate Hanseatic community, certainly promoted the urbanization of the towns in which they resided. They brought with them both capital and expertise, although the Hanseatic merchants at Bergen, Oslo and Tønsberg shipped most of their profits back to Lubeck and the other North German Hanseatic towns. The monarchy granted the German merchants special privileges in 1278, 1285 and 1294 in the form of exemptions from the Town Law (Lunden, p. 359), and for this and other reasons the vast bulk of foreign trade out of Bergen and the other Norwegian towns was in the hands of the foreigners by the 1320s. After this time, native Norwegian merchants were largely reduced to plying the domestic trade and to playing the role of middlemen between the Norwegians and the foreign merchants (Helle & Nedkvitne, pp. 251-52).

By the middle of the fourteenth century, Norway's urban centers had become much more respectable entities than their twelfth-century predecessors had been. While the rudiments of the classic European medieval city were now all in place, however, the Norwegian towns remained diminuitive. Although the Norwegian population reached its zenith in the fourteenth century, no more than 20,000 people lived in towns in the year 1300. The maximum populations for the larger towns were about 7,000 for Bergen, 3,000 for Trondheim, 2,000 for Oslo, and 1,500 for Tønsberg, while the other towns had populations varying between 200 and 500 (Helle & Nedkvitne, p. 262; cf. Lunden, pp. 319-20). Yet, the larger towns had become regional centers in terms not only of trade and handicraft production, but also in terms of administrative and ecclesiastical affairs. By this time, too, King Magnus Lagabøte's legal reforms of the mid-1270s had established a uniform distinction between the Land Law and the Town Law for the whole kingdom, and the towns had developed a system of courts and governing bodies separate from those of the surrounding countryside. However, unlike their counterparts on the Continent, which enjoyed a measure of liberty vis-a-vis royal power, Norwegian towns remained under the supreme legislative and judicial control of the king (Helle & Nedkvitne, p. 272).

IV.   Urban and Economic Decline in the Late Middle Ages; The Disestablishment of the Catholic Church

The history of Norway in the Late Middle Ages is dominated by the demographic and political effects of the Black Death and the other epidemics that swept across the land in 1349 and over the next fifteen years. For Norway's towns, most historians believe that, as one has put it, "stagnation and decline are the principal characteristics of the history of the Norwegian towns in the Late Middle Ages" (Benedictow, p. 159; cf. Helle & Nedkvitne,

p. 278 for a less definite interpretation). The
fortunes of both the monarchy and the Church were
also seriously affected, since the severe loss of
population increased the cost of labor and improved
the bargaining position of tenant farmers. After
King Olav IV died in 1387, no Norwegian would sit on
the throne until 1905, and the steady attrition of
the Norwegian nobility meant that Norway slipped
inexorably deeper into submission to Denmark from
1387 to 1536. The economic fortunes of the Church
also waned after 1349; only five of the fourteen
churches that stood in Trondheim in the early
fourteenth century remained in 1430 and only three
of them remained in 1530 (Helle & Nedkvitne, p.
274).

The formal subordination of Norway to Denmark
came in 1536 with the accession of Christian III as
King of Denmark, but for all practical purposes
Norway had been without its own kings since 1387.
From 1536 to 1814, Norway was governed by the Danish
kings as a province within their realm rather than
as a separate kingdom. Although Norwegian legal
codes remained in effect where not specifically set
aside by Danish decrees, the Danish kings tended at
first to lack the direct interest in Norwegian town
development demonstrated by the former kings of
Norway. Likewise, since Christian III had brought
the Lutheran Reformation to Norway and confiscated
all the property held by the Catholic church,
Norwegian towns also lost the constructive influence
of the Church on their continued development.

TABLE 2.1   Number of Incorporated Towns and
             Recognized Export Harbors 1500-1900

Year	Incorporated Towns	Recognized Export Harbors	Total
1500	7	–	7
1600	7	1	8
1700	12	12	24
1800	23	19	42

Source: Knut Mykland, ed., Norges historie
        (Cappelen)

While the medieval towns in Norway did not languish entirely under Danish rule, their population in the 1530s stood at approximately 10-12,000, with Bergen accounting for approximately half of the total urban population. The disestablishment of the Catholic church as a result of the Reformation left towns such as Stavanger and Hamar without their leading residents and their leading source of revenue (Fladby, p. 54), and the only new town to be founded during the sixteenth century was merely a replacement for the medieval town of Sarpsborg, which had been destroyed by the Swedes during the Nordic Seven Years' War (1563-70). Fredrikstad, established ten kilometers downstream from Sarpsborg, was better situated for the export trade and, perhaps even more importantly, was situated in a more easily defendable location. Indeed, Fredrikstad was the first Norwegian town to be set up as a modern fortified town in the then-prevalent Dutch manner (Sogner, p. 52).

V.   Town Growth in the Mercantilist Period

With the seventeenth century came the first wave of city planning in the early modern Danish state. The widely-held concepts of what we commonly refer to as mercantilism came to dominate royal policy, thus leading to a series of measures designed to maximize exports, minimize imports, and tax both domestic and foreign trade in order to enhance the crown's cash revenues. The Danish kings now founded a series of new towns, giving each of them not only town privileges, but a ready-made physical blueprint, as well. In Norway, the reign of Christian IV (1598-1648) witnessed not only the founding of two mining towns (Kongsberg in 1624, Røros in 1646) and the rebuilding of Oslo as Christiania following a major fire in 1624, but also the founding of Kristiansand in 1641.

The plans for Kristiansand reflected Christian IV's interest in the early Renaissance perspectives on city planning. The new town was to serve as a trading center for the extensive lumber industry that had developed on the south coast and as a naval base for Denmark's expanding royal navy.

The king's plans for the new town envisioned a city of 15-20,000 with streets laid out on a grid pattern typical of many of the new towns elsewhere in the European world of the seventeenth century. Merchants were instructed to build their homes on crown land in the new town in return for monopolistic privileges of trade in the Christiansand region. Within a few years, Kristiansand became both a military garrison and a diocesan center for the Danish state church, as well as a center for trade and the crafts. In the main, the town developed along the lines envisioned by Christian IV (Byplankontoret i Kristiansand, 1978; pp. 1-3).

TABLE 2.2   Population in Incorporated Towns and Densely Populated Areas 1801-1910

Census	Towns		Densely Populated Areas Outside of Towns		Total Population
	Abs.	Pct.	Abs.	Pct.	
1801	77,642	8.8			88,487
1825	114,188	10.9			1,051,381
1845	161,875	12.2	38,060	2.9	1,328,471
1865	266,292	15.6	61,928	3.6	1,701,756
1890	474,129	23.7	112,289	5.6	2,000,917
1900	627,650	28.0	164,085	7.3	2,240,032
1910	689,228	28.8	229,048	9.6	2,391,782

Source: Folketellingen and Historisk Statistikk 1978

These years also saw the publication of Christian IV's Norwegian Law Code, which further restricted trade to the towns. From this point on, it is clear that the royal revenues from customs duties and excise taxes were of such great interest that the royal government was very anxious to promote and exploit the economic interests of merchants and manufacturers in a systematic way. In 1662, for example, the Crown granted a common set of

privileges to all the incorporated Norwegian towns
(Sogner, p. 59). This new royal interest in the
towns led to a centralization of authority through
the provision that town councilors--formerly
appointed by local magistrates upon the approval of
the leading citizens of the towns--were now to be
appointed by the king and by the king alone (Sogner,
p. 75).

Administrative practices and legal measures
in the years following Christian IV's reign
acquiesced to a certain extent to the fact that
Norway's extensive export of timber and other wood
products--an export sector developed mainly in the
decades following 1500 (Fladby, pp. 152-56)--had led
to widespread trade outside the incorporated towns.
While the bulk nature of timber had meant that its
export had been allowed from several rural locations
even earlier, all other trade at those sites had
been strictly forbidden.

In the years after 1640, however, the Crown
allowed merchants from the nearest town to use these
locations to unload goods from and ship goods to
other parts of the Danish realm (Sogner, p. 53).
Responding to local requests and to the growth of
trade, the Crown granted ten of these sites full
town privileges between 1665 and 1752. These new
towns included Drammen (1665), Larvik (1671), Moss
(1720), Molde (1742), and Kristiansund (1742), but
none of them was situated north of Trondheim
(Sogner, pp. 54, 83-84).

Fourteen more towns were granted full town
privileges over the course of the next century, with
the early expansion taking place north of Trondheim
(Hammerfest in 1787, Vardø in 1788, Tromsø in 1794)
and the later expansion taking place primarily in
the southeast and in the eastern valleys (Sogner, p.
54). When the many centuries of Danish rule drew to
a close in 1814, the growth of trade, the impact of
mercantilism, and the Napoleonic wars had brought an
increase in the number of fully incorporated
Norwegian towns from seven in 1500 to twenty-three
in 1814, while the number of ladesteder, or export
harbors with limited trading privileges, had risen
from zero to twelve (Myhre, p. 25).

By 1814, nearly 10% of the Norwegian population lived in towns, with over 16,000 living in Bergen and over 13,000 living in Christiania (Oslo). The period of Danish rule had thus witnessed a major expansion of urban life in Norway, and this expansion was to continue along the same lines over the next thirty years. By 1845, there were thirteen more fully incorporated towns (six of which had been ladesteder) and eight new ladesteder, while the population living in urban areas had grown to over 12% and Christiania's population had grown to 33,000, clearly surpassing that of Bergen (24,000) to become Norway's largest city (Myhre, p. 16 Table 2 & p. 72 Table 16).

Although major constitutional and political changes came in 1814 with the end of Danish rule, with the adoption of a Norwegian constitution (still in effect today), and with Norway's acquiescence in a personal union with Sweden, the real revolution for Norway's towns and cities came as a result of sweeping economic and ideological changes in the years after 1835. One of the first major political reforms inspired by classical economic liberalism and by democratic ideals was the enactment in 1837 of a local self-government act for both rural and urban municipalities (Sejersted, pp. 339-42). Under this act, every municipality was to be governed by a locally elected municipal council, thus freeing the towns and cities from direct central governmental control. The guild system of restricting entrance into the handicrafts began to be dismantled in 1839, and the commercial monopolies granted the incorporated towns in the years of Danish rule were abolished. The vestiges of mercantilist legislation were to disappear by the end of the 1860s (Try, p. 227).

VI. Industrialization, Economic and Urban Growth Up to 1900

It was in the 1840s, in particular, that the institutions of industrialism and capitalism began to make themselves felt in Norwegian towns and cities. The 1840s brought Norway's first railroad construction project, as well as extensive con-

25

struction and improvement of the public roads and the opening of the first industrial factories (Myhre, pp. 14-15). After the first private commercial bank (Christiania Bank og Kreditkasse) opened in 1848, a substantial number of commercial banking institutions developed in the 1850s, thus providing a source of capital for men with plans to build the factories and purchase the raw materials they needed to pursue their plans for new modes of industrial production (Try, pp. 309-10). Long the centers of trade, commerce, administration, and cultural life, cities in Norway were now to emerge as centers of industrial activity, thus attracting thousands of new workers and creating tremendous demands for new housing, public services, and adequate transportation facilities (Myhre, pp. 50-53). In short, the advent of industrialism led to problems and opportunities for Norway's towns and cities that had hardly been dreamed of as late as 1840.

It would be wrong to see the changes taking place in mid-nineteenth century Norwegian towns and cities in isolation. Viewed broadly, these changes were intimately linked to the economic and ideological changes affecting Norwegian society as a whole. During these years, Norwegian farmers were coming to think more and more in terms of markets and of a cash economy. Not only were farmers specializing their production in order to maximize their ability to sell their produce for cash; they were beginning to view the land itself in terms of its market value (Sejersted, pp. 140-45; Try, p. 265). The continuing institution of odel, which limited one's right to sell one's land, limited the actual traffic in land sales, but improvements of one's land (which required investments) were encouraged by this new view of property.

Farmers began to interact more and more with the towns and cities as they sought new markets for their crops, loans for the improvement of their property, and cash with which to pay taxes and buy manufactured goods. This development, in turn, led to the towns and cities competing vigorously for the burgeoning business of the farmers. The 1850s and 1860s have been characterized as a period during

26

which Norway's towns and cities struggled with one another to capture the hinterlands, both in view of the expanding rural markets and in view of the demise of trading monopolies (Myhre, p. 45).

With the new ethos of capitalist competition and with the development of credit institutions requiring tremendous amounts of capital to serve growing industries, the new flurry of urbanization in the second half of the nineteenth and the first decades of the twentieth centuries brought with it a new centralization of power and population to Christiania, the nation's largest city and its political capital. The medieval and early modern privileges granted to cities had attempted to protect the individual towns from the competition of other towns, but with the breakthrough of classical economic thought and with the end of privilege the way had been cleared for the "survival" of the "fittest" cities and the decline of their weaker counterparts. For example, Christiania not only drove the other towns in eastern Norway to the edge of ruin by attracting all the new business, but its phenomenal growth also hurt cities like Trondheim, despite the fact that it was so far away. Christiania's share of Norway's imports was 25% in 1851, but by the late 1890s it had increased to 53% (Myhre, p. 49). In addition, the fact that Christiania was the seat of the Norwegian government also increased its dominant position, since the national government grew in size and in responsibility with the increasing complexity of Norwegian society and with Norway's independence from Sweden in 1905.

The development of Norway's communications network in the nineteenth century also favored Christiania, as the capital became the center of the telegraph system built in the 1850s and the center of the telephone system built from the 1880s on. The railroads, too, were built with Christiania as their principal terminus, thus demonstrating the city's dominant stature, while at the same time promoting its ability to penetrate domestic markets even further. Symbolic of this is the fact that two railroad terminals—one serving the eastern part of the country, and one the western—were built in Christiania rather than one central station.

TABLE 2.3   Population of Norway's Four Largest
             Towns 1300-1920

Year	Bergen	Oslo/ Christiania	Trondheim	Stavanger
1300*	7,000	2,000	3,000	500
1500*	6,000	1,000	1,000	500
1660*	8,000	4,000	2,500	1,500
1801	18,000	9,200	8,800	2,500
1845	23,800	33,000	14,800	9,100
1875	42,200	100,200	23,800	23,500
1900	78,900	250,000	38,500	32,000
1920	103,500	330,000	60,800	50,400

* Estimated guesses, information from different
  sources.
Source: Folketellingen and Historisk Statistikk
         1978

        Thus, it is not surprising that, as the
administrative, political, financial, cultural,
communications, and transportation center of the
country, Christiania's ability to increase its
commercial preponderance and its importance as a
center for industrial development was considerably
enhanced (Myhre, pp. 61-64). While the population
of Christiania grew from 33,000 in 1845 to 100,000
in 1875, 250,000 in 1900, and 330,000 in 1920 (a
tenfold increase), that of Bergen--previously
Norway's largest town and now its second-largest
city--grew only a bit more than fourfold between
1845 and 1920 (from 23,800 in 1845 to 42,200 in
1875, 78,900 in 1900, and 103,500 in 1920). Both
Trondheim and Stavanger grew at rates somewhat
higher than Bergen, but neither came anywhere near
Christiania's tenfold rate of growth (Myhre, p. 72
Table 16).
        Between 1845 and 1900 the population of
Norway's towns and cities grew from 161,875 to
627,650, and the percentage of Norwegians living in
cities and towns grew from 12.2% to 28.0% (Myhre, p.
16 Table 2). This tremendous growth naturally

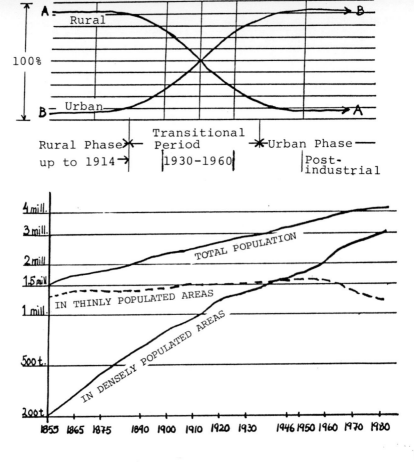

FIGURE 2B   Stages in the Norwegian Urbanization
Process; by Theoretical and Actual
Diagrams.

The first diagram for the theoretical
urbanization process may be regarded as expressing
the transition in terms of people belonging to urban
occupations outnumbering people in rural occupations, or as urban/industrial culture taking over
from rural culture.

The second diagram for the actual urbanization shows an increasing share of the population
living in densely populated areas. (Defined as
built up areas with a population of 200 and more).
Urban population in socioeconomic or cultural terms,
however, exceeds the 70.2% living in densely settled
areas.

Source: Rasmussen (1966) and data from Census 1980
and Historisk Statistikk 1978.

brought with it a complete transformation of urban life in the larger cities and towns such as Christiania, Bergen and Trondheim.

VII. Christiania (Oslo), the Leading City with Emerging Urban Problems

If one considers Christiania--which had the most dramatic increase in population during this period--the following changes would be among the most striking to the resident of that city who had been born there in 1830 and who turned seventy in 1900: the size of the city, the occupational distribution of its citizens, the nature of intra-urban transportation, the growth of public works and the size of the municipal workforce, the trans-formation of the city's social life, and the marked improvement of the material standard of living of most categories of the city's inhabitants. Our imaginary resident's surprise at the nearly eightfold growth of Christiania's population between 1845 and 1900 can easily be understood from the population figures mentioned earlier, but it is useful here to explore the other characteristics of life in Christiania at the turn of the century that would have contrasted so sharply with conditions in 1845.

When our imaginary resident of Christiania was fifteen, the town in which he lived bustled with the activity of merchants, seamen, craftsmen, government civil servants, and the rest of its population, but only a few people were employed in the nascent factories that were developing along the small Akers River on the east side of town. To get from one part of town to another, people either walked or hired a hack, unless they were among the relatively few who were able to maintain their own horse and carriage. Since the great fire of 1624, most buildings in central Christiania had been plastered or built of stone to reduce the risk of fire, and since there was no professional fire department, this remained one of the best defenses against a new catastrophe. When fires did break out, there was no choice but to tap whatever wells, rivers, ponds, or springs that could be had, since 'he city had no water mains to bring fresh water into homes and businesses. For that matter, there were no sewers, either.

With the growth of Norway's population and its resulting increased demand for all sorts of consumer goods, the importing business was growing very rapidly at mid-century. The increase in prosperity that this brought to the local merchants enabled them to hire more help to increase the volume of business they were able to handle, and the subsequent increase in the workforce increased the circulation of money and the demand for goods and services.

As the nascent industries along the Akers River were also hiring more and more workers, housing became difficult to find and more expensive when one did find it, leading several of the wealthier citizens to build and operate apartment buildings to take advantage of this rising demand on the housing market. With the construction of new housing joining the construction of new warehouses and factories, as well as the expansion of government buildings and the remodeling of the homes of many of the wealthier citizens who were profiting from the growth in trade, the construction trades experienced a boom in the second half of the nineteenth century that transformed them into a veritable industry. Many men were recruited from far and near to help build these houses and factories, thus bringing hundreds of more people into the growing city and increasing the demands on housing and other necessities even further.

The threefold growth in population between 1845 and 1875 put tremendous pressures on the ability of the inhabitants to obtain sufficient amounts of fresh water and to dispose of their refuse and their sewage. This caused the city to invest large amounts of money in a system of water and sewage mains, for which it had to hire many workers and raise taxes in order to be able to finance the project (Myhre, pp. 85-87).

In a similar vein, by 1875 it was more and more difficult for people to move around town in a timely manner, since residential and business sections were rapidly becoming segregated from one

31

another. In order for people to arrive at work on time and to devote the major portion of their energy to their jobs, it became necessary--and profitable-- to build a system of horsedrawn streetcars, which was later electrified just before the turn of the century (Myhre, p. 65). Then, too, the growth of the city led many of its more wealthy citizens to seek the calmer and less smokey surroundings offered by suburban areas that could be serviced by the railroads which had recently been built (Try, p. 105). Both streetcar lines and suburban railroad service required drivers, conductors and maintenance workers, thus further increasing the demands for new in-migrants from rural and small-town Norway.

The tens of thousands of new workers moving into the city brought with them not only a need for housing, fresh water, and transportation, but also a need for food and drink. With so many people in Christiania having work schedules and family situations that did not permit them to do their own baking, bakeries in the capital city did a thriving business and began to achieve efficiencies of scale by introducing mass production of bread for distribution to shops that served as retail outlets. This parallels the rise of breweries to produce the beer that was the reliable alternative to both milk and water in an urban setting. The manufacture of beer and bread, their distribution to retail shops, and the retail shops themselves all created a demand for new employees, thus adding to the growth of the city's population and the demands on the city's developing infrastructure of utilities, public transportation, and so on.

No longer was it possible to get by with volunteer firemen and a nominal police force; the growing population and the anonymity of the large city resulted in a higher rate of petty crime and public disorder--thus requiring a professional police force--just as the number of fires and their potential threat to dwellings and workplaces justified the professionalization of fire protection (Myhre, pp. 85-86).

With the great growth in the level of employment, many underemployed or unemployed residents of rural areas began to seek work in the city even when there were no positions available (Fuglum, p. 462). Thus, underemployment and poverty became a problem in Christiania even as the boom continued. Even when one did find work, the level of pay was often lower than would have been the case had the Norwegian population in general not been growing by leaps and bounds (Fuglum, pp. 315-24). Underemployment or unemployment sometimes--i.e., in hundreds of cases--drove women to casual or habitual prostitution, while the same difficulties drove many of both sexes to drown their troubles in alcohol (Semmingsen et al., pp. 123-25, 140).

Both retreats, drink and prostitution, were somewhat easier to cope with because of the anonymity of the city. Yet, this very anonymity was a major problem for new arrivals used to the close-knit and predictable (although not necessarily pleasant) village or farm societies from which they had come. Indeed, Christiania had become a much more anonymous world even for those who, like our imaginary seventy-year-old, had been born in the city, but they--and those who had spent five or more years in the city--were more likely to have found a meaningful context for their lives in an urban neighborhood, in a church congregation, or in a club or labor union (Fuglum, pp. 368-417).

VIII. Emerging Urban Policies Up to 1939

By 1900--and even more so by 1920--life in Christiania and the other larger cities in Norway had grown to resemble what we know as city life much more than it resembled town life in Norway in the mid-nineteenth century. By 1920, too, the political system we know today had emerged and begun to cope with the practical, social, and economic problems presented by the modern city. The need for a rational, long-range approach to city management and urban planning had already made itself evident to many in the professions and in city government, although the ideology of classical economic liberalism--in its reaction against the regulated state of the preceding period--still balked somewhat at any expansion of municipal or state powers.

One area in which the mechanisms of the marketplace had clearly failed to meet the needs of the growing cities was that of housing. Since private construction did not satisfy the growing needs of the working population at an affordable price, the larger cities began in the years after 1903 to stimulate such construction. Finding that even this did not produce the desired results, these municipalities began in the years after 1910 to construct such housing themselves (Valheim, p. 268). It is indeed significant that Harald Hals, the architect of Norway's first garden town at Ullevål Hageby, which was built by the city of Christiania (Oslo) in the late 1910s, came to serve as head of the Oslo city planning office from 1926 until 1947 after first serving as director of housing for the city (from 1918) and for the national government (from 1920) (Brochmann, p. 445).

With the spread of voting rights to adult men in 1898 and to adult women in 1913, the politics of Norwegian cities began to reflect their social composition more directly. In 1915, for example, the socialist parties received 39% of the urban vote, and in 1924 they received 43%. As a result, many new social policies were introduced in cities with strong socialist representation, and the cities began to lead Norway toward what we today refer to as the welfare state (Baldersheim, pp. 17-18).

There was also greater receptivity to the need for city management and urban planning, although the economic crises of the 1920s and 1930s placed serious obstacles in the way of any ambitious urban planning schemes; during the depression years of the 1930s, Oslo even experienced a slight decline in population. The political settlement reached during the mid-1930s between the Labor Party and the Agrarian Party, however, created the necessary political framework within which urban planning could come into its own.

By the late 1930s, Norwegian cities were experiencing the opportunities and problems presented by modern urban life. Communication, sanitation, transportation, housing and social welfare had all become the everyday concerns of city governments over the course of less than a century.

34

Examples of urban planning initiatives in other European countries and the emergence of a broad political base supportive of public policy in the field of urban affairs had paved the way for the development of new urban planning policies, although the economic resources necessary for such initiatives were in short supply because of the depressed economy. In the end, it was the crisis of Germany's wartime occupation of Norway between 1940 and 1945 and the subsequent need to plan for national recovery in the postwar period that ultimately paved the way for urban planning activities in Norway on the scale discussed in the following chapters. (For the political preconditions for these planning policies, see Chapter Eight.)

REFERENCES

Baldersheim, Harald (ed.). Bypolitikk i Norge. Historie, planlegging styring, framtid (Oslo: Gyldendal Norsk Forlag, 1983)

Benedictow, Ole Jørgen. Fra rike til provins 1448-1536, Vol. 5 of Knut Mykland (ed.), Norges historie (Oslo: J. W. Cappelens forlag, 1977)

Brochmann, Odd. "Harald Hals," in Olaf Kortner et al. (eds.), Aschehougs og Gyldendals Store norske leksikon, Vol. 5 (Oslo: 1979)

Byplankontoret i Kristiansand. Forslag til Sentrumsplan for Kristiansand. (Kristiansand: Byplankontoret, 1978)

Fladby, Rolf. Gjenreisning 1536-1648, Vol. 6 of Knut Mykland (ed.), Norges historie (Oslo: J. W. Cappelens forlag, 1977)

Fuglum, Per. Norge i støpeskjeen 1884-1920, Vol. 12 of Knut Mykland (ed.), Norges historie (Oslo: J. W. Cappelens forlag, 1978)

Gunnes, Erik. Rikssamling og kristning 800–1177,
Vol. 2 of Knut Mykland (ed.), Norges historie
(Oslo: J. W. Cappelens forlag, 1976)

Helle, Knut & Nedkvitne, Arne. "Sentrumsdannelser
og byutvikling i norsk middelalder," in Grethe
Authén Blom (ed.), Urbaniseringsprosessen i
Norden, Vol. 1 Middelaldersteder (Oslo:
Universitetsforlaget, 1977)

Lunden, Kåre. Norge under Sverreaetten 1177–1319,
Vol. 3 of Knut Mykland (ed.), Norges historie
(Oslo: J. W. Cappelens forlag, 1976)

Myhre, Jan Eivind. "Urbaniseringen i Norge i
industrialiseringens første fase ca. 1850–
1914," in Grethe Authén Blom (ed.),
Urbaniseringsprosessen i Norden, Vol. 3
Industrialiseringens første fase (Oslo:
Universitets-forlaget, 1977)

Sejersted, Francis. Den vanskelige frihet 1814–
1851, Vol. 10 of Knut Mykland (ed.), Norges
historie (Oslo: J. W. Cappelens forlag, 1978)

Semmingsen, Ingrid et al. (eds.) Brytningsår
blomstringstid, Vol. 5 of Norges kultur-
historie (Oslo: 1980)

Sogner, Bjørn. "De 'anlagte' byer i Norge," in
Grethe Authén Blom (ed.), Urbaniseringsprosessen in Norden, Vol. 2. De anlagte
steder på 1600–1700 tallet (Oslo:
Universitetsforlaget, 1977)

Try, Hans. To kulturer-En stat 1851–1884, Vol. 11
of Knut Mylkand (ed.), Norges historie (Oslo:
J. W. Cappelens forlag, 1979)

Valheim, Ragnald. "Boligpolitikk," in Olaf Kortner
et al. (eds.), Aschehougs og Gyldendals
Store norske leksikon, Vol. 2 (Oslo: 1978)

CHAPTER THREE: POST-WAR URBANIZATION IN TWENTIETH CENTURY NORWAY: THE EMERGING HABITAT AND BACKGROUND FORCES

"Human settlements embody a nation's social, economic and environmental attributes. They also symbolize a nation's political will and cultural heritage." (United Nation's Recommendations for National Action. In preparation for Habitat Conference, 1976.)

I. A Conceptual Framework: Five Main Regions and a Number of City Regions.

In the preceding chapter, urbanization of Norway was described in the context of a long historical development indicating some of the important influences of the medieval, the pre-industrial modern, and the later industrial periods on the shape and character of Norway's developing urban life. As in other parts of the world, the spatial form and the cultural character of urban life as shaped by the medieval and industrial influences are rapidly being transformed in contemporary Norway. The historic centripetal movement of people into a few leading urban centers is being followed by a centrifugal movement into the peripheral areas surrounding the central cities. In other words, contemporary Norway is experiencing a "new urbanization" similar to that of other countries of Europe, and shares with them a similar preoccupation with the problems and possibilities associated with expanding metro-urban regions (Berry 1973, pp. 142-143). Since many of modern Norway's urban and environmental policies are prompted by this "new urbanization" it is important to understand some of its major attributes.

The most comprehensive description of this development in Norway has been made by Tor Rasmussen in his book, Byregioner i Norge: Den Regionale Konsentrasjon i Bosettingsmønsteret, published in 1969 (Rasmussen 1969). In this book, and subsequent writings, Professor Rasmussen has made a penetrating analysis of the transformation of Norway's settlement patterns in the twentieth century. Because of his broad experience in teaching and research in both Norway and Sweden as well as the U.S.A., his analysis sheds light on both the similarities and contrasts between the urban developments in Norway and other parts of Scandinavia and the Western World.

The uniqueness of the Scandinavian approach, according to Rasmussen, is reflected in the kinds of regional levels that have been developed in the Nordic countries. The regional divisions found most helpful have been, first, a division of the country into three to six main regions, and secondly, a sub-division of those into a number of "city regions" (Rasmussen 1979, p. 401). In the case of Norway, the country is divided into five main regions, which reflect both the physiographical and socio-cultural distinctions among them. Each has its own identity and specialized economic functions within the Norwegian economy (Rasmussen 1979, pp. 403-4). Each main region contains several counties, which have become increasingly important for regional planning, as well as a number of expanding "city-regions." Figure 3A provides a helpful visual picture of the five main regions and the leading city-regions of the country.

Although there is some variation among scholars concerning the criteria used for delineating city regions, Rasmussen's criteria serve well the purposes of this book. The 21 city regions that are indicated on the map consist of one or more central cores with a commuting hinterland extending outward 25 to 30 kilometers from those centers. All of these city regions contain 30,000 or more inhabitants. Nine of those city regions are relatively small, with populations from 30,000 to 50,000 inhabitants. six have populations from 50,000 to 100,000, and six have populations over 100,000. Because Norway's definition of city regions includes all urban areas with 10,000 or more inhabitants, the map might also have included thirteen additional city regions. Even though they are not indicated on the map, Rasmussen has taken them into account in his analysis of Norway's urban and regional development.

39

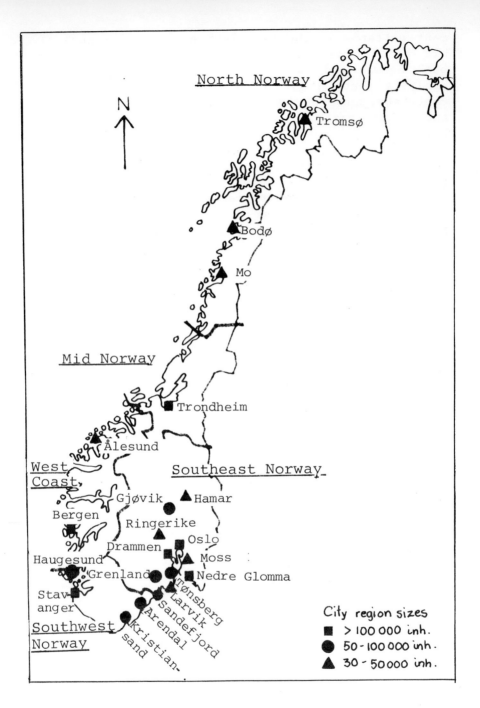

FIGURE 3A   Five Main Regions in Norway and City
            Regions with more than 30,000 Inhabitants

II.   Population Growth Among the Main Regions

Since one of the most controversial policy questions in postwar Norway has been focused on the twin problems of declining populations in some regions and the rapid growth of others, Rasmussen has examined both the comparative growth of the five main regions as well as of the urban areas within those regions. Table 3.1 presents a summary of his findings concerning the proportion of Norway's population and growth rate within the five main regions of Norway from 1910 to 1980.

TABLE 3.1   Distribution of Population in Norway within Five Main Regions 1910-1980

Region	Proportion of Population					Annual Rate of Growth (%)			
	1910	1950	1960	1970	1980	1910-1950	1951-1960	1961-1970	1971-1980
South East	46.7	48.3	48.7	49.1	48.6	1.04	1.04	0.88	0.38
South West	12.5	11.7	11.8	12.2	12.8	0.71	1.05	1.33	1.14
West Coast	19.1	18.3	18.2	18.0	18.0	0.78	0.9	0.65	0.48
Middle Norway	9.8	9.4	9.1	9.1	9.1	0.80	0.67	0.67	0.48
Northern Norway	11.9	12.3	12.2	11.7	11.5	1.05	0.82	0.36	0.32
Percent	100	100	100	100	100	0.93	0.96	0.82	0.49
Population	2,391,782		3,591,234		4,035,365				

Source: Rasmussen, Tor. The Distribution of Population in Norway (1979) and later additions for 1980.

In the light of the controversy over unbalanced regional growth, it is interesting to note that the percentage distribution of the population among the main regions of Norway has remained rather stable throughout the twentieth century. Professor Rasmussen observes that compared to other Nordic countries this is rather remarkable. He notes that Finland and Sweden had substantial population drain from the forested northern areas to the south and that Denmark had a drain from the agricultural areas of the north and from west Jutland, to Copenhagen and East Jutland (Rasmussen 1979, p. 404). It is likely that Norway's fishing

41

industry and other coastal activities have provided
a better base for local development than the
agricultural and forest industries of the other
countries.

But despite this relative stability of
Norway's regional population distribution, a closer
examination of each of the main regions reveal
striking--and from the Norwegian perspective--
troublesome differences. Southeast Norway, consisting of 8 counties and by far the largest number
of city regions has contained close to 50% of
Norway's population throughout the twentieth century. Its percentage of Norway's population shows
some sign of receding, however, during the decade of
the 1970s. Southwest Norway lost part of its population during the depression years after World
War I, when its shipping industry declined and
larger shipping companies in Oslo took leadership in
the industry. But during the decades of the 1960s
and the 1970s this region has bounced back and
experienced the highest average annual population
growth of all of Norway.

The West Coast with three counties, Mid-
Norway with two counties, and North Norway with
three counties, are the regions where economic
growth has been considered most inadequate. But, as
Professor Rasmussen points out, they too have
nevertheless succeeded fairly well in keeping their
share of the country's population (Rasmussen 1979,
p. 404).

III.   Population Growth in City Regions

It is when one examines the population growth
in Norway's city regions that one gets the clearest
picture of the nature and extent of Norway's
twentieth century urbanization. Table 3.2 provides
a helpful summary of this urban growth.

As the data indicate, the twelve larger city
regions with over 50,000 inhabitants have absorbed
most of the increase in Norway's urban population.
They increased their share of the nation's popula-
lation from 39.9% in 1910 to 50.2% in 1980. The
percent of Norway's population living in urban
centers increased from 51.7% in 1910 to 70.0% in

TABLE 3.2   Population Growth Rate and Proportion of
             Population in the Urbanized Areas of
             Norway 1910–1980

	Population Number			Percent of Population in Whole Country			Rate of Growth(%) Annual Average	
							1961-1971-	
	1910	1970	1980	1910	1970	1980	1970	1980
12 largest city regions (more than 50,000)	955,367	1,948,863	1,047,124	39.9	50.0	50.2	1.4	0.5
18 medium sized city regions (20,000-50,000)	249,463	512,121	544,224	10.5	13.2	13.3	1.3	0.6
5 smaller city regions (10,000-20,000)	31,409	73,676	76,589	1.3	1.9	1.9	0.7	0.4
25 fringe municipalities		163,762	185,849		4.3	4.6		1.4
Total	1,236,239	2,698,422	2,853,786	51.7	69.4	70.0	1.4	0.6
Population in 10 new smaller city regions		147,773	166,604		3.8	4.0		1.3
Population of the rest of Norway (Rural Norway)	1,155,543	1,042,113	1,058,510	48.3	26.8	26.0	-0.9	0.1
The Whole Country	2,391,782	3,888,308	4,078,900	100	100	100	0.8	0.5

Source: Rasmussen 1979, p. 409 and later additions
           for 1980.

1980.   After 1970 their rate of annual growth has
declined somewhat, giving rise to considerable
discussion concerning its portent for the future.
Some interpret it as a reaction against urbanization
and a desire to return to smaller rural and more
romantic settlements.   The data do not, however,
strongly support such a thesis.   The percentage of
the population in the "rest of Norway," i.e., the

43

unurbanized part, continued to decline rather than increase.

What appears to be happening is that more people are becoming residents of the medium and smaller city regions. This gives continued support to Professor Hallstein Myklebost's thesis that one of the distinctive features of urbanization in Norway has been an expansion of many rather small places throughout the country; and that "the strongest growth takes place in peripheral areas where the degree of urbanization has been low." Professor Myklebost had found this trend toward the expansion of smaller city regions beginning as early as the decade of the 1950s (Myklebost 1968). As will be noted later, this kind of urban development is in harmony with official Norwegian policies. What is not as compatible with those policies is the increasing growth of the fringe municipalities around the larger urban centers that has occurred in recent decades.

The demographic trends of the 1970s do indicate that the process of urban concentration was slower than that of the previous decades. This is partly a reflection of a declining population growth in the country as a whole from an annual rate of growth of 0.8% in the decade of 1960s to a rate of only 0.5% in the 1970s. It is also evident that commuting has increased greatly in recent years, so that many people are living outside the boundaries drawn for the city regions. The largest cities of Oslo and Bergen have experienced a less than average increase, while the medium-sized cities have experienced a strong increase. This is likely influenced by a Norwegian preference for such cities as well as by the national policies of decentralizing public services and administrative structures. This is particularly evident in the county capitals of the country.

It is, of course, obvious that the city regions vary greatly in size, and considerably in the rate of growth. Table 3.3 provides a detailed picture of those variations among Norway's largest city regions. The largest metro-urban region is that of Oslo, whose population of 848,091 in 1980 made up approximately 20.7% of all of Norway's urban

TABLE 3.3   Population and Growth Rate 1910 - 1980
             for City Regions with more than 30,000
             Inhabitants in 1980

Population — Growth rate — Annual Average (%)				
	1980	1911–1950	1951–1960	1961–1970	1971–1980
Oslo	848,091	1.4	1.5	1.3	0.2
Bergen	250,320	1.3	1.5	1.4	0.3
Stavanger	170,571	1.5	1.8	1.7	1.5
Trondheim	157,182	1.4	1.4	2.1	0.7
Drammen	113,538	0.9	1.2	1.3	1.0
Nedre Glomma	109,934	0.5	1.2	1.0	0.2
Skien/Porsgrunn	93,773	0.9	1.8	1.3	0.5
Kristiansand	82,013	1.4	2.5	2.2	1.0
Haugesund	58,831	1.2	7.3	7.2	0.7
Tönsberg	58,287	1.1	1.4	1.1	0.4
Gjövik	53,481	1.2	0.9	0.8	0.5
Arendal	52,103	1.0	0.5	1.1	1.1
City Regions over 50,000	2,047,124	1.2	1.4	1.4	0.5
Tromsø	45,833	1.1	1.9	2.7	1.7
Ålesund	43,497	1.1	1.7	1.1	0.6
Hamar	42,554	0.9	1.1	1.2	0.1
Moss	41,938	1.5	2.0	2.3	0.7
Larvik	35,202	0.5	1.0	0.9	0.4
Sandefjord	34,758	1.9	1.7	1.0	0.8
Bodö	32,567	1.4	4.0	2.4	1.2
Ringerike	30,883	0.7	1.3	0.7	0.6
Mo	30,835	2.0	3.8	2.7	0.1
City Regions 30,000-50,000	338,073	1.1	1.7	1.3	0.6
City Regions over 30,000	2,385,197				

Source: Rasmussen 1979, p. 408 and later additions
          for 1980

45

population. While it has grown steadily throughout the twentieth century, there is evidence of a declining growth rate in the 1970s.

The next three in size--Bergen, Stavanger, and Trondheim with a total population of 578,073 inhabitants in 1981--contain about 14% of Norway's total population. Together with Kristiansand in Southwest Norway and Tromsø in North Norway, they serve as the dominant urban centers of their respective counties. Several other city regions throughout Norway have experienced growth not unlike that of these regional capitals. Some have even exceeded their growth rate, providing evidence of dispersed urbanization in the country.

Altogether, the city regions over 30,000 inhabitants account for 58.5% of Norway's population in 1980. It appears that the process of concentration has been slower in the decade of the 1970s than in previous years. While there was an absolute decline of the rural population from 1961 to 1970, this was reversed to a very slight increase during the decade of the 1970s. This is likely explained by increased long-distance commuting to city centers, since in terms of life style, consumption patterns, and other urbanizing attributes, Norway is more urbanized than ever.

IV.   Urbanization and the Five Main Regions of Norway.

The extent of urbanization varies considerably among the five main regions of Norway. As would be expected, Southeast Norway which hosts the nation's capital is by far the most urbanized, with about 85% of its population residing in urban settings. The extent of urbanization decreases steadily as one moves from East and South to West and North, until one reaches North Norway where only about 28% of its population in 1960 lived in the city regions, as over against 73% in Southeast Norway at that time (Rasmussen 1969, p. 58). Figure 3B provides a helpful graphic illustration of these regional differences in urban growth.

As already noted, in North Norway only about 28% lived in city regions. It should also be noted

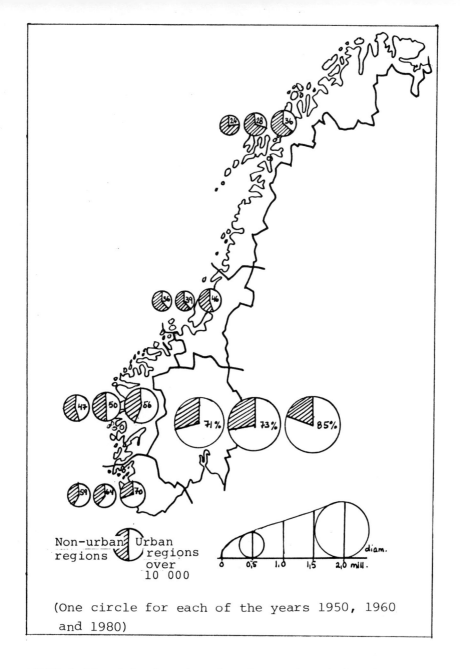

Non-urban regions

Urban regions over 10 000

(One circle for each of the years 1950, 1960 and 1980)

FIGURE 3B   Urbanization in Five Main Regions as identified by number of people living in city regions in percentage of total population in respective regions.

that those city regions are relatively small. The
largest, Tromsø, had a population of only 27,000
inhabitants in 1960. What is interesting however,
is that this city region north of the Arctic Circle
continued to grow until it reached 45,833 inhabitants by 1980. A similar relatively strong growth
has occurred in such other city regions of North
Norway as Bodø, Mo, and Harstad which by 1980 had
populations of 32,567, 30,835 and 27,605 respectively. As Professor Rasmussen has noted, it is the
economic vitality of its city regions that has made
it possible for North Norway to preserve its percentage share of the nation's population. That
part of North Norway that falls outside of the six
city regions of more than 10,000 inhabitants has
declined (Rasmussen 1969, p. 63).

Moving southward to Mid-Norway, one finds
that the urban population had reached 39% by 1960
with projected upward growth to 46% by 1980. The
principal city region here is, of course, Trondheim,
with a population of 121,116 in 1960 and which grew
to a population of 157,181 by 1980. The other city
region was Steinkjer which had a population of
20,509 by 1980. As in North Norway, those city
regions increased on the average of 13% every decade
between 1910 and 1960 compared with an average 4.1%
per decade for the rest of Mid-Norway.

West Norway is more urban than either North
Norway or Mid-Norway. By 1960 about 50% of its
population was urban. The largest of its city
regions is Bergen with a population of 213,349 in
1960 and 250,320 by 1980. The other city regions
with populations of over 20,000 are Ålesund,
Kristiansund, and Molde. In this part of Norway
too, the growth of its city regions played the most
important role in keeping the region's percentage of
the nation's population at a relatively stable
level.

Southwest Norway's growth of the urban
population comes closest to that of Southeast
Norway, reaching about 64% by 1960. According to
Rasmussen, this region has experienced the most
concentration of its population in a few city
regions. The leading city is Stavanger, which has
in recent decades become the nation's oil capital.

48

It is now Norway's third largest city region with a population of 170,571 inhabitants in 1980. The second largest city region of Southwest Norway is Kristiansand which by 1980 reached a population of 82,013 inhabitants. Haugesund with a population of 58,837 and Arendal with 52,103 inhabitants constitute the other two principal city regions. In Southwest Norway, too, it has been the city regions that have experienced by far the greatest population growth.

V.   Urbanization of 1970s

As noted earlier, demographic data indicate that by 1970 the concentration of Norway's population into urban centers may have largely come to an end. While the predominant part of Norway's population growth in the 1960s had occurred in its urban centers, this part declined to 81% for the period from 1970-74 and to 65% from 1975-77. In 1978 the city regions absorbed only about 44% of the nation's population growth. It appears that municipalities outside of the urban centers are now experiencing the fastest growth. Most central cities are experiencing declines which are not fully compensated for by the population growth in their inner ring of suburbs (Helvig 1979, p. 216). Magne Helvig, professor of Geography at the University of Bergen's Geographical Institute, suggests that what is happening in present-day Norway may not be too unlike what is occurring in other western countries as described in Charles L. Leven's book The Mature Metropolis (Leven 1978). In his study of Bergen, he documents a centrifugal population shift from the central city to its expanding metropolitan periphery, including increasingly urbanized municipalities beyond boundaries of the Bergen city region (Helvig 1979). Similar developments are occurring in most of the other city regions.

These developments of the 1970s have caused some to challenge the assumption of "inevitable urbanization" and argue that Norway is experiencing a bit of a rural renaissance. Others, such as Tor Rasmussen, suggest that the changing settlement patterns of the 1970s can best be interpreted as an expansion or penetration of urban life further into the peripheries of the city regions of the country. He suggested that a good case can be made for the claim that even the 25% of Norwegians living in the so-called non-urbanized part of Norway have also become urbanized (Rasmussen 1977). Many of them are likely to be related in some way to one of the city regions developing throughout the nation.

VI.   Tertiary Activities and the New Industrialization

To understand the reasons for the concentration of Norway's population into urban-centered regions, it is necessary to examine some of the major economic, technological, and socio-cultural changes that have led to the transformation of the country's habitat.

As has already been noted, one of the most general economic changes has been the transformation of the occupational structure, i.e., the sharp decline in the number of people engaged in the primary industries of farming, fishing, and forestry and even more precipituous increase in the number of people engaged in such tertiary industries as commerce, transportation, and other service industries. As can be seen from Table 3.4 the percentage of people engaged in the primary industries dropped from 35.3% in 1930 to 11.6% in 1970, while the percentage engaged in the tertiary industries increased from 38.2% to 51.1%.

These data indicate clearly the dramatic decline in the number of people engaged in the primary industries and the sharp increase in the number of people engaged in governmental services, education, commerce, communications and other public and private service occupations. These trends continued in the 1970s so that by 1980 only 8% were engaged in primary occupations, and 62.7% in the tertiary. In the secondary industries--i.e., manufacturing--the percentages rose sharply from 26.5% in 1930 to 36.4% in 1950. From that time it grew only slightly to 37.4% by 1970, after which it began to decline again to 29.3% by 1980.

50

TABLE 3.4 Occupational Populations in three Main Groupings in 1930, 1950 1970 and 1980.

Industries/ Sectors	Numbers			Per cent			
	1930	1950	1970	1930	1950	1970	1980*
Primary	412,341	359,575	170,019	35.3	25.8	11.6	8.0
Secondary	309,813	506,680	545,228	26.5	36.4	37.3	29.3
Tertiary	445,360	527,437	746,912	38.2	37.9	51.1	62.7

* In 1980, the definition of occupational population was changed to also include part-time workers, which gives a larger number of occupied persons than in previous censuses. However, the percentage distribution between the three sectors may still be compared with previous censuses.

Source: Census Reports

In describing these dramatic structural changes in Norway's economic and occupational life, Jan Christian Eckhoff has noted their striking similarities with changes occurring in Sweden, Great Britain and the U.S.A. These similarities support the thesis that even if the size and scale of metro-urban developments in Norway are smaller than that of most urbanized western nations, the substantive socio-economic and cultural realities of urbanization are similar (Eckhoff 1969, pp. 19-21). Although the growth of tertiary industries constitutes the major distinctive occupational concomitant of contemporary urbanization, it is important to note some changes in the secondary industries that contribute to Norway's emerging urban habitat. One of the most important influences has been the harnessing of its vast water resources for the development of a highly efficient hydro-electric energy system. "Harnessing the water to turn turbines and spark generators," say Jerman and Nyquist, "is Norway's major modern adventure, involving thousands of engineers and construction workers . . ." (Jerman and Nyquist 1970, p. 22). It has been an adventure of immensely complex and highly technical engineering achievements in a wide variety of topographical and geological conditions.

51

One index of the success of this development is the fact that this small nation of approximately 4 million people is second only to the Soviet Union in terms of hydro-electric power production in Europe.

This vast new energy resource has altered virtually every arena of Norway's economic life, including the production, processing, and distribution technologies related to such historic industries as agriculture, forestry, fishing and international trade. Of particular importance to this study of modern urbanization, however, are the new industrial spin-offs from the hydro-electric energy system. One such spin-off has been the development of the electrometallurgical industries. Metals now rank first among the exports from Norway. Such exports are principally ferro-silicon and other ferro-alloys, iron and steel, aluminum, copper, zinc, and most recently, magnesium. Already Norway ranks among the world's biggest exporters of ferro-silicon, aluminum, and magnesium (Royal Ministry of Foreign Affairs 1969, Reference Paper No. 213). It has the largest output in Western Europe of ferro-silicon, ferro-silicon-manganese and silicon carbide (Royal Norwegian Ministry of Industry 1975, p. 27).

A similar hydro-electric spin-off has been the growth of Norway's electro-chemical industries. The Nation's leading industrial firm, Norsk Hydro, was launched from this development. It reported a year's production of 443,000 tons of nitrogen in 1967. Nitrogen products on this basis were: 899,000 tons of calcium nitrate, 588,000 tons of complex fertilizers, 179,000 tons of urea, 60,000 tons of liquid ammonia, 23,000 tons of ammonium nitrate, and 15,000 tons of nitric acid. (Royal Ministry of Foreign Affairs 1968, No. 212). In its annual report for 1978/79 Norsk Hydro's Nitrogen division registered a sales volume of nearly 54 million dollars.

Norsk Hydro's influence is felt throughout Norway, providing evidence of the importance of hydro-electric power for the decentralization of both industry and urban settlements. In the far north, its Glomford factory is the main supplier of fertilizers for the domestic market. In 1978, this

52

factory employed 585 people. On the west coast, its large aluminum plant at Karmøy has a production capacity of 110,000 tons of light aluminum a year, and as of 1978 had 1,300 employees. Its factory complex in Porsgrunn at Herøya in Telemark, with about 4,600 employees, is now Norway's largest industrial complex. Its most important products are fertilizers, magnesium, and PVC resins. In the small city of Rjukan, snuggled in a deep and narrow mountain valley of Telemark, Norsk Hydro produces electric power, ammonia, and ammonium nitrate. The total number of Hydro employees at Rjukan was 770 in 1978.

In recent years Norsk Hydro has taken part in the exploration for oil and gas in the North Sea and is now co-owner of several oil and gas finds. Out of this modern energy source, the company has launched new ventures in various petro-chemical activities, including a refinery at Mongstad in North Hordaland, and a petrochemical plant at Rafnes in Telemark. Hydro's national office is located at Oslo, where all its activities are coordinated. They are organized into the following seven special divisions: aluminum, electric power, engineering, magnesium, nitrogen, petroleum, and petro-chemicals. Beyond Norway, Norsk Hydro has an extensive foreign market and is engaged in productive activities in Denmark, Sweden, Great Britain, Spain, Hong Kong, Brazil, and the U.S.A. (Norsk-Hydro No. 4, 1978).

The preceding litany about Norsk Hydro was presented to illustrate two main points: one, the dynamism of Hydro-electric power, which has provided the basis for Norway's "new industrialism"; and two, the consequence of this energy system for decentralized urbanization into many relatively small city regions throughout the country.

Closely rivaling Norsk Hydro's status as Norway's largest industrial firm is Elkem, the world's largest company engaged in ferro-alloys. Founded in 1904 for the purpose of utilizing water power for the creaton of industry on a large scale, it pioneered in developing new processes and techniques for harnessing Norway's enormous hydro-electric energy resources. One of its early successes, the Soderberg electrode, has made it the

world's largest supplier of electric furnaces for
the smelting industries. Besides its extensive
steel mills, Elkem has become one of the world's
leading ferro-alloy concerns in the world market.
Among its products are ferro-silicon, silicon metal,
manganese alloys, and electrode paste for the
smelting furnaces.

Its steadily increasing and highly diversified activities have thrust it into extensive
international economic involvements. It owns or has
substantial stock holdings in 40 production plants
in Norway, Denmark, Iceland, Great Britain, the
Netherlands, the United States, and Brazil. In 1981
it purchased five Union Carbide Corporation ferro-
alloy plants in the United States and Norway, and
has set up an Elkem Metals Company subsidiary in
the United States. With nearly 10,000 employees,
Elkem has become one of Norway's biggest employers
of an increasingly sophisticated work force (Skog
1981, pp. 94-96 and "Metallurgical Industry in
Norway" 1981, p. 33).

There are, of course, many other modern
industrial corporations who have had similar
influences on Norway's urban life. Perhaps no
industrial spin-off from the hydro-electric
techno-culture has played a greater role in
transforming Norway's social relations and life
styles than the development of electronic and
telecomunications industries. Norway's entry into
these fields after World War II symbolized the
country's shift from an economy relying primarily on
the production of raw materials and semifinished
goods to one increasingly dependent on turning out
and marketing sophisticated consumer products, such
as radios, televisions, tape recorders, computers,
and a wide variety of other electronic devices.
Their impact on Norway's communication system has,
of course, been very important. The development of
a national radio and television system has served to
break down the physical barriers that had separated
Norwegians and their communities from each other for
centuries (Jerman and Nyquist 1970, pp. 104-111).

Without attempting to document all the
consequences of these industrial developments on
Norway's life, a few comments concerning their

influence on urbanization are relevant for this study. In the first place, they have provided greatly expanded work opportunities in Norway's industrial communities. Secondly, because of the distributive nature of electric energy, new factories have been widely dispersed throughout the country, thereby contributing to the vitality of regional urban growth centers in many parts of Norway. Furthermore, the highly technical aspects of the "new industrialization" have led to an ever increasing demand for highly trained technical personnel to design, manage, and operate the new power-intensive industries. The related engineering industries, for example, employed about a third of all the industrial workers of Norway by 1973 (Royal Norwegian Ministry of Industry 1975, Report No. 67., p. 28). People employed in these, as well as the other new power-intensive industrial activities have become "new artisans" requiring new education and training.

With the discovery and development of the rich oil resources of the North sea, another new "power-intensive" industrial development has been added to Norway's socioeconomic milieu. Some perception of its impact can be gleaned from the fact that the production of crude oil from the Norwegian sector of the North Sea Continental Shelf grew from less than 2 million tons in 1974 to 17 million tons in 1978 and 30 million tons in 1983. Natural gas production increased from 3 billion normal cubic meters in 1977 to 15 billion in 1978 and 26 billion in 1983 (Statistisk Sentralbyra Årbok 1984). Since only 5% of the Norwegian Continental Shelf has so far been explored, this production is but the beginning of Norway's entry into the age of oil. Parliamentary sources estimate that the petroleum sector will generate one-tenth of Norway's GNP by the mid-1980s. This estimate was based on the assumption of a moderate petroleum production growth to around 90 million tons a year (Interna-tional Herald Tribune October, 1979).

The impact of this new industry is most dramatically evident in the city region of Stavanger on Norway's west coast. From a relatively serene historic sea coast fishing and sailing center, it has been catapulted into a throbbing international city. People from 74 nations now have their homes in Stavanger, numbering 6,000 foreigners and 81,000 natives. Perhaps in no city region in Norway can the transformation of urban life be more dramatically witnessed today than in this relatively small Stavanger metropolis. The capital-intensive oil activities have added a new dimension to its economy, increased the demand for new technical and economic knowledge, and given impetus to a campaign for transforming Stavanger's regional college into a national university with special research and educational programs related to the oil industry (Hatløy 1978, pp. 10-13).

But the spin-offs are not limited to Stavanger. The building of off-shore oil drilling platforms and all the other technical equipment needed for the new industry, plus the development of refineries and other petro-chemical activities, have brought new related industrial ventures to other urban areas as well.

All these industrial developments have led to an expansion of both theoretical and applied scientific research. Such research activities have been typically organized as partnership ventures between industrial firms and institutions of higher learning together with considerable support from public funding. The Norwegian Central Institute for Industrial Research is an example. Since these activities are closely related to institutions of higher learning, the industries involved have sometimes been referred to as "intelligence industries." People who are active in them have, of course, become part of that growing number of Norwegians engaged in the tertiary sector of the economy.

VII. Education, Specialization, and Social Mobility

The inevitable dependence of the new industrialism's technology upon science and an increasingly skilled labor force had important consequences for the entire educational system of Norway. Higher education expanded its basic programs in all the sciences, both at the leading universities and at new and expanded colleges and technical institutes. Elementary and secondary schools were altered and expanded to prepare a growing number of young people for admission to these new programs in higher education. As Professor Rasmussen has pointed out, these educational developments had a two-sided impact on settlements in Norway. In the first place, communities large enough to host what the Norwegians now call the "Videregående Skole," including both the historic "realgymnasium" and the vocationally-oriented trade schools, became increasingly important. In the past, it was thought a "gymnas" district ought to have a population between 20 to 30,000 inhabitants. Since the number pursuing "gymnas" and technical trade schools has increased sharply, their locations enhance the importance of the larger city centers (Rasmussen 1969, pp. 114-115).

In like manner, the increasing importance of higher education has led to the establishment of more institutions of higher learning. As part of its national policy of providing equal opportunity in education in all parts of the country, Norway has established "distrikthøgskoler" (regional colleges) strategically dispersed throughout the country. The map in Figure 3C shows the distribution of the first eleven such colleges. Each of the cities in which they are located have become growth centers, partly because of their location. In 1975 these new colleges were brought into a national regional college system, into which the previously established teacher training colleges, technical colleges and social work colleges were incorporated. In 1981, health service training was also incorporated into the system, so that the total number of institutions with formal regional college status reached about 150 (News of Norway. Vol. 41, No. 3, 1984).

In addition to these colleges, Norway supports post-graduate universities at Tromsø in North Norway, Trondheim, Bergen, and Oslo. The decision to launch a university and a medical school in Tromsø is a striking example of how Norway treats locational planning of educational institutions as

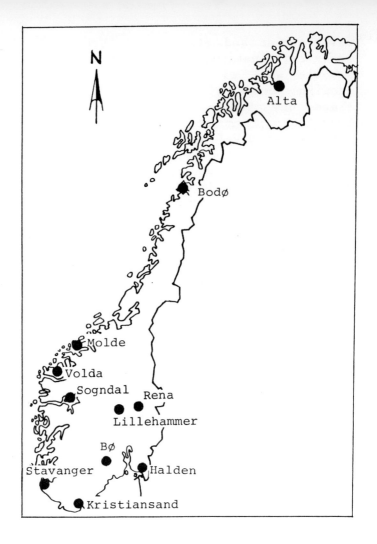

FIGURE 3C Eleven Regional Colleges (Distrikt-shøgskoler) were established in the years 1969-1980 in order to provide institutions for higher education outside the four university cities (Oslo, Bergen, Trondheim, Tromsø). The "Distrikt-shøgskole" in Stavanger is gradually being upgraded to a technical university while that in Bodø is being upgraded to a business school.

58

part of its regional policy. All these educational institutions tended to promote the growth of urban centers.

The second impact that Rasmussen noted, is that young people who have acquired advanced professional and technical education inevitably seek employment not typically found in the smaller scattered settlements of the country. Smaller centers simply cannot provide the variety of employment opportunities for specialists that the larger centers can. The result is a growing concentration of professional and technical elites in the larger urban centers that runs somewhat counter to some of Norway's democratic ideals. What has been said about professionalization in education and research also applies to the fields of public health and social services that have developed in modern Norway. As in other parts of the western world, the organizational structures and profes- sional services of the growing public sector of socioeconomic life contribute greatly to the tertiary occupations characteristically found in urban centers.

Another concomitant of greater specialization and an increasingly skilled labor force has been a rapid growth of Norway's gross national produc- tivity. Professor Greve noted that between 1950 and 1963, its GNP (at constant prices) rose by 67.7%--an average of 2.8% a year from 1900 to 1950 (Greve 1969, p. 12). This growth in GNP, he noted, was translated into increased spending and related changes in consumer wants and life styles. The biggest increase in spending was on goods and services which most people had hitherto regarded as luxuries or semi-luxuries. Spending on things related to leisure-time activities, such as motor cars, boats and camping paraphernalia increased sharply. Travel and transport, leisure and educa- tion were the areas where the sharpest increase in consumer spending occurred. The spending for home furnishings and equipment also rose sharply. Such increases in consumer spending have continued ever since. Professor Greve is no doubt right in saying that Norway "has entered a new era and people are crowding to join the revolution of rising expectations" (Greve 1969, pp. 12-13).

The "revolution of rising expectations" was also reflected in the distribution and use of the health and welfare services that developed out of Norway's commitment to the values of a "welfare state." Here, too, specialization and increasing technical and professional expertise have made larger urban centers more attractive to both practioners and their potential clients.

All of the above-mentioned factors have contributed to an increased social mobility in modern Norway, both vertical and horizontal. And what is perhaps most important for an understanding of the dynamics of metro-urban development, all have contributed importantly to the growing geographical migration from scattered small rural settlements to more concentrated regional urban centers throughout the country (Rasumssen 1969, pp. 117-121).

VIII. Compelling Challenges of Twentieth Century Urbanization

Virtually every aspect of Norway's life has been influenced by the changes associated with twentieth century urbanization. Where people live, how they make their living, what they expect out of life, what happens to their family relationships, where and when they go to school--all these and many other personal concerns have been affected by the transformation. The impact on the public life of the nation has perhaps been even more dramatic. The expanding urban areas have spilled-out over historic municipal boundaries; threatening to absorb lands formerly used for agriculture, forestry, or attractive recreational open spaces. Every major city since World War II has faced the problem of housing its growing populations and providing the social services and community amenities demanded by a citizenry of ever-increasing living standards and life expectations. The remote regions of the country are faced with problems of declining populations, diminishing opportunities, and all the other traumatic pains associated with community decline.

The following chapter will examine how modern Norway has responded to these complex and compelling challenges of urbanization: how it has fashioned national policies for guiding urban growth; how it has developed regional and municipal structures for governance, planning and community building throughout the country; how it sought to protect the country's rich environmental resources from the potentially destructive forces of technological growth and urban expansion; and how it has sought to secure for the people of every region of the nation all of the basic human needs articulated by its welfare-oriented social democratic philosophy.

REFERENCES

Berry, Brian J. L. 1973. The Human Consequences of Urbanization. New York: St. Martin's Press.

Eckhoff, Jan Christian 1969. Byplan: Norske Bysamfunn i Vekst-Mot Hva? Oslo: Pax Forlag.

Greve, John 1965. Boligpolitikk og Økonomisk Vekst. Oslo: Norges Byggforskningsinstitutt.

Greve, John 1969. Housing, Planning and Change in Norway. Oslo: Norwegian Building Research Institute.

Hatløy, Odd 1978. "We Must Make Good Use of Our Opportunities." Norsk Hydro Nr. 4. Oslo: Norsk Hydro.

Helvig, Magne 1979. "Byene Blir Stadig Mer Problemfylde." Bedriftsøkonomen Nr. 4

International Herald Tribune, October 1979. "Norway's Entry Into Age of Oil." Special October Edition on "Scandinavia: Banking and Finance." Paris.

Jerman, Gunnar and Finn P. Nyquist 1970. New Norway: An Introduction to Norwegian Industry on Entering the 1970s. Oslo: The Export Council of Norway and Grøndahl og Søn.

Leven, Charles L. 1978. The Mature Metropolis. Lexington, Massachusetts: Lexington Books

Myklebost, Hallstein 1968. "Urbanization and Regional Concentration in the 1950s and 1960s" Norsk Geografisk Tidskrift, 22, 227-244.

News of Norway Vol. 41, No. 3, 1984. New York: Norwegian Information Service in the United States.

Norsk Hydro No. 4. 1978. "A Report of Norsk Hydro's 1978 activities at home and abroad, with special concentration on its activities in the county of Rogaland." Oslo: Norsk Hydro.

Norsk Hydro No. 4. 1979. 1978-1979 Årsberetning og regnskap. Oslo.

Norges Offentilige Utredninger 1979: 5. Bypolitikk. Oslo: Universitetsforlag.

Rasmussen, Tor 1969. Byregioner i Norge: Den Regionale Konsentrasjon i Bosettingsmøns-teret. Oslo: Norsk Institutt for By-Og Regionsforskning.

Rasmussen, Tor 1977. "Befolkningsutvikling og Bosettingsendringer." A paper presented at a conference of the Norwegian Society of Civil Engineers in Bergen.

Rasmussen, Tor 1978. Regional Development Planning, Regional Science and Regional Analyses in the Nordic Countries in the Post-War years. A manuscript prepared for later publication in NOROREFO's Journal.

Rasmussen, Tor 1979. "The Distribution of Population in Norway, Regional Changes and Regional Policy." Reprint from Antoni Kuhlinski and Olli Kultalahti and Britta Koskiaho (eds.) Regional Dynamics of Socio-economic Change. Tampere: Finn publishers.

Royal Ministry of Foreign Affairs 1968, No. 212. "Electro-Chemical Industries, Chemicals, Plastics." Oslo: Press Department of Royal Ministry of Foreign Affairs

Royal Ministry of Foreign Affairs 1968, No. 213. "Electrometallurgical Industries-Alloys Metals." Oslo: Press Department of Royal Ministry of Foreign Affairs.

Royal Ministry of Industry 1975. "Norwegian Industry's Development and Future." Unofficial

translation of Report No. 67 to the Norwegian Parliament.

Skog, Jon 1981. "Project Tiger Completed," The Norseman. No. 4, pp. 94-96.

Statistisk Sentralbyra 1979. Ekonomisk Utsyn over Året 1978. Oslo

The Cooperation Committee for Oslo and Akershus 1969. Oslo/Akershus - A Regional Development Plan. Oslo.

Thorsnæs, Geir 1972. "Arbeidsplassenes Utvikling og Arealbruk i Osloregionen," in Anker, Erik et al. 1972. Planlegging i Byer og Tettsteder. Oslo: Norsk Forening For Bolig-Og Planlegging.

CHAPTER FOUR: NORWAY'S RESPONSE TO METRO-URBAN CHALLENGES

I. The Cultural Base for Norway's Policy Development

Any nation's response to its compelling challenges will inevitably be mediated through its distinctive culture. As was suggested in the first chapter of this book, Norway's reaction to urbanization would be influenced by some of the distinctive cultural attributes it shares with other members of the Scandinavian cultural region. At the outset of this chapter, therefore, it is appropriate to examine some of the major orientations of that cultural region which has helped shape Norway's perceptions of both the challenges of urbanization and the most constructive responses to them.

Democratic Values and Political Traditions

Perhaps no aspect of Norway's culture is more significantly related to its developing national policies than its democratic values and political traditions. Most students of Norway's political life will probably agree with Harry Eckstein that Norwegian democracy has been both stable and durable (Eckstein 1966 pp. 11-32). During most of the nineteenth century it had all the familiar features of an emerging democracy to a degree unrivaled among other European nations. Its national constitution of 1814 was perhaps more democratic than that of any European nation at that time. Since then, the rudiments of democratic participation have been extended to an ever-increasing part of the adult population; establishing universal male suffrage in 1898, partial female suffrage in 1907, and achieving formal political equality of the sexes in 1913.

In spite of the many political conflicts that have contributed to deep divisions in the country, none of them have produced serious crises of legitimacy. This was true even during the nation's transformation from an essentially agrarian society to one which was predominantly urban and industrial. Its democratic parliamentary system has been

65

flexible enough to accommodate this shifting political dominance from a coalition of civil servants, farmers, and free professionals to that of the Labor Party which became politically dominant in 1935.

Another essential element in Norway's democratic creed is its longstanding commitment to municipal self-government. In 1837, parliament enacted legislation delegating extensive jurisdiction and power to all local municipalities and providing legal structures for democratic political life at the local levels of polity. The persistent nurturing of vigorous local democracy since that time, together with an affirmative faith in the rightness and efficacy of government by law on both national and local levels, set the stage for the development of the legal structures and procedures essential for dealing with the complex urban and environmental issues of contemporary Norway.

As noted earlier, the Labor Party became the dominant party in Norway's parliament in 1935. Its origins had been heavily weighted with the ideology of a class-conscious socialism that had gained ascendancy in much of Europe in the early part of the twentieth century. But as it became the majority party of the country, its earlier commitments to the class-struggle ideology were superseded by a more pragmatic politics based on a larger national community consciousness (Kjeldstadli and Keul 1973, pp. 97-98). Instead of pursuing a doctrinaire policy aimed at socialization of the economy, the new government adopted a more Keynesian-like program of directing the economy so as to achieve such national goals as full employment, greater equalization of income, and a comprehensive social security and welfare system. What is of particular importance for the purposes of this chapter is that the new governemnt of Norway was prepared to assume a leading role in directing the nation's response to challenges of urbanization.

Cooperatives and the Democratic Creed

Norway's democratic creed was not limited to political democracy. During the last half of the nineteenth century and the first half of twentieth, Norwegians developed an extensive cooperative movement through which the average Norseman came to have first hand experience with democratic procedures in managing important aspects of both their economic and socio-cultural existence. Farmers developed extensive cooperative systems for the marketing and processing of virtually all their agricultural products. Local cooperatives became the principal structures for the marketing of dairy products throughout the country. These local cooperatives in turn formed regional and national organizations for the marketing and processing of such products. Similar systems were developed for the marketing and processing of poultry, meat, and other agricultural products. Cooperative organizations were also developed by fishermen, albeit with less success (Grimley 1937, pp. 75-100). Consumer cooperatives also flourished. Hundreds of local consumer cooperative societies emerged throughout the country, typically one in each rural community and several in the larger cities. Like the producer cooperatives, these societies established a national organization--the Cooperative Union and Wholesale Society.

That the cooperative movement of Norway was related to similar developments in the rest of Scandinavia is indicated by the fact that this society was an active member of the Scandinavian Cooperative Society--an association of consumer cooperative societies from Denmark, Finland, Sweden, and Norway (Grimley 1937, p. 104). Cooperative organizations have also been active in the fields of credit. The Cooperative Union and Wholesale Society developed its own cooperative bank (Samvirkebanken) and the producers cooperatives developed their Farmers Bank ("Bondernes Bank"). Similar developments have occurred in the insurance field (Grimley 1937, pp. 101-108).

That the cooperative movement has enjoyed substantial public favor is reflected in the fact that the Norwegian government has consistently encouraged its growth and defended it from its adversaries. Courses in cooperation are taught in agricultural schools, and agricultural agents who

draw part of their salaries from the State are
professional experts and promoters of cooperative
selling and buying (Grimley 1937, pp. 109-110). In
the context of this cooperative legacy it is understandable that when the country was faced with
critical needs for housing and urban expansion it
should find cooperative housing to be one of the
strategies for meeting such needs.

Egalitarianism and the Welfare State Ethos

For whatever historic reasons, the values of
mutual aid and cooperation have permeated much of
Norway's culture and laid a philosophical basis for
what has come to be known as its "welfare state"
ethos. Since that ethos inevitably influenced
Norway's perceptions of both the problems of an
urban society as well as possible solutions of
them, some elaboration of it is important.

The programs and policies of the welfare state
emerged crescively through time rather than by any
all-inclusive legislative enactment sponsored by any
particular political party. No leading political
party--not even the historic conservative (Høyre)
party--has opposed its basic assumptions. Most
Norwegians think of their nation as a welfare state
in a positive way. A Gallup Poll taken in 1967
showed that 85% of the Norwegians understood their
country from such a perspective (Sosialdepartementet
og Norges Almenvitenskapelige Forskningsråd 1970, p.
24). According to a recent analytical account of
Norway's welfare system, its ethos is grounded in
the following basic value assumptions (Sosialdepartementet og Norges Almenvitenskapelige
Forskningsrad 1970, pp. 20-21):

1. Every individual shall be given all
   possibilities for personal development and
   self-realization in proportion to
   abilities.
2. Society, as a collective whole, should be
   so developed as to promote good social
   relations and to control damaging social
   obstacles to such a society.
3. Society should make secure both individual
   and collective welfare, giving thought to

maintaining a balance between them.

4. Every person must be given "full citizenship" status.
5. Equality is an important value that needs to be planned for and secured by law.
6. Economic planning and control are essential.
7. The social security system is an integral part of the welfare system.

Dr. Karl Evang, the well-known "architect" (and for many years the Director General) of Norway's National Health Service has referred to Norway's welfare state system as a democratic middle-way option between a free enterprise system and totalitarianism (Evang 1973). Economically, he has argued, it redistributes the gross national product each year in the interest of equality and helping prevent economic recessions. Its strongest argument, he has insisted, is the humanitarian one that flows from the assumptions that "we are all our brother's keeper" and that the services of the welfare system are basic human rights. In tracing the development of Norway's health system, Dr. Evang grounds it in the early nurture of the social conscience in the local communities of the nation. Support for it, has come from virtually every segment of Norwegian society, including all political parties, trade unions, churches and cooperatives, etc. (Evang 1970, pp. 14-22).

These assumptions of the welfare state ideology imply that every person in Norway should be provided such fundamental human needs as a good public education, sound health care, good housing in wholesome communities, and basic economic and cultural opportunities for human growth and development. They also imply that the national government and the local municipalities are jointly responsible for providing them. That this widespread concensus about such assumptions would influence Norway's urban and environmental policies, seems irrefutable.

Norway's Nature-Oriented Culture

Norway's culture has also been informed by the nation's historic encounter with nature. For

69

centuries its life and culture have been intimately related to the sea, the mountains, the forests, the waterfalls, the valleys, and the very limited but precious tillable soil (Schilliaas 1950, p. 29). Many have speculated about their impact on the Norwegian character. While such speculations might be somewhat treacherous, it can be safely asserted that a consciousness of their dependence upon and intimate relationship with nature is a widely-shared perspective among Norwegians. This is reflected in much of Norway's painting, music, and literature (Haugstøl and Vegel 1949, pp. 10-13).

That this love of and concern for nature should manifest itself in Norway's response to the urban technological transformations of their life and habitat was inevitable. It is instructive to note that the first official guidebook on planning, prepared for the elected officials charged with implementing the 1965 national planning act, begins with a section entitled "Norge--fra naturlandskap til kulturlandskap." The guidebook sharply accents the ways in which much of Norway's natural environment is being transformed by urbanization and related technological changes. It asserts that serenity, clean air, pure water, and an undisturbed nature will become the major assets that need to be protected in the future. It emphasizes that careful thought of how Norway is to use its land areas--whether on the mountains, along the coast, in the lowlands, or in the cities--will be of greatest importance in the years ahead (Johnsen 1970, pp. 11-33).

In a later book on urban planning, Professor Egil Gabrielsen presents a philosophical treatise on the importance of the natural milieu in towns and large cities. The chapter begins with a negative reaction to an American urban planner's statement that "the city is not a tree." It suggests metaphorically that if the city might be permitted to "be a tree," it could become the urban community in which humankind might survive. From this premise he proceeds to describe the physical, biological, esthetic, and recreational functions of the natural environment in the city; and concludes with a section describing guidelines for developing the

70

best possible natural milieu within the urban habitat (Gabrielsen 1972, pp. 53-60).

For Norway, urban life should not mean that nature must capitulate to the culture of technology. In 1971, Norway's Ministry of Local Government and Labor issued a brochure summarizing the government's official position on the conservation of the natural environment. The brochure was prepared as a basic document to be used at conferences set up in all of the 18 counties of the country. The document begins with a statement of the importance of nature for Norwegian health and well-being. It points out how technological developments threaten to alienate people from the rhythms of nature, and how changes in the settlement patterns are jeopardizing values which Norwegians have historically assumed to be both free and unlimited--such as pure water, clean air, serenity, safe travel, and the possibility of living in natural and cultural landscapes that are surrounded by birds, animals, and copious vegetation. The conservation of outdoor environments-- from the playgrounds, parks, and beaches of the cities to the forests, mountains, and seacoasts of the country--was given a very high priority as a basic goal for all governmental authorities in the land. The rest of the official brochure described the means for implementing the nation's environmental policies through legislation, planning, and social implementation (Kommunal-og Arbeids-departementet 19 71, pp. 5-29).

Popular support for such official policies, is in no small way related to Norway's literary heritage. Like other Nordic countries, Norway has a long and rich literary tradition coupled with a high degree of popular literacy. The "renaissance" literature of the nineteenth century helped to fashion a Norwegian culture which nurtured a love and awe of nature intermingled with a romantic nationalism and love of country. Its penetrating realism, such as reflected in Henrick Ibsen's plays, exposed the potential sham and perversity of human kind. His <u>Master Builder</u> is as penetrating a critique of modern man's insensitive abuse of nature as the contemporary environmentalists could wish for. His <u>Peer Gynt</u> is as devastating an expose of

71

all the rationalization that people employ to justify their exploitive self-indulgence as any contemporary "protest" literature. His artistic and creative use of Norway's troll folklore to animate the bad manners, the poor judgments, the careless insensitivity, and all-around potential meanness of people is as germane to the contemporary situation as to that of the nineteenth century (Stavig and Svendsen 1977). It is impossible that such a literary legacy would not influence Norway's response to the environmental challenges of urbanization.

Norway's Moral Culture

All these cultural attributes may be perceived as parts of the nation's moral order, providing the consensus needed for developing and implementing its national policies and programs. Another component of that moral order is Norway's religious heritage. Like the rest of Scandinavia, Lutheranism is the established religion of the country. More than 90% of its population belong to the Lutheran Church. The Church is administered through the Ministry of Church and Education, and religious education is an integral part of the public school curriculum. Consequently the Judeo-Christian legacy as mediated (since the Reformation in 1536) through Lutheran perspectives becomes one of the basic understandings of self and society.

Although there is a scarcity of research data on religion's impact on Norway's community life, there is no doubt but that the Church plays an important role in both national and local affairs. As one document points out, "it is difficult to name any aspect of society that the church has not influenced." The clearest illustrations are its social responsibilities in education, health care, and concern for the poor (Norges Offentlige Utredninger 1975:30, p. 139). As Tor Rasmussen has suggested, the ethical imperatives derived from religion are supportive of the goals of a solidary society wherein the fortunate have responsibility for helping the less fortunate. From such a premise there is but a short distance to the equalitarian

72

ideology that played a central role in the politics and policies of the Labor Party (Norges Offentlige Utredninger 1979:5, p. 141). Similarly, it can be reasonably surmised that the Lutheran ethics of stewardship has been supportive of the national environmental policies as well as those related to commuity development and nurture.

II. National and Regional Settlement Policies

One of the central policy questions that accompanied urbanization and economic growth in Norway was how to deal with the twin problems of depopulation of some regions and the rapid growth and expansion of others. The manifest inequalities implicit in these regional imbalances ran acutely counter to the nation's egalitarian values. Since virtually every other aspect of Norway's urban policies have been influenced by this concern about regional imbalances, a fairly detailed analysis of the nation's regional policies provides an essential background for understanding other policies and programs.

Pre-War Regional Activities

Prior to World War II, the government under the Labor Party leadership, sought to deal with the problems of economic inequality in the context of an over-all response to the great depression. It was clear that the local communities could not by themselves solve the problems of unemployment, poverty, and related crumbling world markets. It launched a national program of support for the building of highways and other communications networks, for the expansion of hydro-electric power systems, and for housing. Special aids were given to the primary industries which at that time were still employing about 40% of Norway's labor force. These programs were favorably disposed to the continued vitality of the small local communities throughout the country. They were oriented toward a kind of town and country development in which local populism might flourish (Hersoug og Leonardsen 1979, pp. 14-22). It was a program which won for the

Labor Party both rural and urban support. The Nazi invasion of April 9, 1940 brought an abrupt end to these programs for the next five years.

Post-War Regional Policies--The North Norway Program

The post-war period presented a vastly different situation. In the first place, concerns of post-war reconstruction brought Norway into new international relationships through Western Europe's Organization for Economic and Cooperative Development (OECD) and the American Marshall Plan. Domestic planning and development had to be reconciled with world market concerns implicit in these new relationships. Hence, the earlier pre-occupation with the nurture of the primary industries which only produced 15% of the gross national product even if they employed about 30% of the labor force seemed no longer adequate. Instead, the government placed a greater emphasis upon the promotion of the secondary and tertiary industries; and on the development of larger local centers in which they might best be nurtured (Hersoug og Leonardsen 1979, pp. 44-50).

The most pressing post-war situation demanding attention was the reconstruction of Northern Norway, which had suffered the brunt of the war-time devastation. The scorched earth strategy adopted by the retreating Germans left widespread destruction throughout the region. The city of Bodø was destroyed by bombing in 1940. Hammerfest, Kirkenes and all other settlements in Finmark were destroyed in the winter of 1944-45. The rebuilding of this part of Norway provided the setting for Norway's first comprehensive regional development program, which was destined to inform later regional policies for the rest of the country.

After much debate concerning appropriate approaches to regional development, Parliament established a "Development Program for North Norway" in 1952. The dominant goal of the program was to increase productivity and employment opportunities through increased economic growth in the region. Emphasis was placed upon developing a more capital-intensive economy--i.e., a change from the small

74

local labor-intensive fishing and farming activities to larger industries compatible with special circumstances in North Norway.

The three principal means for implementing the program were (1) the establishment of a North Norway Fund, (2) the development of special tax programs for the region, and (3) extraordinary national initiatives for the building of its infrastructure. All these strategies were directed towards promoting economic activities which would insure continued growth in production and stable employment opportunities. The program supported the development of hyro-electric power for strategic new industrial activities, expansion of existing industries, the establishment of regional branches of southern Norway firms, and the development of smaller industries and commercial enterprises oriented toward the local market. It gave special support for the shipping, mining, and housing industries; and promoted socio-cultural and educational programs for the area.

These socioeconomic stimuli were coordinated with an over-all settlement policy which fostered the development of local growth centers which would provide the setting needed for the nurture of the socio-cultural life of the region as well as for its economic vitality. Special beneficiaries of the Program were such cities as Hammerfest and Kirkenes in the northern-most county of the area, and such other northern cities as Tromsø, Harstad and Bodø. In effect, this first Norwegian regional program launched what might well be characterized as a policy of "decentralized centralization" (Hersoug og Leonardsen 1979, pp. 112-124).

The Nationwide Regional Development Program

In 1960, Norway launched a nation-wide regional development program in which many of the features of the North Norway Program were extended to other underdeveloped areas of the country. The following quotation from the statute establishing the nation-wide Regional Development Fund provides a clear indication of its principal objectives:

It is the aim of the Regional Development Fund to promote measures which will ensure increased, permanent and profitable employment in districts with special employment problems or where underdeveloped industrial conditions prevail. In this respect, the Board and the Secretariat of the Fund shall assist with the investigation of the industrial possibilities in such districts and shall--by way of initiative, organization, planning and coordination--ensure that the possibilities are utilized to the full. In its activities the Fund shall contribute to the development of expanding centers and other local centers in the districts as mentioned in the first section (Carlson 1976, p. 5).

The fact that the Fund does not support measures in the larger urban municipalities in South Norway nor in heavily urbanized counties in Southeastern Norway provides unmistakable evidence of the government's goal of achieving a regional balance with respect to demographic, economic, cultural, and environmental development throughout the country.

Although there is considerable anti-urban sentiment in many parts of Norway, the basic goals of "distriktpolitikken," as the new regional program was called, has not been to restore a romantic rural past; but rather to develop such local small cities and regional growth centers in all parts of the country so as to slow down what has been perceived as an unhealthy overconcentration in the largest urban areas of the country. In a sense, it can be said that the regional policy sought to foster a decentralized urbanization throughout the whole of Norway. This is reflected in Norway's definition of the minimum size of its regional cities. While in Sweden, the emphasis has been upon city regions of 30,000 or more inhabitants, in Norway the city regions have been defined to include areas of only 10,000 inhabitants. Furthermore, much attention has also been paid to a large number of even smaller settlements in Norway's regional policy (Rasmussen

1979, pp. 400–406).

During the period between 1965 and 1970 the government created five Inter-County Committees charged with the task of submitting proposals for the development of the five major areas (regions) of Norway. The boundaries for these Inter-County Committee planning areas were the same as delineated in Figs. 3A and 3B as five functional main subregions in Norway.

All the reports of the Inter-County Committees have been considered by the government and have contributed to the formulation of guidelines for a national policy with respect to regional and rural development. The original task assigned these committees and the responsibility for inter-county planning have now been transferred to the Ministry of Environment in cooperation with county authorities (Stokke, p. 32).

Principal Strategies of "Distriktpolitikken"

Over the years since the inception of the Regional Development Fund in 1960, Parliament has developed a comprehensive coordinated threefold strategy for the achievement of its goals:
1. The planning and development of appropriate settlement patterns.
2. A program for stimulating and strengthening the economy of lagging areas.
3. The nurturing of a general socio-cultural environment in the various centers throughout the country.

The Ministry of Local Government and Labor was assigned the major responsibility for coordinating the activities of the central government in these strategies, and relating them to the local and county planning systems throughout the country.

As already noted, the settlement pattern strategy has sought to create a variety of centers throughout the country appropriate for containing the socioeconomic and cultural developments of modern Norway. Local centers have been strengthened and further developed in the lagging areas so as to provide all the essential social services, the

77

institutions for elementary and adult education, community centers and recreational programs, and the commercial and communications institutions needed for a thriving small town centered community life.

Similarly, larger regional growth centers have been developed in each area, which can serve as transportation and communications stations, including a regional airport. Such centers are designed to provide a broader spectrum of commercial services and sites for a variety of medium-sized industries and where appropriate, some larger industries. They should also contain such larger public institutions as hospitals, geriatric centers, secondary schools, district colleges, and vocational schools; as well as regional theaters and art centers. These centers are usually referred to as regional growth centers.

The third type of center promoted in the program were the major regional city centers, which were expected to provide a broader spectrum of specialized social, cultural and economic activities and serve as the leading urban centers in each of the inter-county areas. They would host such institutions as universities, research centers, specialized medical programs as well as important commercial and industrial establishments. All the centers--local, regional, and district--were to be planned and developed in cooperation with the municipal, regional and county planning authorities.

The second major strategy of "Distrikt-politikken" involved the stimulation of economic growth and increased employment opportunities in the areas of the country with a lagging economy, including an encouragement and modernization of the primary industries and the nurture of new economic activities related to them, research in and development of new industrial activities, and the prolif-eration of expanded commercial and other tertiary services. Both the public and private sectors of the economy have been involved in these economic developments.

The third major strategy has been to nurture a vital social and cultural milieu in all the municipalities and developing centers. This has involved the strategic location, planning, and

78

development of cultural, recreational, educational, and social institutions, and programs appropriate for the various types of centers. It was intended that such centers would provide good health services, convenient access to the social services, possibilities for participation in a variety of cultural activities, attractive recreational programs and outdoor activities, and sound and comfortable housing in well-designed environmental surroundings (Kommunal og Arbeidsdepartementet 1972, pp. 23-24). The administrative system which had given the municipalities their independent economic power, provided the precondition for implementing such a policy within a local democratic framework. In order to make the municipalities able to deal with all the tasks laid on them by the Government, the number was reduced from approximately 1,200 to 450.

Tools and Techniques of "Distriktpolitikken"

The principal thrust of the Regional Development Fund has been to promote the economic growth of the disadvantaged area of Norway. A wide variety of tools and techniques have been developed for this purpose, including the following (Carlson 1976, pp. 11-13):

1. Loans for investments in buildings, machinery and equipment, including loans for the erection of municipally-owned leasable industrial buildings and other types of buildings.
2. Guarantees for loans raised through banks or other credit agencies.
3. Investment Grants to promote localization or expansion of economic activities which may reinforce the economic base and increase employment in economically weak regions. The size of these grants varies from region to region in relation to need.
4. Training Grants to cover the cost of special training of the manpower needed in the new industries located in the developing regions.
5. Relocation Grants to enterprises reloca-

ting from well-developed areas to the disadvantaged areas.

6. <u>Grants</u> for the surveying and planning needed before launching new enterprises.

The Fund's total annual financial support commitments grew from approximately 80 million Norwegian kroner in 1961 to more than a billion kroner in 1975. Of the 1975 commitments, 58% were in loans, 13% in loan guarantees, 3% in relocation grants and 26% in investment grants. From 1961 to 1975 the Fund granted support for a total of 5.5 billion kroner (Carlson 1976, pp. 14-16). After 1975 the financial support up to 1984 has been kept at a slightly declining level in deflated prices. However, direct grants to industry in the "districts" have increased.

The extensive activities of the Regional Development Fund are significantly supplemented by many other official or semi-official financial institutions or programs which assist in the financing of projects in the economically under-developed areas. The following list is indicative of their variety (Carlson 1976, pp. 22-24):

1. <u>Norwegian Bank for Industry</u> to provide long-term investment loans to industrial concerns, power stations and hotels, as well as for leasable industrial buildings.

2. <u>The Fund for Handicrafts and Small-scale Industry.</u>

3. <u>The Fund for Industrial Growth and Adaptation</u> for encouraging mergers or other structural readaptation in industry.

4. <u>The National Bank for Fisheries</u> for financing fishing and sealing vessels, processing plants for fish and fish products etc.

5. <u>The National Bank for Agriculture</u> to cover the financing of undertakings in agriculture and forestry.

6. <u>The Industrial Estates Corporation</u> which is a government-owned company formed for purchasing industrial sites and con-structing industrial buildings for leasing to business firms.

7. <u>The National Institute of Technology</u> which

provides an advisory service for industrial firms offering courses in technology and business economics.

8. The Committee for Industrial Location.
9. The Municipal Bank granting loans for site preparation and the purchase of land for special infrastructural investments in centers of expansion.
10. Appropriations from the National Fiscal Budget to finance schools, construct roads and bridges, and power supply projects which are of direct or indirect significance for regional development.
11. The Regional Taxation Law which provides special tax incentives for firms investing in the developing areas.
12. The National Housing Bank which plays a leading role in financing new housing construction.

Administration of "Distriktpolitikken"

The Regional Development Fund is administered by a 10-member Board, appointed by the Government (The King in Council) for four-year terms. The Board directs the Fund's activities and administers its resources. It is assisted in its work by a Secretariat and its staff. The Development Fund also has a twenty-one-member Council of which fourteen are appointed by the Parliament and seven by the Government. The members of the Council are appointed for two-year terms and are as far as possible representative of various districts and branches of industries involved with the program. While the Regional Development Fund clearly reflects a national initiative and direction, its activities are coordinated with the local, county, and municipal planning and governmental authorities. Its activities are also coordinated with the other expanding services of the national government to the local municipalities in such a way as to enhance the regional development objectives.

III. Planning Legislation and Structure

As the policies and programs of "Distrikt-politikken" were modifying Norway's habitat, con-current changes were altering the planning and governmental structures of the country--changes which in many ways were supportive of its developing regional policies. But before describing these changes, some clarification of the political and administrative system of Norway is appropriate.

There are essentially three levels of government in Norway: the national, the county, and the municipal. Since the Norwegian county called the "fylke" is equivalent to neither the American nor the English county, its status and functions are not fully reflected by that term. In some respects the Norwegian "fylke" might be more appropriately perceived as a "province" or a "state," but such translations would also present some problems. In this book the term "county" will be used, trusting that the reader would be aware of its limitations as a translation for the Norwegian "fylke."

Administrative units for planning

There are eighteen such counties in Norway. Each has a capital city which has historically functioned as an administrative center for the national government, with a county governor and administative staff appointed by and responsible to the central government. In recent years, the governance of the county has become increasingly democratic with a locally-elected council and an executive and administrative structure responsible to that council.

The predominant activities of counties are concentrated on education, health care institutions and certain building projects--foremost of which are the county highways. The counties are also engaged in other economic activities, such as the supplying of electricity. Apart from these, they have assumed increasingly important functions in physical and economic planning which are the principal concerns of this chapter. Figure 4A provides a picture of the populations of Norway's counties in 1978.

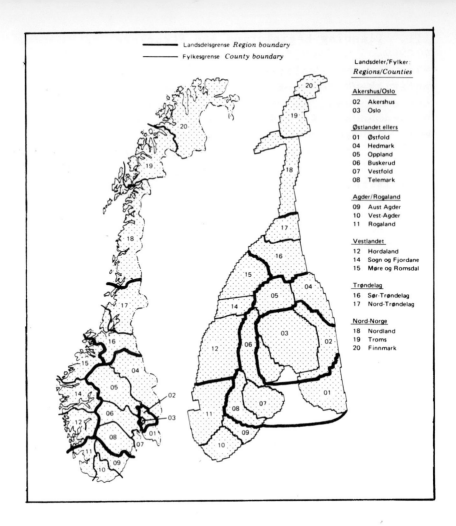

Legend:
— Landsdelsgrense *Region boundary*
— Fylkesgrense *County boundary*

Landsdeler/Fylker:
Regions/Counties

Akershus/Oslo
02 Akershus
03 Oslo

Østlandet ellers
01 Østfold
04 Hedmark
05 Oppland
06 Buskerud
07 Vestfold
08 Telemark

Agder/Rogaland
09 Aust Agder
10 Vest-Agder
11 Rogaland

Vestlandet
12 Hordaland
14 Sogn og Fjordane
15 Møre og Romsdal

Trøndelag
16 Sør-Trøndelag
17 Nord-Trøndelag

Nord-Norge
18 Nordland
19 Troms
20 Finnmark

FIGURE 4A   Real areas in a "normal" map over Norway with Counties and Five Main Regions and Map with Areas Proportional with Population. Distribution of population is very uneven in Norway. One sees, for example, that Oslo/Akershus and Vestfold Counties have a small territory on the map to the left, and a large area on the map to the right. With Finmark it is the opposite.

Source: Miljøstatistisk 1978 SAM 37, Statistisk Sentralbyra, Oslo

The Norwegian municipalities have long been of
central importance and power in Norway's political
system. Their strong tradition of local autonomy
helps inform the planning system that has emerged in
recent times. Their size and number have, however,
been significantly altered by the National government in order to make them more congruent with the
changing settlement patterns. Their number was
reduced from 744 in the early 1950s to 445 by 1976.

The 1965 Building Act

Perhaps the most important changes were made
in the Planning and Building legislation of the
country. In Norway this legislation has been
primarily contained in one law--the Building Act
which was originally enacted in 1924. Although it
had been amended frequently to make it more appropriate for changing circumstances, its inadequacies
led to a substantial revision in 1965.

Deliberations concerning this revised Building
Act began in the early 1950s. A Parliamentary
Committee was appointed in 1954 to prepare recommendations for the new legislation. The Committee's
recommendations of 1960 became the basis for a long,
extensive parliamentary debate which culminated in
the enactment of the 1965 Building Act. Its major
purposes and provisions, even though somewhat
comparable with earlier legislation in other
countries of Europe, reflect distinctive characteristics related to Norway's historic traditions.

The Act recognizes Norway's long commitment to
local autonomy and the values of local participation
in democratic decision-making. The entire legislation stipulates that the municipalities themselves
solve important planning and development problems.
It provides for comprehensive planning in the
context of municipal, regional and national
perspectives.

The Act was designed to create a planning
structure on both the local and national levels
which would not only deal with the traditional
issues of urban planning, but also those of
population loss, conservation and economic planning
related to balanced regional growth. A basic goal

was to integrate community planning with planning for the needs of the country as a whole (Stokke 1976, pp. 3-5). According to a recent publication of the Ministry of Environment, the following are some of its principal characteristics:

1. The Act applies throughout the country and requires every municipality to prepare a comprehensive municipal plan which outlines the main features of the land use pattern and indicates a proposed investment program.

2. It also requires that municipalities supplement these general comprehensive plans with detailed local plans for areas to be used for building purposes.

3. The "general" and "local" plans should be based on regional plans in cases where joint planning between two or more municipalities is deemed necessary.

4. The Act leaves it to the municipal authorities to decide whether there is a need for such cooperation. The Ministry or County Governor can, however take the initiative in preparing a regional plan, should the municipalities fail to do so.

5. Local plans are legally binding. The general municipal and regional plans serve only as guides.

6. The general municipal and the regional plans can be made binding for all or part of the planning areas bv adopting a bylaw to the plans to this effect. This also applies to county plans which were mandated by a later revision of the Building Act.

7. As later amended, the Act authorizes the Ministry of Environment to require cooperation between two or more counties when this is considered appropriate (Stokke 1976, p. 5).

An examination of the various plans required by the Building Act clearly indicates the comprehensiveness of the new legislation. The County Plan which became a part of the Building Act after 1973, is a "comprehensive plan for the coordination of state, county, and municipal planning with regard to the utilization of the natural resources in a county and other questions of common interest for the promotion of economic growth and welfare in the county." According to the Building Act, the County Plan should include the following (Stokke 1976, p. 7):

1. Provisions for comprehensive utilization of natural resources, including sea and water-course utilization, and the use of land for building areas, agriculture or forestry areas, nature areas and traffic arteries and other transportation facilities.
2. Setting goals for population development and settlement patterns.
3. An evaluation of the labour market situation and general business trends.
4. A general survey of needed public developments in the county, such as roads, harbors, airports, schools, hospitals, nursing homes and welfare institutions, economic ventures, energy and water systems and environmental protection.

The County Plan provides the foundation upon which county and municipal development activity is based and is meant to serve as a guideline for the preparation of regional, municipal and local plans.

The Regional Plan provided for in the Building Act is a comprehensive plan for coordinating land use and joint solution of problems concerning developments of two or more municipalities. It should not be confused with the regional planning associated with "Distriktpolitikken," which is more similar to regional planning as usually perceived. The Norwegian "Regional Plan" is more small-scale and more localized.

The municipal "General Plan" is perhaps the most significant plan provided for in the Building Act. It is a plan for the utilization of land within a municipality and for the solution of problems regarding public utilities and community facilities to meet the overall requirements of the municipality. It indicates the main features of its land use such as building sites, agriculture or

86

forestry areas, nature areas, traffic arteries, and other transportation facilities. It suggests solutions to problems of water supply, sewage disposal, and other measures necessary for meeting the general welfare requirements of the municipality.

The "Local Plan" is prepared for areas set aside for building purposes--such as housing areas with sites for local shops and stores; areas for offices, industry, recreational activities and public institutions; and area commitments to form transportation systems, markets and public squares, etc. The Local Plans become binding when ratified by the County Governor, or, in the case of a possible complaint against the Governor's decision, by the Ministry of Environment.

The Structure of the Planning Organization

The Building Act, as it was originally enacted and modified through later revisions, established the basic planning and development structure for all of Norway. At the outset in 1965, the principal emphasis was upon physical and economic planning at the local level and such intermunicipal regional planning as seemed necessary. But by 1973, the Building Act had been amended to reflect the incremental development of planning at other levels of government as well. As amended, the act now provides that the three principal levels in planning and development in Norway shall be: the national level, the county level and the municipal level.

As noted earlier, these planning activities at the various levels of government were to be integrated. The diagram on page 88 provides a helpful visual representation of the relationship between the responsible political and planning bodies at the various levels of authority.

The chief planning authority at the national level was initially the Ministry of Local Government and Labor, but after the establishment of the Ministry of Environment in 1972, the authority was transferred to that department. This Ministry has assumed a two-fold function with respect to planning. On the one hand, it is the highest

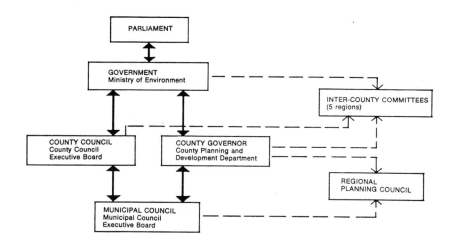

Source: Stokke 1976, p. 32.

planning authority for the adoption of the municipal
and county plans, as well as the authority which can
grant dispensations regarding them. On the other
hand, the Ministry takes part in the planning work
at the national and inter-county levels, and deals
with concrete efforts aimed at solving the many
problems which localization and changing settlement
patterns create (Stokke 1976, p. 33).

Placing the authority for planning and development in the Ministry of the Environment reflects
the national decision to locate planning bodies at
all levels of government in the public administrative structure; with the assumption that they have
the best means for implementing the plans proposed.
It also reflects that the "dominant view in Norway
has been to guarantee that the really important
questions of community development not be delegated
to bodies which were more or less remote from the
responsible political authorities" (Stokke 1976, p.
33).

By making national planning activities a part
of the central administration and by emphasizing
inter-ministry cooperation, it was hoped that
planning would be better coordinated and more
effectively implemented. To assist the efforts at
Inter-Ministry cooperation and coordination, the
government has created a committee of senior

officials with representatives from those ministries particularly involved in planning work. The funcctions of this committee are indicated by its title: "The Inter-Ministry Coordinating Committee for Resource Management, Environmental Questions, and Regional Planning."

The Building Act of 1965 expanded the functions and importance of the county unit of government. It delegated to it important planning duties and responsibilities. The county governor was given the responsibility of supervising the planning activities in the county and ensuring that comprehensive general and local plans were prepared as required by law. He was also to aid the municipalities with their planning and developmental tasks, as well as make certain that appropriate public hearings were held concerning them.

To assist the governor in these functions, the Act provided for the establishment of a planning and development department for each county. The department's most important duties were (Stokke 1976, p. 36):

1. To assist the county governor with the duties assigned him under the Building Act-- especially to supervise and initiate physical and economic planning and implement the development plans for the county.
2. To facilitate the coordination of public investments and private developments so as to strengthen the economy and promote a harmonious settlement pattern in the county.
3. To consider applications for financial aid to planning and development activities where such aid can be given.
4. To serve as a secretariat for the work of preparing maps of the county.
5. To make proposals for dealing with matters of interest to the department.
6. To contribute to the municipal planning work by giving lectures or conducting other educational functions.
7. To participate in educational activities requested by the county governor or the National Ministry.

It is evident from the above that the county planning and development departments were to play a very important role in the planning work of the country.

Since 1965, important changes have taken place in the political structure of the county government. Starting in 1975, the County Council has been chosen by direct elections by the inhabitants of the county. The County Mayor, elected by the Council from amongst its members, has become the county's highest political leader. Starting in 1976, the county had its own administrative system separate from that of the County Governor's office and the County Planning and Development Department was transferred from the County Governor's office to that of the County Administration. One of the important new planning functions of the county planning and development departments is to prepare a county "Kommuneplan" with which the municipal plans are to be articulated.

At the local level, the Building Act gives full responsibility for land use and investment planning to the elected political authorities, i.e, the Municipal Council and its Executive Board. The diagram on the following page illustrates the organization of the planning structure in the municipalities.

It should be noted that all municipal authority is concentrated in the municipal council which is elected to serve for a four-year term. This Council elects its chairman, who serves as mayor of the municipality, and an executive board that assumes the executive functions of municipal government. It should also be noted that the Council has dominion over virtually every aspect of public life; including public health, education, recreation and park services, social welfare, agriculture, forestry, and many more.

This represents a marked contrast to the more fragmented political situation that prevails in many municipalities of the U.S.A.; where one typically finds school boards, park boards, health and welfare agencies etc. with their own political autonomy. The memberships of the municipal councils varies according to the size of the municipalities. Those

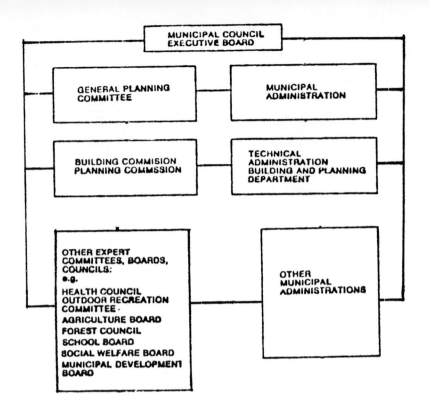

not over 3,000 are by law expected to have at least 13 and not more than 21. Those with more than 100,000 inhabitants have not less than 59 nor more than 85, which is the size of Oslo's City Council.

It has been noted that one of the reasons for transferring the responsibility for planning from professional groups to the elected political bodies was to ensure better coordination of physical and economic planning, and to improve communication between the planning professionals and the political decision-makers in the planning process. It has also been observed that this transfer has brought about "a stronger interest and greater understanding for the necessity of long-term planning among the political bodies of the municipality" (Stokke 1976, p. 37).

The principal responsibility of the General Planning Committee is to prepare the municipal plan. It can appoint trained officials and others who are not members of the Council to participate in this work, but they do not have the right to vote. The implementation of the plan is assigned to the main building authority in the municipality--the Building Commission. Every municipality has such a Commission which is responsible for developing the detailed local plans and helping to implement them. All members of the Commission are elected by the Municipal Council which also appoints its chairman and deputy chairman. The Commission, by design, has the character of a politically elected coordinating body that has close association with other important political bodies of the municipality. The larger municipalities typically establish a Planning Commission to carry out many of the planning functions of the Building Commission.

The Urban Renewal Act

Although the Building Act of 1965 was applicable to both city and country, it did not adequately deal with the specially acute city problems requiring urban renewal. Hence, Parliament in 1967 enacted the Urban Renewal Law, for the purpose of assisting urban municipalities in the revitalization of their city centers. It authorized such municipalities to define and declare the areas to be renewed. After appropriate public hearings and deliberations, and after the resolution designating such areas had been approved by the Municipal Council and the Ministry of Local Government and Labor, the property rights of owners in such areas were temporarily restricted. They could neither build nor subdivide lots or make other changes of property ownership which would make renewal difficult.

The act also made it possible for the municipality to group the properties in the area to be renewed so that renewal could be more easily carried out according to principles which provide for a satisfactory aesthetic and functional environment and an effective pattern of development. The municipality was authorized to expropriate real estate in renewal areas during the time limit designated (Stokke 1976, pp. 20-21). In 1976 the law was thoroughly revised, after which urban renewal has been speeded up considerably.

IV. Special Environmental Legislation

Norway's historic concern for its natural environment has already been noted. Its limited agricultural land, its cherished wonderland of mountains, fjords, forests, and sea coasts, have long been considered essential national assets for the country's life and culture. It is therefore quite understandable that special legislation for their protection and nurture should be enacted to supplement and be integrated with other legislation pertaining to urban and regional affairs.

The Agriculture Act

Perhaps in no country has the conservation of agricultural land become more closely related to urban development than in Norway. In spite of its relatively low population density, it has the lowest amount of cultivated land per person of all the countries of Europe. Only 3% of the total land area is arable. The nation's degree of self-sufficiency for agricultural products is only 40%.

What is particularly noteworthy, is that most recent urban expansion has occurred precisely in areas containing these highly valued agricultural lands. Strong public reaction to this developed at the end of the 1940s. In 1955, Parliament revised an older Agricultural Act to deal more decisively with the issue (Stokke 1976, p. 21).

The revised Agricultural Act stipulates that cultivated lands may not be used for other purposes without consent of the authorities administering the Act. Such consent is also required for the subdividing of agricultural land. Such consent can only be given if such subdivision is justifiable with respect to the economic returns or if important community interests warrant it. The two bodies primarily responsible for administering the Agricultural Act are the Municipal Agricultural Board and the County Agricultural Board. Provisions are made for ultimate appeal to the National

93

Ministry of Agriculture in case of unresolved conflict.

Because of the intrinsic expansive nature of modern urbanization, this Act effects the planning and development of virtually every city in the country. Even in Oslo, there is a Department of Agriculture that watches over the disposition of arable land.

Nature Conservation Legislation

Similar actions have been taken with respect to the conservation of other resources of nature. A "Protection of National Resources Act" was enacted in 1910 to protect plant and animal environments of scientific interest. In 1954 a new Nature Conservation Act was enacted, providing a more extensive conservation of nature than merely protecting certain natural phenomena. It provided authority for establishing national parks for recreational purposes in addition to reserves for plant and animal life and geological deposits.

The scope of Norway's nature conservation legislation was further expanded by the Nature Conservation Act of 1970. Calling attention to the accelerating exploitation of natural resources and the urgency of preserving the natural environment for human health and well-being, the Act lays down provisions for protecting the natural environments and distinctive landscapes. In accordance with the Act, such areas of beauty may be designated "landscape protection areas" where developments endangering their quality will be prohibited.

According to the Act, the planner of large developments or installations which may involve substantial alterations of the natural environment shall, before proceeding, submit the plans to the authority concerned for comment in accordance with the Act. "The Act also contains rules concerning a ban on placing advertising posters outside of built-up areas, and a ban on depositing or emptying refuse and the like in such a way as to harm the landscape or the natural environment in general" (Stokke 1976, p. 23 and Smith 1972, pp. 11-12).

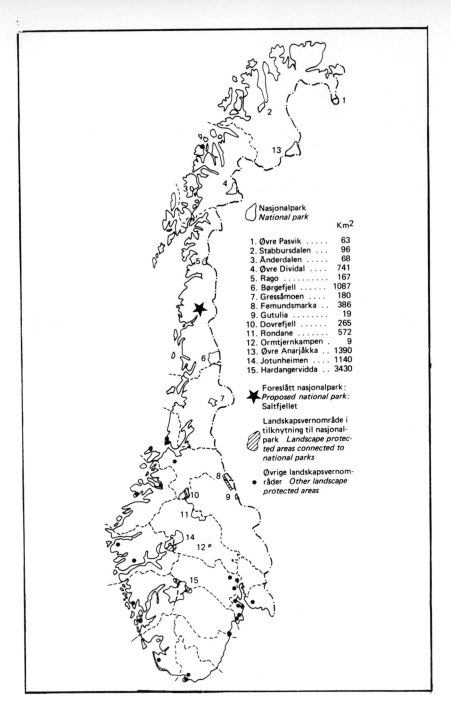

Nasjonalpark
National park

Km²

1. Øvre Pasvik   63
2. Stabbursdalen . . .   96
3. Ånderdalen   68
4. Øvre Dividal 741
5. Rago 167
6. Børgefjell 1087
7. Gressåmoen 180
8. Femundsmarka . . 386
9. Gutulia   19
10. Dovrefjell 265
11. Rondane 572
12. Ormtjernkampen .   9
13. Øvre Anarjåkka . . 1390
14. Jotunheimen 1140
15. Hardangervidda . . 3430

Foreslått nasjonalpark:
Proposed national park:
Saltfjellet

Landskapsvernområde i
tilknytning til nasjonal-
park *Landscape protec-
ted areas connected to
national parks*

Øvrige landskapsvernom-
råder *Other landscape
protected areas*

FIGURE 4B   National Parks and Location of Landscape
Protected Areas

Source: Ministry of Environment.

The Act provides for the creation of a National Council for the Conservation of Nature to serve as an advisory body for the ministry responsible for administering the Act. The most comprehensive project resulting from the Act has been the development of a National Plan for National Parks. This Plan now covers seventeen large wilderness areas, stretching from the country's northernmost county of Finnmark to the famous inter-county "Hardangervidda" in the south. Most of these areas are now established national parks.

The Outdoor Recreation Act, 1957

A somewhat related legislation--The Outdoor Recreation Act--was enacted in 1957. In many ways it established by law what had long prevailed by custom, the right of public access to privately-owned but uncultivated land and to lakes and rivers for such recreational purposes as picnicing, camping, berry-picking, swimming, and hunting. It provided for a National Outdoor Recreation Board with responsibility for improving and developing outdoor recreation throughout the country.

The Act also mandates the creation of similar boards or committees at the county level and makes optional similar arrangements at the municipal level. The provisions of the act impinge on environmental planning at all levels of political authority and have had important environmental consequences throughout Norway.

The Shore and Mountain Planning Act

The seacoast of Norway has for centuries been a vital natural resource, both for life's basic sustenance and for the nurture of the more esthetic and recreational concerns. The southern seacoast, in particular, because of its good summer climate and coastline inlets and islands, has been highly cherished for its excellent opportunities for recreation. Consequently, extensive construction of cottages took place, occupying large parts of the seacoast and blocking public access to the sea from the inland areas.

This problem became increasingly acute as Norway's living standards steadily increased. By 1969, Norway had 178,000 vacation homes scattered along its seacoast and in the mountains, and was adding about 10,000 more a year (Langdalen 1969, p. 96).

Out of consideration for the national environment and in order to ensure appropriate forms of development along the coast, legislation was adopted regulating seashore developments. In 1965, a provisional seashore act prohibited the building of cottages and other structures within a 100-meter wide strip along the entire coast. A major purpose of the act was to allow the general public free access to the seashore. This act was followed by the Shore and Mountain Planning Act of 1971 and its amendments of 1973 and 1976.

Under this law as amended, developments along the seashore can only occur in accordance with officially-approved seashore plans. Similarly, restrictions are established for developments along water courses and in the mountains. Following a proposal from the county authorities, the Ministry may decide that the construction of buildings in any such areas must be reported to the country governor who may demand a shore plan or mountain plan as the case may be. Such plans must be in conformity with the comprehensive plans of the municipalities in the area (Stokke 1976, pp. 17-19).

Pollution Legislation

Like other modern nations, Norway has become perturbed over the growing problems of industrial pollution. Air, water, and noise pollution have all become exacerbating problems. The familiar tensions between the forces of industrial growth and environmental protection have led to innovative ventures in environmental planning. Such planning innovations were embodied in the Building Act of 1965, which provided that municipal and regional plans had to meet certain environmental standards.

When in 1970 Parliament adopted the Water Pollution Act, one of its sections related the Act back to the Planning and Building Act of 1965 and noted the desirability of coordinating pollution control with regional land use planning. Under the new act no municipal or regional land utilization plans could be approved without acceptable arrangements for water supply and sewage. Acceptability was judged in terms of municipal and regional land use and the quality of affected water bodies (Smith 1972, p. 13).

The Water Pollution Act imposes on everyone responsibility for preventing pollution of water and "lays down a general prohibition on starting or pursuing any activity--which may cause water pollution, without permission from authorities" (Stokke 1976, p. 26). The Act is applicable to all inland bodies of water, and to all estuaries as well as to the sea and ground water near industrial and built-up areas.

Regulations regarding air and noise pollution had been developed through enactment of The Neighbor's Act of 1961, which prohibits the initiation of any industry or other activity which spreads pollutents into the air, unless they have been granted special official permission or concession to do so. Since enterprises which were already operational were exempt from its mandate, the law was amended in 1973 empowering the government to introduce compulsory licensing of enterprises--including those begun prior to the Act's enactment. A later amendment expanded the Act so as to make the same licensing procedure applicable to noise pollution (Norges Offentlige Utredninger 1976: No. 47, pp. 25-27).

According to a recent account, "All new industries are now subject to stringent requirements with regard to treatment of discharges into air and water, and emergency services for possible accidents causing pollution." For existing industries a comprehensive 10-year clean-up program was launched in 1974, costing an estimated 5 billion Norwegian "kroner"; most of the effort to be focused upon the pulp and paper, the ferro-alloy, and the chemical industries.

Already, these efforts have led to significant reduction in pollutant discharges into the natural environment. A comparable program has been launched

to clean up pollution from municipal sewage systems.
Special pollution control programs have also
been fashioned for the oil industry in the North
Sea. Since 1975, the Ministry of the Environment
has been responsible for oil pollution control
emergency services and other measures against
pollution from ships and from other activities on
the continental shelf. Measures to prevent oil
spills and other hazards are taken care of by other
ministries (Fort 1979: No.4, pp. 96-97).

The Establishment of the Ministry of Environment

The preceding account of Norway's planning and
environmental legislation, clearly demonstrates that
the problems of physical and economic planning,
pollution control, and environmental protection were
perceived to be closely inter-related. They were
also perceived as demanding administrative machinery
that could integrate these related parts and
coordinate the actions of the county and municipal
levels of government with the long-term comprehensive policy goals of the national government.
In 1972, after exhaustive studies of the
administrative requirements for achieving such
integration and coordination, Parliament established
the new cabinet-level Ministry of Environment. In
it were lodged the following areas of administrative
responsibility:
1. Urban and regional planning
2. Coordinated planning and management of
    land and water resources (municipal,
    county, and national)
3. Pollution control, noise abatement, and
    waste disposal
4. Conservation of nature and recreation
    areas
5. Preservation of cultural environments in
    town and country
6. Coordination of research and international
    cooperation in the field of environment
7. Long-term management of the country's
    natural environment (this added later)
In addition to its five administrative departments, the Ministry had the following official admi-

nistrative agencies subordinated to it:
1. The State Pollution Control Authority
2. The Smoke Control Council
3. The Council on Oil Pollution
4. The Directorate for Wildlife and Fresh-water Fish
5. The State Council for Open-Air Activities
6. The State Council for the Conservation of Nature
7. The Central Office of Historic Monuments
8. The Geographical Survey of Norway
9. The Hydrographic Office of Norway
10. The Norwegian Polar Institute

The size, scope, and comprehensiveness of the Ministry is impressive. It has approximately 200 full-time employees in the Ministry itself, and about 1,200 full-time employees in the subordinated institutions. The structure reflects Norway's growing commitment to nation-wide, comprehensive and coordinated planning and management of its physical, social, and environmental resources.

V. Changing Perspectives and Strategies for Future Planning and Development

The preceding account of planning and environmental legislation--while far from complete--provides a reasonably clear picture of the planning system that Norway has developed in response to twentieth century urbanization. It is obvious that it has not been a product of a singular grand design--but rather of an incremental growth resulting from pragmatic political responses to critical problems as they arose.

But even as the basic system was put into place by the Building Act of 1965, and implemented throughout the country, new and complex social forces were at work challenging some of the premises that had inspired the architects of that system. In a sense, the establishment of the Ministry of the Environment in 1972 reflects a turning point in Norway's post-war response to urbanization. Even though the post-war policies and programs had led to unparalleled achievements in the 1950s and 1960s and the goals of economic growth and full employment had been realized beyond expectations, the very achievement of those goals left in its wake new problems and challenges which could scarcely have been foreseen in the late 1940s.

Heightened Environmental Consciousness

Perhaps the most apparent and pervasive challenge came out of an intensified and expanded environmental consciousness. The environmental movement has had a long and significant influence in Norway. "Norges Naturvernforbund" (Society for the Protection of Nature) had been established in the early part of the twentieth century. It has grown into a nation-wide organization of 60,000 members belonging to 19 branch societies throughout the country. It publishes a journal called Norsk Natur as well as a companion publication called Natur og Ungdom (Nature and Youth) for the members of its youth organization.

This society had long been a champion for the protection of nature's esthetic, recreational, and scientific values. It had also been greatly concerned about the protection of natural areas and landscapes for the habitation of animals and vegetation. But in its response to new environmental threats accompanying post-war industrial expansion, it focused increasing attention upon technology's threat to Norway's most important energy resource--its natural waterfalls, and upon the growing problems of air and water pollution.

In recent years, the perspectives of the environmental movement have expanded to embrace a more social-symbiotic consciousness nurtured by the ecological movement. This was dramatically demonstrated in 1979 in the controversy over the hydro-electric power development project in the Alta river area in Northern Norway. The natural environmental issues were joined with the complex socio-cultural issue of the project's potential threat to the Lapland subculture.

The psychological and political vitality of this new environmentalist protest led to a Parliamentary decision to postpone its carefully designed project for an expanded hydro-electric power system at Alta (<u>Arbeiderbladet</u>, October 17, 1979, p. 6 and <u>Aftenposten</u> September 8, 1979, p. 40). By 1983 the power plant was under construction but at a reduced scale compared to the original plans and proposals.

In these and similar activities, the environmentalists were challenging the post-war confidence in economic growth and technological innovation as the central formula for achieving the good life. These new ecological perspectives had also been stimulated by Norway's participation in international conferences such as the U.N. Conference on Environment held in Stockholm in 1972. They added further impetus to the global perspectives which have become an important ingredient in Norway's environmental approach. That these concerns were being shared by the Norwegian populace is indicated by a nation-wide poll before the parliamentary election of 1977, which indicated that the considerations of Norway's environment and the use of its resources had become their most important social concerns (Gustavsen 1979, p. 16).

Growing Concerns about the Expanding Role of Government and Bureaucracy

The proliferation of planning and environmental legislation and their implementation led inevitably to a greatly expanded role of government at all levels, together with a growing bureaucratization of public life. While most Norwegians agreed that unlimited individual free enterprise was unthinkable and that certain forms of public planning and control were necessary in modern society, there was, nevertheless, a growing apprehension about the government's encroachments upon individual freedom. The classic dilemmas of "freedom versus organization" which had preoccupied Bertrand Russell and other scholars had become increasingly troublesome (Gustavsen 1979, pp. 94-99).

While very few would risk surrendering their socioeconomic and environmental concerns to the unlimited sovereignty of the market mechanism, many believed the time had come to critically re-examine the drift toward centralization and bureau-

102

cratization that had accompanied the building of Norway's welfare state. All the classic complaints about the cumbersome, impersonal, and irresponsive public bureaucracies were becoming a part of commonplace conversation.

The Rise of a Post-Industrial Individualism

This growing critique of government found considerable support from a new generation of Norwegians who had been the beneficiaries of the "good society" which had been orchestrated by the architects of post-war Norway's public policies. Their very socioeconomic well-being had shifted their preoccupation from concerns about social and economic justice to more individual concerns about personal and human development. Their attention was increasingly oriented toward socio-psychological aspects of the "good life."

It can perhaps be said that their growing affluence prompted an increasing interest in what the psychologist A. H. Maslow has called the "higher wants of social esteem and self realization" (Maslow 1943). It is likely that these new perspectives were especially congenial to the growing number of professional employees in Norway's emerging post-industrial, service-oriented society. For such, the concerns of the intimate milieu of the neighborhood, the work place, the school, and other settings for interpersonal relationships, had become increasingly important.

The New Program for a "Qualitatively Better Society"

That these changing perspectives were impacting the policy deliberations of the national government was clearly reflected in its proposed Long-Term Program for 1978-1981. While re-affirming its historic commitments to fostering a productive economy with full employment, it noted that this long-term program was "to a large extent focused on the human environment and tasks relating to the family, the work place, and the local community" (Royal Norwegian Ministry of Finance, Parliamentary Report No. 75: 1976-77, p. 9).

The challenge in the years ahead, says the report, "lies in making a good society better." It asserts that "an active policy of reform must be developed in close cooperation with the large organizations in society, with the aim of gradually creating a qualitatively better society." It emphasizes that the "freedom to choose a life style and the opportunity to influence decisions relating to oneself are of fundamental importance for well-being and welfare." To secure such a freedom and opportunity, the Report notes that Norway's society must be based on a decentralized decision-making system. The Report accented the achievement of the following eight national goals for the pursuit of a qualitatively better society:

1. Security and good living conditions.
2. Greater solidarity and equality.
3. Strengthening the family and the local community
4. Employment for everyone.
5. Better working environment.
6. Sound management of natural resource and the environment.
7. Freedom, democracy and legal protection.
8. International solidarity.

Source: Royal Norwegian Ministry of Finance, Norwegian Long-Term Programme 1978-1981. (Unofficial Translation). Parliamentary Report No. 75 (1976-77), p. 11

Some of the goals represent the government's continued support of past objectives such as Social Security and good living conditions, greater solidarity and equality, and employment for everyone. Others reflect the government's sensitivity to the changing perspectives discussed earlier; such as the goals of strengthening the family and the local community, improved working environments, sound management of natural resources and the environment.

In its elaboration of the implications of all the rudiments for a qualitatively better society, it becomes even clearer that the majority party has sought to develop a long-term program which takes into account the changing perspectives in contemporary Norway (Royal Norwegian Ministry of Finance, Parliamentary Report No. 75: 1976-77, pp. 31-101).

The government's response to the growing concerns about expanding roles of government and bureaucracy, is especially noteworthy. To improve the relationships between public administration and the individual, the Report proposed more decentralized structures and procedures for decision-making, reduced administrative details in less important fields, and simplification of the system of rules and regulations (Royal Norwegian Ministry of Finance 1967-77, p. 91).

New Strategies and Structures for Future Planning and Development

By the beginning of the 1980s, Parliament had enacted a "New Planning Law" which incorporated many of the new perspectives and goals enunciated in the Long-Term Program for 1978-1981. It was a comprehensive law; encompassing virtually every aspect of resource utilization, environmental protection, economic development, and community planning which had been addressed in the many disparate laws enacted in the past. It has been referred to as Norway's "Basic Planning Law Number Two"--superseding the Building Act of 1965. It was designed to provide the legal basis for a coordinated planning system that would consolidate many of the special planning and administrative structures that had been developing in recent decades.

Many of the laws and regulations restricting private developments for the sake of environmental protection were modified or nullified; including such important laws as the Shore and Mountain Act and the Nature Conservation Act. The planning goals and administrative structures of such special laws were consolidated with and integrated into the more all-encompassing planning system created by the new legislation. It was hoped that within such a system, a more holistic, better coordinated, and less bureaucratically burdensome planning and development would be possible.

The new legislation also sought to considerably decentralize the planning system. It enunciated the principle that planning activities and decisions should be made at that level of government where the plans involved would be implemented. Problems which did not have significant bearing on national policies were to be solved either at the municipal or county levels of public authority.

At the municipal level, a less extensive and detailed "kommuneplan" (municipal plan) replaced the more complex and comprehensive "general plan" that had been mandated by the Building Act of 1965. The law provided that such a plan should be developed at least once within each four-year term of municipal government. One of the principal objectives of such planning was to provide an overview coordinating land use and environmental conservation policies with other aspects of municipal planning and development. When any extensive development was to be contemplated for some area within a municipality, the law provided that a more detailed "komunedel-plan" (a plan for a municipal sub-area or sub-community) should be prepared.

In the interest of strengthening local autonomy, all these plans were to require formal approval only from the Municipal Council. It was, however, mandated that the "kommuneplan" and the "kommundelplan" should not run counter to the plans of the county or the national government (Miljø-verndepartementet 1977, pp. 10-12).

The new law also made provisions for more effective local neighborhood participation in municipal planning and community building, as well as for more meaningful public information and hearings concerning projected developments. Major developments involving extensive construction and substantial impacts on the environment would require environmental impact analyses. The enforcement of such impact assessments is placed in the hands of the public planning authorities (Norges Offentlige Utredninger 1977:1, pp. 30-33).

The incremental growth in democratic planning at the county level that has already been alluded to, were incorporated into the new legislation. Under the law, the county must update its County

Plan at least once within each four-year term between elections. Such county plans were expected to coordinate the national, county, and municipal plans with regard to resource utilization, economic and community development, and environmental conservation. Each county plan would be officially approved by its elected council and accepted by Norway's National Ministry of Environment.

Under the new legislation, the national government was required to prepare for Parliament a national planning document depicting the nation's planning and development relating to natural resources, employment, settlement patterns, and the developments of the various regions of the country. The plan would clarify the major national goals and policies pertaining to such matters. One of the objectives of the new law was to achieve more effective coordination between the various sectors of national planning. The Ministry of Environment continues to be given a leading role in this effort. It is given the major administrative responsibility for the nation's planning activities. Provisions are made for an interdepartmental coordination committee to assist the Ministry in this work (Norges Offentlige Utredninger 1977:1, pp. 99-100). The Ministry is also given the responsibility for initiating inter-county regional planning.

Because of the governmental changes brought about by the national election of 1980, bringing a Non-Labor government into power, this new planning law has not been put into effect. The new government will prepare a revised planning law. It is not expected, however, that the revised law will significantly break with the main principles developed by the previous government.

REFERENCES

Aftenposten. The daily newapaper of the Conservative Party.

Arbeiderbladet. The daily newspaper of the Labor Party.

Carlson, Reidar. 1976. The Regional Development Fund Oslo: The Regional Development Fund.

Eckhoff, Jan Chr. 1969. Byplan: Norske Bysamfunn i Vekst-Mot Hva? Oslo: Pax Forlag.

Eckstein, Harry. 1966. Division and Cohesion in Democracy: A Study of Norway.

Princeton: Princeton University Press.

Evang, Karl. 1970. Health Services in Norway. Oslo: S. Hammerstad Boktrykkeri.

Evang, Karl. 1973. Lecture to classes enrolled in the Scandinavian Urban Studies Term at the University of Oslo, Blindern.

Fort, Richard. 1979. "Environmental Approaches in Norway." The Norseman (Nos. 4 & 5.) Oslo: Nordmanns-Forbundet.

Gabrielsen, Egil. 1972. "Naturmiljøet i byer og tettsteder" pp. 53-62 in Planlegging i Byer og Tettsteder edited by Erik Anker, Øivind Linseth, and Egil Lund. Oslo: Norsk Forening For Bolig-og Byplanlegging.

Grimley, O. B. 1937. The New Norway: A People with the Spirit of Cooperation. Oslo: Griff-Forlaget.

Gustavsen, Øyvind. 1979. Naturresurser og Samfunn. Oslo: Tiden Norsk Forlag.

Haugstøl, Henrik and Jon Vegel, 1949. This is Norway. Arne Gimnea Forlag A/S.

Hersoug, Bjørn og Dag Leonardsen. 1979. Bygger de Landet? Distriktpolitikk og Sosialdomokrati 1945-1975. Oslo: Pax Forlag.

Johnsen, Ingvar. 1970. Planlegging: Hvordan Planlegger vi Arealbruk og Utbygging. Oslo: Johan Grundt Tanums Forlag.

Kjeldstadli, Knut og Vidar Keul (red). 1973. DNA- Fra folkebevegelse til statsstøtte. Oslo: Johan Grundt Tanums Forlag.

Kommunal-og Arbeidsdepartementet. 1972. Stortingsmelding Number 13 Om Mäl og Midler i Distriktsut-byggingen.

Kommunal-og Arbeidsdepartementet. 1971. Vern Om Naturmiljøet. Oslo: Norsk Institutt for By-og Regionsforskning.

Langdalen, Erik. 1969. Naturvern og Fritidsbebyggelse. Reprint from AD NOVAS No. 8, pp. 96-106. Oslo: Universitetsforlaget.

Maslow, A. H. 1943. "A Theory of Motivation." Psychological Review. 50, pp. 370-396.

Miljøverndepartementet. 1977. Den Nye Planleggings-loven. Spesialnummer av Miljønytt No. 4.

Ministry of the Environment. 1976. National Report of Norway to Habitat: United Nations Conference on Human Settlement. Oslo.

Norges Offentlige Utredninger. 1976; 47. Miljøvern-politikken. Oslo: Universitetsforlaget.

Norges Offentlige Utredninger. 1977; 1. Ny Planleggingslov. Oslo: Universitetsforlaget.

Norges Offentlige Utredninger. 1975: 30. Stat og Kirke. Oslo: Universitetsforlaget.

Norges Offentlige Utredninger, 1979:5. Bypolitikk. Oslo: Universitetsforlaget.

Rasmussen, Tor. 1979. The Distribution of Population in Norway, Regional Changes and Regional Policy. Reprint from Antoni Kuuklinski et al. (eds.) Regional Dynamics of Socioeconomic Change. Tampere: Finn-publishers.

Royal Norwegion Ministry of Finance, Parliamentary Report No. 75; 1976-77. Norwegian Long-Term Programme 1978-1981. Unofficial translation from Norwegian.

Schilliaas, Magne. 1950. Norskdom og kristendom. Namsos: Joh. Røberg Vik.

Smith, Douglas V. 1972. Norway Innovates in Environmental Planning. Oslo: Norwegian Institute of Urban and Regional Research.

Sosialdepartementet og Norges Almenvitenskapelige Forskningräd. 1970. Sosialpolitikken og Samfunns-forskningen. Oslo: Universitets-forlaget.

Stavig, Arthur and Svendsen, Inger. 1977. Trolls, The Whipping-boy of Norwegian Folklore. Freeman, So. Dak. Hill Press.

Stokke, Aaamond. 1976. Survey of Norwegian Planning Legislation and Organization. Oslo: Ministry of Environment. Translated into English by Peter Thomas and Richard Frost.

CHAPTER FIVE: PLANNING AND COMMUNITY BUILDING IN METROPOLITAN OSLO

Even though Norway's national policy has sought to limit the growth of Oslo and its metropolitan region in the interest of maintaining a regional balance in the urban development of the country, its growth and development has made it the leading metropolitan center of the nation. As was indicated in Chapter Three, it has become the leading administrative center for Norway's financial, commercial and industrial firms; as well as for education, research, and government. Hence, an examination of planning and community building in metropolitan Oslo, provides a uniquely helpful illumination of their dynamics and the issues involved.

Although similar social and community changes are at work in other urbanizing regions of Norway, their scale and visibility are nowhere as great as in Oslo. In no other urbanized region of Norway, have the post-industrial tertiary industries exerted such a pervasive influence. Furthermore, as the nation's capital city, its planning and community building become in a unique way integrally related to the nation's over-all urban and environmental policies.

I.   The Growth and Development of the Oslo Region

Demographic Growth

As was noted in an earlier chapter, the Oslo region contains the largest population concentration in all of Norway. The city of Oslo had been growing steadily in the first half of the twentieth century from a population of 227,600 in 1900 to 286,200 in 1946. By 1950 the number had increased to 434,000 largely as a result of Oslo's merger with the neighboring municipality of Aker. The city continued to grow during the following two decades until it reached its peak population of 478,000. Since 1970 its population has begun to decline, dropping to 446,000 by 1984.

These data about Oslo's growth do not, however, adequately reflect its growth as the center of Norway's largest metropolitan region. If one takes in the growth beyond the administrative boundaries of Oslo, the metropolis has grown from a population of 487,702 in 1930 to 801,187 in 1974 (Brækus 1976, p. 130). By 1980 it had grown to a metropolis of 850,000 inhabitants.

For the purpose of explaining the nature and dynamics of this growth, Professor Brækhus has divided the metropolis into the following zones: (1) The City (core); (2) The Inner Zones (West and East of the Aker River); (3) The Outer Zones (West and East from the municipality of Aker which became part of Oslo in 1948); (4) The Near Zone (made up of the suburban municipalities of Nesodden, Oppegård, Ski, Lørenskog, Rælingen, Skedsmo, Nittedal, Bærum and Asker); and (5) The Far Zone (made up of Frogn, Ås, Vestby, Enebakk, Aurskog, Høland, Fet, Sørum, Nes, Ullensaker, Gjerdrum, Nannestad, and Lunner as delimited in 1970. The following table reveals the differential growth of these various zones from 1920 to 1974.

Table 5.1: Population Growth of the Oslo Metropolis

Year	City (Core)	Inner Zone of Oslo West	East	Outer Zone of Oslo West	East	Near Zone	Far Zone	Total
1920	45,800	75,576	139,546	26,184	26,762	57,439	59,991	431,298
1930	46,964	83,059	131,516	41,660	44,295	78,094	62,114	487,702
1946	39,113	103,020	142,306	66,321	63,411	92,724	67,835	574,730
1950	37,382	98,554	141,864	76,225	74,864	102,267	70,923	602,079
1960	23,964	83,609	113,246	86,575	162,832	145,300	78,481	694,007
1970	13,365	65,091	97,266	85,046	203,820	215,106	96,984	778,678
1974	10,833	63,288	78,185	85,222	223,669	234,005	105,985	801,187
1982	7,000	62,000	77,000	83,000	219,000	249,000	116,000	873,000

Source: Brækus, Kjeld 1976. "Oslo: past, present, future." Norsk geografisk tidskrift. 30, p. 131 and later additions.

As Professor Brækhus points out, the data demonstrate an almost classical outward expansion of the metropolis with a corresponding decrease of the inner city core and the central city. The popula-

tion of the city core declined steadily from its
peak of 46,964 in 1930 to a low of 7,000 in 1972,
and the inner zone of the city thinned out from a
peak population of 245,326 in 1946 to a low of
139,000 in 1982.

Only in Oslo's Outer Zone East, formerly the
Aker municipality, did Oslo's population continue to
grow after 1950. The phenomenal growth of this zone
from a population of 74,864 in 1950 to 223,669 in
1974 reflects Oslo's extensive planning and community building in the newly acquired rural municipality of Aker. After 1975, however, declines in
population have come also in the Outer Zone of Oslo,
as revealed in Table 5.1.

The municipalities beyond Oslo's administrative boundaries have experienced a substantial
growth since 1950. The Near Zone municipalities
grew from 102,267 inhabitants in 1950 to 249,000 in
1972 attributable to developments of nine municipalities near Oslo but located in the Akershus
"Fylke" (county). It should be noted that the rate
of growth in this zone has accelerated sharply
during the last two decades.

The growth in the Far Zone has been steady but
at a much lower rate. Based on Professor Brækhus'
data, the total metropolitan population beyond
Oslo's city boundary had reached nearly 340,000 by
1974. This was approximately 42% of the total population of the metropolis. After 1975, population in
these zones has continued to grow, but at a slower
rate than before.

These general population trends have continued
through the decade of the 1970s. The population of
Oslo has declined from 478,000 at the beginning of
the decade to about 446,000 in 1984. The urban
population in Akershus during that time continued to
grow until it comes close to that of Oslo (Oslo
Byplankontoret 1979, pp. 4-5).

Expanding Functions of Oslo

The demographic growth of Oslo was of course
associated with an expansion and transformation of
its economic, socio-cultural, and civic functions.
Like other metropolitan regions of Norway, only more

113

so, Oslo experienced a decisive shift from the primary and secondary occupations to the tertiary or service-oriented industries. From 1960 to 1975 employment primary in industries declined from 5% to 2%. During the same period, employment in tertiary occupations grew from 65.0% to 72.8% (Norges Offentlige Utredninger 1979:5, pp. 28-29). Table 5.2 provides a summary of the occupational growth and transformation of the Oslo-Akershus area from 1950 to 1980. It indicates that employment in the primary industries had declined to 1.7% by 1980, and that employment in the tertiary industries had increased to 76.6%.

It should be noted that the number employed increased considerably between 1950 and 1980. Most of the increase occurred in the tertiary occupations of commerce, finance, public administration and other service industries. Even of the nearly 73,000 industrial workers, less than half were operators. All the data clearly indicate that Oslo was becoming predominantly an office and administrative-oriented city.

This predominance of tertiary employment was of course significantly related to Oslo's role as the nation's capital. In 1974 nearly 40,000 Osloites were employed in the nation's governmental services. Although less obvious than the expansion of direct governmental services, Oslo's multiple role as a leading center for higher education and research; for the administrative headquarters of many of Norway's major industries; for the central offices of the leading banks and insurance companies; for the headquarters of national fraternal and professional organizations; for museums, theaters, and opera; and for the nation's railroad, radio, and television systems have all contributed to the growth of the tertiary occupations. By 1970 more that 70% of the work places in the center core and inner zones of Oslo were involved in such functions.

It was inevitable that these developments should bring to the fore a whole series of acute problems for planning and community building, many of which would have both local and national significance. Perhaps the paramount problem and all-

114

Table 5.2 Occupational Distribution in Oslo and
Akershus Area 1950 - 1980.

Occupational Categories	Total		Percent of Total			
	1950	1980	1950	1960	1970	1980
Agriculture, Forestry & Fishing, etc. (Primary)	18,905	7,513	6.4	4.3	2.1	1.7
Mining & Industry, etc.	92,904	72,961	31.7	28.8	25.9	16.2
Construction Industry	24,848	24,755	8.5	8.1	6.5	5.5
Finance	9,038	14,186	3.1	3.6	4.4	3.2
Communication & Transportation	30,671	41,128	10.4	11.2	10.5	9.2
Public Administration, Public & Private Service	49,950	177,756	17.0	20.4	27.3	39.7
Personal Service & Other	26,259	13,574	7.9	6.3	4.4	3.0
Commerce	44,125	96,250	15.0	17.3	18.9	21.5
TOTAL	296,700	448,123	100.0	100.0	100.0	100.0

Source: Oslo Kommunes Administrasjon 1975, Oslo
Kommuneplan 1976 - 1985, p. 40 and
additions for 1980.

The definition for "occupied person" was wider in
1980 than in 1950, as part-time employees were not
included in 1950.   However, the percentage distribution between occupational categories reflects the
real situation fairly well.

encompassing challenge was to create what Lewis Mumford calls "an adequate urban container" for all the people and their activities in the developing metropolis (Mumford 1968, p. 144). This would require a system and program for managing its growth and development, involving the public acquisition of the needed areas for expansion and the planning of community structures within them. It would also involve controlling urban density and land use for the whole metropolis. It would require the re-shaping of Oslo's historic city from one adapted to its pre-industrial and industrial past, to one more suitable for the life and culture of a post-industrial capital city. This would involve providing adequate and suitable locations in central Oslo for the expanding post-industrial occupations and building an appropriate transportation network linking them to the growing residential communities surrounding the city's center.

II. Capital City Planning and National Policies in the Post-war Period

Oslo's response to these challenges were inevitably influenced by the political developments in Norway at the time. By the close of World War II, the Labor Party had become the dominant power in both national political affairs and in Oslo's muni-cipal government. Becoming a majority parliamentary party, its earlier commitments to a working-class consciousness was superseded by a more pragmatic politics based on a larger national community consciousness (Kjeldstadli and Keul 1973, pp. 97-98). Even though the roots of that community consciousness lay deep in Norway's history, there can be no doubt that Norway's struggle with the Nazi invaders had intensified it.

After the war the problems of reconstruction required the united support from the whole national community. This served to strengthen the political influence of those who sought to direct the Labor Party's ideology toward a form of regulated capital-ism which could support Norway's ambitious social service systems. Thus the Labor Party's major post-war objectives were developed around (1) a

116

dynamic program of post-war reconstruction; (2) a continual increase in the gross national product; (3) full employment; and (4) a policy of equalization of income and services for all Norwegians. In the pursuit of these objectives, the Labor Party secured the cooperation of the liberal, center, and conservative parties of the country (Kjeldstadli and Keul 1973, p. 166).

Out of such a political climate growth, prosperity, and the general welfare, tended to be perceived as synonymous concepts (Johnsen 1973, p. 26). It was assumed that the national government would have the responsibility for establishing the ways in which the local municipalities should help promote such economic growth and social welfare. Municipal policies and programs were perceived as integral parts of the developing national community politics. Thus the early response to Oslo's rapid growth was generally positive on both the national and local levels of government.

One of the most important early steps taken by the national government was the creation of a Housing Bank (Husbanken) in 1946 to provide long-term low-interest bearing loans to housing ventures all over Norway. Although not limited to cooperative housing societies, the Housing Bank looked with special favor upon them, and provided the major financial support for the extensive activities of Oslo's cooperative housing societies.

Two years later (in 1948), the national parliament took a decisive step toward expanding Oslo's boundaries by incorporating the large rural municipality of Aker into the City. This changed the size of Oslo from a very limited 6.6 square miles to a large metro area of 175 square miles; making it geographically the fifth largest city in the world (Karevold 1980, p. 5). It provided the city of Oslo a unique opportunity for controlling and shaping its metropolitan future; including its housing and community developments, its use of the vast open forests and agricultural areas, the location and promotion of industrial and commercial activities, and the development of a communications system for the entire metropolis. In other words—developing an appropriate container for Oslo's future metropolis.

III. Comprehensive Planning for an Expanding Metropolis

The first master plan encompassing Oslo's boundaries as expanded by the incorporation of Aker, had been developed in 1934. This plan established the basic directions for Oslo's later development. It envisioned the expansion of the city in three principal directions: (1) to the North and West, (2) to the North and East, and (3) to the South. It identified boundaries separating "Oslomarka" (Oslo Forests and Fields) from the land set aside for city building. The plan reflected an optimistic perspective for the City's growth to a population of 700,000 inhabitants. It set aside housing and industrial areas to accommodate such an expanding population.

Planning For A Plurinuclear Metropolis

The end of the war and the great expansion of Oslo in 1948, made comprehensive planning for the metropolitan development increasingly urgent. Particularly critical was the need for clear and decisive plans for developing the outer zones resulting from Aker's merger with Oslo. The City Planning Department published in 1950 a new plan for these areas.

This plan reflected a continued pro-growth perspective for a population of 700,000. But for the large areas of new undeveloped land, the plan abandoned the "concentric principle" of the preceding plans which presumed a gradual decrease in building density with the lengthening distance from the City's Center. Instead, the plan envisaged a plurinuclear metropolis involving the development of sub-centers; each of which should be surrounded by tributary residential areas. Instead of "dormitory" suburban development typical in the United States, these sub-centers would take the form of "satellite towns," as they were sometimes called. These towns were to be comprehensive, relatively compact units linked with Oslo's Center by a public rail transit system. According to the plan the towns should be economically, socially, and politically integral parts of Oslo even if somewhat self-sufficient town

communities (Oslo Planning Department 1960, p. 34).
A more detailed description of these satellite towns
and their central importance for shaping Oslo's
future is provided in the following chapter.

The Master Plan of 1960

While planning and community building in
Oslo's newly acquired area were taking place, the
City Planning Department was actively developing
zoning plans and a revised master plan for the
entire city which culminated in the 1960 Master
Plan. This planning activity was based on Norway's
General Building Law of 1924 and Oslo's Building
Ordinances. The Legislation mandated the
preparation of a complete plan for the city and its
future development. The following paragraph from
the Master Plan of 1960 provides a good summary of
its central features:

"Broadly speaking the plan envisages a central
business and commercial district--surrounded by a
dense residential area--which is in turn surrounded
by an outer residential area of varying building
density. Industrial zones are located near the
harbor, in the Grorud Valley in the east, along the
Aker River and at local centers. The whole development area is surrounded by Oslomarka (Oslo Forests),
to which the central parts of the town are connected
by a system of greenways and parks. A system of
suburban railways, other railways, arterial highways
and ringroads, and public bus and tram services
provide internal and external communication." (Oslo
Planning Department 1960, p. 33).

Of the total city area of 175 square miles,
only 54 square miles were scheduled for development
in the Plan. The remaining 121 square miles make up
the famous "Oslomarka"; comprising large areas of
forest, lakes, and streams. This was to be kept
intact and utilized in its present condition, and
serve as catchment areas for the city's reservoirs
and as recreational areas for the entire Oslo
population.

Within the total development area, land was
designated for a population of 600,000 people. This
projection was based on maintaining the past housing

densities as much as possible in the Inner Zone and the Centrum, and in anticipated large scale housing development in the new Outer Zones. Figure 5A provides a helpful map of the various developmental zones as well as of the vast open space areas.

Land zoned for industry made up 10% of the total development area, or about 4,000 acres. The location of such land for future industrial use accented the pre-war location in eastern Oslo. Although there was considerable opportunity for industrial expansion in the Outer Zone North, West, and South, the only remaining areas in Oslo with extensive stretches of fairly level unbuilt land readily useful for industrial activities were in eastern Oslo. Hence, 55% of the land zoned for industry was located there in the Grorud Valley through which the main railway lines to East and North Norway and to Sweden run. In an attempt to reduce the problems of the journey to work, the sides of Grorud Valley were zoned for residential use (Oslo Planning Department 1960, pp. 33-34).

Communications and Transportation Plans

The most important elements in the Master Plan for transportation were the main national railways, the suburban railway network, and the system of ring roads and traffic arteries. One of the major items in the Plan was the proposal to connect the railways to the East and West by a tunnel under the City Center, and the replacement of the two terminal railway stations by a new Central Station on the site of the existing East Railway Station.

The Master Plan for suburban railway network was based on the assumption that the population of the Outer Zone would travel primarily by public transport. For areas not covered by the rail network, bus connections to local suburban railway stations or bus routes direct to central Oslo were planned. As will be described in greater detail in the next chapter, the extension of the suburban railway system was to be coordinated with the development of the satellite towns in the new areas of Oslo.

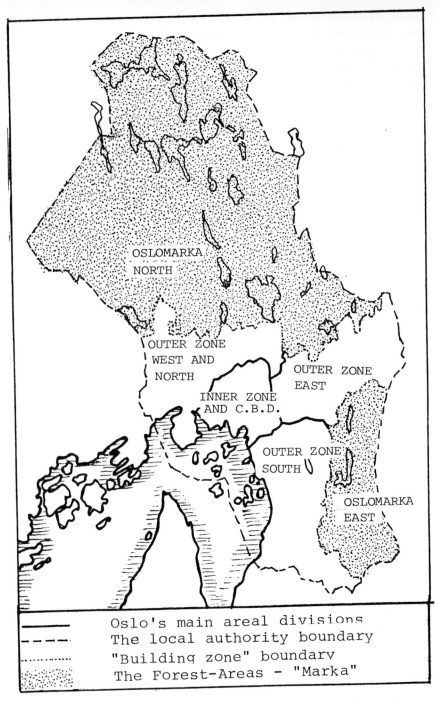

Figure 5A: The Municipal Area of Oslo with four
Urban Zones and Oslomarka.

121

The main road system provided for in the plan
included a main thoroughfare along the shore of the
Oslo harbor to connect the main highways into Oslo
from the West and the South, and a system of ring
roads connecting the main arterial roads radiating
out.

Large parking facilities were planned for the
intersections of the inner ring roads and the
arterial roads so that motorists entering the City's
center could park their automobiles and use public
transport or walk within one kilometer radius of the
Center (Oslo Planning and Development 1960, pp.
36-37).

Recreational Areas

Recreational and public open spaces play a
prominent role in the Master Plan. In terms of the
area set aside for such purposes, it was the
dominant land use of the Plan. The vast forest and
lake areas of Oslomarka surrounding the development
area embraced two thirds of all of Oslo's land.
According to the Plan, the Inner part of Oslo was to
be connected with these vast areas by "tongues" of
"green open spaces" which should thread their way
through the Outer Zone, dividing residential areas
into separate clusters and separating housing from
industrial activities. They should also provide
easy access to and from the recreational areas for
the population via the famous "turveier" system.
(See Figure 5B.)

This plan for parks and "turveier" had been
approved in 1953. Fifty of the fifty-six miles of
"turveier" had been planned in detail, preventing
any other developments on them. By 1960 about half
of the land for them had been acquired by the City
for implementation of the plan. To secure the
City's use of Oslomarka for recreational and other
public uses, the Oslo Municipality had also purchased 25,000 acres of land and established
restrictions against developments on 75,000
additional acres.

For the central core of Oslo, the Plan for the
most part involved the preservation of the historic
parks, squares and green areas around public

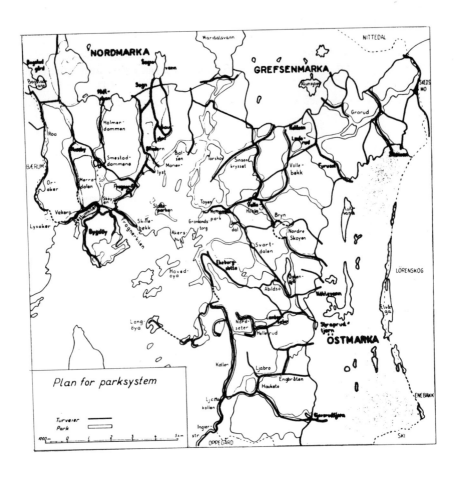

Figure 5B   Parks and green tour routes ("turveier")
in the built-up area according to master
plan of 1960.

institutions such as the Parliament, the Palace and the Akershus Castle. Similarly, for the rest of the Inner Zone the Plan involved the preservation of such recreational areas as the famous Frogner Park, sports fields, church grounds, and other public open space areas.

In addition, the Plan included a commitment to an Aker River redevelopment program begun before the war. The Program was designed to change the river back to the clear stream it had been before the industrial development in its valley. A chain of parks were to be created along the river through which it would be possible to walk from Oslo's Center, through the heart of Oslo, to the large Lake Maridal five miles to the North. This would involve the removal of several of the industries still located here even if they no longer used the water power generated by the Aker River. In 1984 this work is almost completed. A salmon was caught in the river in 1983 for the first time in almost 100 years.

The Center and Inner Zone

For the most part, the Master Plan continued the pre-1960 land use for Oslo's Center. Except for the public buildings, squares and parks, it was mostly zoned for such commercial uses as shops and offices. Some reference was made, however, to areas around the central business district where the age of the buildings and other factors had led to an invasion of new commercial uses and blight. These areas were designated for renewal as high density residential areas. The Plan alludes to the changes in land use from residential to office and commercial uses which "have complicated the picture and caused serious problems" in the Center (Oslo Planning Department 1960, p. 82).

For the Inner Zone, commercial activities were largely confined to local centers in accordance with the sub-center principle. Such centers should provide locations for offices, community centers, cinemas, etc., as well as the typical small town commercial activities. In historic commercial streets with a tradition of residential functions in upper stories combined with first story commercial activities, mixed land uses would be continued. Most of the Inner Zone area was, however, zoned for residential use.

It was noted that much research and planning remained to be done for Oslo's Center and Inner Zone and that "the preparation of a program for the next 20-30 years development in Inner Oslo, form the most important task in the forthcoming years" (Oslo Planning Department 1960, p. 40).

From the preceding description of planning developments in post-war Oslo, it is clear that Norway's capital city was developing ideas for an urban size and form which could provide a more adequate container for the metropolitan realities that were emerging. A review of some of the major developments of post-war Oslo will indicate how those ideas were translated into new metropolitan realities.

IV.   Post-war Developments of the Oslo Metropolis

The Shaping of a Polycentric Metropolis

As already noted, the annexation of Aker in 1948 provided Oslo a strategic opportunity for controlling and shaping its metropolitan growth. Its 1950 Master Plan outlined the City's commitment to a kind of multinuclear metropolis based on the development of satellite towns and other planned-unit developments. Since a fairly comprehensive account of such developments is provided in the following chapter, only a few comments regarding them need to be made here.

In the largely undeveloped areas of the Outer Zone East and the Outer Zone South, the building of satellite towns plus the development of a public transit system linking them with the expanding metropolis happened at a rather rapid pace. The 1950 plan for continued development of Outer Zone West and North according to more traditional housing and community building also took place. There too, attempts were made to cluster housing around commercial centers and public transit stations.

125

The extent of the developments in the Outer Zone--i.e., the area from the original Aker municipality--is indicated by the growth of its population from 129,732 in 1946 to 288,866 in 1970. By 1970 the population in this Outer Zone exceeded the population of Inner City Oslo by more than a hundred thousand. It should also be noted that of the 288,866 inhabitants in the Outer Zone in 1970, over 200,000 were in Outer Zone East where the satellite town strategy was most rigorously pursued. Thus a very substantial portion of Oslo's expanding population became residents of the new satellite towns.

Housing Development

Closely related to the development of the new towns was a rapid expansion of the housing supply. By 1960 some 50,000 new housing units had been built since the close of the war. Most of them--42,000-- were built in the Outer Zones (Oslo Planning Department 1960, p. 55). Approximately 35,000 more were added the following decade, and another 40,000 dwelling in the 1970s.

As will be described in more detail in the following chapter, the municipality of Oslo usually acquired the land and developed the building sites. The National Housing Bank provided much of the financial capital at low interest rates, and the substantial part of the housing development was done by cooperative societies--particularly the Oslo Bolig og Sparelag (OBOS). OBOS became, in fact, the principal agent for implementing both Oslo's housing policy and its satellite town ideas.

By this time Norway had come to regard the application of the principles of Consumer Cooperation to housing as the most effective way of implementing its idea that a suitable dwelling was a human right to be secured for all its citizens. In 1928, sixteen national trade unions had gone together to form a cooperative, non-profit building association. This became the prototype for OBOS which became the nation's largest cooperative housing society.

The fact that about 80% of all new housing in Oslo was financed through the Housing Bank played an important role in keeping the costs of new housing for families with children at a relatively moderate level (Nestor 1979, p. 29). The majority in both Norway's Parliament and Oslo's City Council strongly favored cooperative housing as a means of making it possible to secure suitable dwellings in mass produced housing. Thus OBOS was favored by both the National Housing Bank and the City Council (Nestor 1979, p. 12). Ironically, the people who were best able to take advantage of the favored cooperative housing opportunities were not the very poor, but the better educated white collar workers in the growing tertiary occupations. Of the new OBOS members around 1970, about 70% were academics, and 50% of the total membership came from this population (Nestor 1979, p. 125).

The prominence of cooperative housing in Oslo's developing metropolis is clearly seen by the fact that OBOS alone built almost 50% of all the post-war housing in Oslo (Norway's State Housing Directorate 1968, p. 22). It had played an important role in implementing the goal of home ownership and housing security for Osloites. When OBOS began, two thirds of the housing was in rental units. By 1978 that proportion had been reduced to one third of the dwelling units (Nestor 1979, p. 176).

Industrial and Commercial Development

Even as in housing, post-war Oslo also experienced an acute shortage of industrial space for industry for harbor facilities and railways, for warehousing and for sewage treatment plants. Important strides were taken to improve the situation from 1948 to 1959. During that time, 82 million square feet of floor space were created for such uses. Even as in housing most of the space-- nearly two thirds--was developed in the Outer Zone, near Lake Østensjø and in the Grorud Valley. The city acquired the land and leased it to private firms for development--chiefly of light industry. In the Inner Zone much of the industrial expansion took the form of expanding established industrial

127

plants along the Aker River. Manufacturing had shown a marked tendency to decentralize from the Inner City to the Outer Zone. In addition, it had been losing in relative importance to other occupations (Oslo Planning Department 1960, pp. 59-64).

Building for commercial and office uses, on the other hand, was concentrated in Oslo's Center. Some 80% of the offices and 85% of the hotels and restaurants were built in the Center. There was also an increase in commercial shops in the Center during the post-war years; although about two thirds of the increase was constructed in the Outer Zone in the satellite towns and neighborhood centers.

One of the most striking changes in Oslo's centrum was a sharp increase in office buildings to accommodate expanding governmental services, financial and commercial institutions, and other corporate centers of activity. While these new structures were presumably congruent with Oslo's development as a post-industrial metropolis, they threatened the continued existence of the historic residential areas near the heart of the city. As one student has noted, these new developments amounted to a decisive transformation of the cityscape of Oslo's core area (Satterness 1978).

Other post-war structures especially appropriate to a post-industrial age were a wide variety of buildings for social, educational, and cultural activities. Some of these, such as the new Concert Hall were appropriately located in the center. Others such as schools and health and welfare centers were located in the new sub-centers of Oslo.

V.   Change and Special Planning Challenges in the 1970s and 1980s

From Growth to Decline

By 1970 the post-war, pro-growth optimism was being tempered by a growing skepticism about both the continued growth projections as well as of their qualitative merits.

In the first place, the City's rapid population growth had largely come to an end by 1960. During the decade of the 1960s it only grew from

476,000 to 478,000 when it reached its highest point. During the following seven years its population declined to 460,000 (Norges Offentlige Redninger 1979:5, pp. 18-89). By 1982 the population was down to 448,000. This decline was similar to that experienced by other large cities of Norway.

While some anti-city romanticist sought to interpret this decline as evidence of a "greening of Norway" momentum and an end to urban growth, a careful analysis of the population changes suggests rather that the urban areas were spreading out beyond their boundaries. In Oslo, it was clear that the thinning out of the population in the inner city was accompanied by a rapid growth in the periphery.

While the population in the Outer Zone more than doubled between 1946 and 1982, the Inner Zone experienced a decline of over a 140,000 inhabitants. During that same period the Center of the city declined from 39,113 to about 10,800. Not only were people moving out from the City's Center to the new developments in the Outer Zone; but they were also moving out beyond the City's 1948 boundaries to the neighboring communities and municipalities of Akershus and other counties around Oslo. Thus, the population decline of inner city Oslo does not mean a decline of urbanism, but rather a spreading out of the metropolitan community.

The Expanding Metropolis as Gigantic Separator

In this process of population change and outward expansion the metropolis has functioned as a gigantic "centripetal--centrifugal separator" to borrow a metaphor from the American political scientist, Bert E. Swanson (Swanson 1970, p. 58). The Inner Zone of Oslo has become increasingly over-represented by the elderly and under-represented by young children. In 1976, the people over 65 years of age made up 31% of the population of the Inner Zone of Oslo--more than twice the 14% of Norway's population at this age.

In the same year, the number of children from 5 to 14 years of age in the Inner Zone made up only 5.5% of its population compared with 16.2% of Norway's population for that age category (Norges

Offentlige Utredninger 1979:5, p. 23). In the Outer Zones and beyond, families with children and people in the occupationally productive years are more predominant.

One of the most significant changes in Oslo's Inner Zone has been the concentration of work places at its Center. In spite of a declining employment in industry, Oslo has experienced a striking growth in employment. Most of this growth has been in tertiary occupations. The City's roles as a national capital and "Fylke" center; as a national center for cultural affairs; as a shipping and commercial center; and a center for Norway's largest metropolitan region have made Oslo a magnet for a highly diverse employment.

Of the 100 largest industrial institutions in Norway, some forty had their central offices in Oslo. Of the three largest banking institutions in the country, two have their headquarters in Oslo. More than 70% of Norway's population engaged in the nation's commercial, professional, political, and ideological organizations work in Oslo; and 50% of those engaged in the educational and research organizations of the country. Specialization, technological innovation, and public administration are characteristic attributes of work in the City's Center (Norges Offentlige Utredninger 1979:5, pp. 36-38).

This concentration of work places, coupled with a thinning out of the residential population in the Inner Zone has made for many new and complex problems of planning and policy development in contemporary Oslo.

VI.   Transport Planning and Development in the Oslo Region

Perhaps no problem was more pressing than that of planning and developing an appropriate transportation system. The continuing expansion of the urbanized areas both within and beyond the City's boundaries coupled with an ever increasing imbalance between workplace concentration and residential dispersion led inevitably to acute problems of traffic management and all the environmental issues related to it.

Oslo's Developing Public Transit System

As has already been noted, the 1950 master plan for Oslo's outward growth provided for the development and expansion of its public transit system. In many ways transportation planning was combined with community planning much as Wilfred Owen describes and defends in his eloquent book, The Accessible City (Owen 1972). The new satellite towns were linked to Oslo's center by new subway trains similar to the Stockholm pattern which Wilfred Owen described so favorably in his book. In other parts of Oslo, the extension of older streetcar lines and bus routes insured that most residential districts in the outer areas would be served by public transit.

Oslo's 1960 master plan clearly reflected the City's continued commitment to an extensive public transportation network articulating the services of its new subway trains, its older light rail system, the major national railways, and a supplementary bus system. One of the major items in the plan was the proposed connection of the rail system of eastern Oslo and those of western Oslo by a tunnel under the city center, and the replacement of the two terminal stations by a new central station at the site of the East Railway Station. Similarly, the plan called for an underground connection of the eastern subway system with the western light rail system and the building of appropriate subway stations in the City's center. That these complex and costly plans for a future modern transit system were more than wishes is attested to by the fact that most of them have by now been implemented. (See Figure 5C).

The Challenge of the Automobile Culture

But transportation problems continue to be a compelling challenge for Oslo. Like other cities of the western world, it has experienced a phenomenal growth of "bilismen"--an adept Norwegian word for an "automobile culture." Oslo planners, public officials, and its population at large have become keenly conscious of what Wilfred Owen describes as the

131

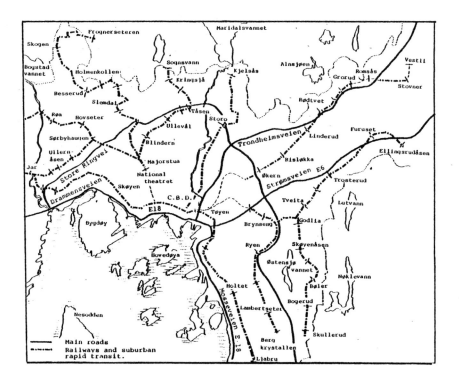

Figure 5C Oslo's Subway System and Main Roads.

The first line on the Western branches of the subway
system was built in 1898, and gradually extended.
The municipalities of Oslo and Aker were the greatest shareholders. The lines were built at the same
time as construction of one-family houses took place
over the wide areas. To build the eastern branches
was proposed in the master plan of 1952, in order to
serve the satellite towns that were also proposed.
The first lines were opened in 1966. The system has
been extended up to 1980. The names of the stations
shows the location of some of the satellite towns.

"conflict between cars and cities" (Owen 1972, pp. 1-23).

One of the most visible signs of Norway's dramatic post-war prosperity, was the rapid increase of automobile ownership. During the decade of the 1960s, for example, motor vehicle ownership increased from 301,000 to 849,000--an increase of 182.1%. This rate of increase exceeded that of West Germany, France, Belgium, Denmark, and the United Kingdom (Owen 1972, p. 17). The total number of automobiles in Oslo increased from about 22,000 in 1948 to approximately 158,000 in 1977--an increase of about 600%. The number of personal automobiles grew from 13,000 to 138,000. Translated into the number of private persons per auto, this meant a decrease from 29 per auto in 1948 to 3 per auto in 1977 (Nestor 1979, p. 223). In 1981 the number of personal automobiles in Oslo was 150,000, indicating that the increase has reached a peak. However, in the commuting hinterland, the number of private cars in still increasing, causing continuous problems in the inner city area.

This phenomenal growth inevitably challenged Oslo's early commitment to a tranportation system handled predominantly by public transit. Increased automobile usage led to new and improved thoroughfares, which in turn led to increased automobile use. Streets and highways began to fill up with cars, and the City's center became increasingly plagued by more and more cars, parking lots, and ramps. As more and more space was demanded for cars, less became available for the development of an environment suitable for the functions of a capital city. Traffic jams, air and noise pollution, and unsafe streets became familiar problems for both the centrum and the rest of the Inner Zone of the City. This despite the fact that Oslo continued its support of the public transit system anticipated in 1950.

Comprehensive Transportation Planning in the Oslo Area

In response to these growing challenges, the Oslo Planning Office undertook from 1961-1965 a

comprehensive transportation analysis for the Oslo
area, consisting of Oslo and the neighboring municipality of Bærum. The study was aimed at finding the
most rational transportation plan possible for
Oslo's future as envisaged by its 1960 master plan
(Tombre 1965). It sought, in other words, to
coordinate transportation planning with community
planning in ways recommended by Wilfred Owen. After
a systematic analysis the study presented several
possible alternative solutions but recommended for
adoption a "maximal balance" proposal containing the
following basic elements:

1. Reduction of the rate of work place
   concentration in the city center.
2. Concentration of centrum functions
   related to cultural and public institutions, restaurants and entertainment
   establishments, offices and work places
   for specialized services, and commercial
   activities of regional and national
   significance.
3. Locating high traffic-generating activities in the Outer Zones of the city or
   region.
4. Developing urban renewal plans aimed at
   maintaining, and if possible increasing,
   the population of the central city area.
5. Depending on public transit as the main
   vehicle for transporting the working
   people into the centrum.
6. Improving the services of the main
   automobile arteries in the Oslo region.

This "maximal balance" proposal was in essence
adopted by the city council in 1967 and became a
part of Oslo's Master Plan (Eckhoff 1969, pp.
68-79).

As in other matters, the national government
was also concerned about Oslo's transportation
problems. In 1968, it appointed an Oslo Transport
Commission to consider the needs and possibilities
of a transportation system appropriate for its
capital city. The Commission was charged to consider whether the public transportation system could
more favorably compete with private transport
through a better coordination of the various parts

of the system and an improved standard of its service.   It was asked to pay attention to road safety,
air pollution, noise and other environmental factors.   It analyzed the public transit system for the
larger Oslo region, including besides the city of
Oslo the western municipalities of Bærum and Asker,
the eastern area municipalities of Lørenskog,
Skedsmo and Nittedal as well as the southern area
municipalities of Nesodden, Oppegård, Ski, Ås and
Frogn (Oslo Urban Transport commission 1971).   The
areal scope of the study is indicated in Figure 5D.
     It is clear from that map that the Oslo metro-
polis had continued to expand extensively beyond the
city boundaries of 1948.   It is also noteworthy that
this expansion beyond Oslo's city jurisdiction made
increasingly important the involvement of the
national government in the study and planning of the
area's transportation future.   In the appointment of
the Commission members, the government put particular emphasis upon the varied composition of
members representing the public transport industry,
the City of Oslo, county of Akershus, and representatives from each of the three adjacent areas
(Oslo Urban Transport Commission, 1971).
     The Transport Commission Report affirmed the
goals of an Oslo-Akershus Regional Planning
Organization which involved (1) connecting the whole
metro area into one large coherent market for labor,
housing, and service; (2) exercising the greatest
possible geographical restraint on urban growth in
the three directions radiating from central Oslo;
(3) a concentration on work places in Sandvika,
Lillestrøm, and Ski; (4) better relationships
between work places and housing within certain parts
of the metro region; and (5) urban renewal and
rehabilitation in the older areas.   The Commission
regarded the prevailing 70:30 distribution between
public and individual transport for work journeys to
the central City as too low; thinking that an 80:20
ratio would be more optimal.   They noted that the
car owner is covering far less of the costs he
brings upon society than a bus passenger.
     The following quote from the report indicates
the kinds of social costs they had in mind: "If the
reduction in amenities and the disadvantages of

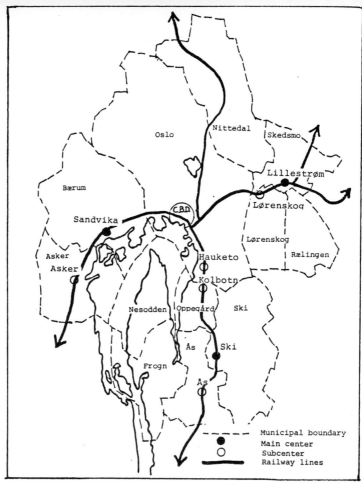

Figure 5D The Central Region of Metropolitan Oslo
with the Suburban Railway Lines and main
subcenters (stations) along the Lines.

The Central region comprises the city of Oslo and 11
municipalities in the Akershus County. From a planning point of view, the area is naturally subdivided
into the west, northeast and south corridors. The
regional plans aim at strengthening one center in
each direction, Sandvika, Lillestrøm, and Ski. The
tunnel under the center of Oslo for connecting the
western, eastern and southern railway lines was
completed in 1980, from which year rapid railway
traffic runs between Lillestrøm and Asker.

Source: Oslo   Urban   Transport   Commission,   A
Summary of the Report on Urban Transport
in the Oslo Region, p. 7. Oslo: The
Ministry of Transport, 1971.

traffic are also considered--noise, air pollution, and traffic accidents--the desire for a higher collective transit percentage is stressed even further" (Oslo Urban Transport Commission, 1971, p. 6). To promote such increased use of public transportation, the Commission laid down some norms for the standard of service that should be sought for the Central Region of Oslo.

The Commission viewed favorably the City's construction of a new subway tunnel through Central Oslo and recommended that when that was completed the regular trains to Asker, Lillestrøm and Ski be reduced from 30 to 20 minutes travel time. It insisted that the mainline railways and the suburban trains should constitute the backbone of the public transportation system and that the public bus system must be brought into harmony with them. In order to increase the supply of services in the surburban areas, the Commission recommended that bus routes coordinated with the railways be further developed.

Other recommendations of the Commission dealt with proposed changes in the organizational structures of the transportation system, modification of fare policies, parking facilities, etc. In order that the recommendations might be implemented, the Commission proposed a system of financing, involving principally the national government, the city of Oslo, and the county of Akershus. They requested that the National Government establish an office to act as a secretariat for the municipal committee set up to negotiate new arrangements for a proposed new joint organization. Norway's Ministry of Transport agreed to this proposal and set up such an office which was linked administratively to the city of Oslo and the county of Akershus (Oslo Urban Transport Commission 1971, p. 11).

Transport Planning and Oslo's Inner City

No part of Oslo was more vulnerable to the environmental assaults of the automobile than the inner city. Like most of Norway's cities, Oslo's fjord-oriented site was more suitable for marine communication than for motor transport. The development of the latter disrupted the historic City's charm; transformed "people" streets into car-filled thoroughways; turned residential areas into parking lots; and brought all the environmental hazards of air pollution, noise, traffic accidents, and general insecurity into the heart of the City. The extent of the environmental assault became so great as to prompt some students of the problem to say that air pollution in the Oslo center had become as bad as that of Los Angeles (Jensen 1979, p. 3).

One of the major ironies of the situation was that it had developed despite Oslo's continued support of its public transit system. Some notion of the extent of that support can be seen from Oslo's transportation budget for 1979, which indicates a city subsidy of 327 million Norwegian Crowns or about 66 million dollars (Prosjekt-Gruppen for Samferdsel, 1979). The irony is compounded by the fact that compared to cities of similar size in the U.S.A., public transit does indeed carry a large part of the people traffic in and out of the City center.

An official report in 1979 indicated that of 200,000 persons entering the Centrum each day, 54% traveled by public transit, 15% by bicycle or by walking, and only 31% by car. Of those who journeyed to work in the Centrum, 70% did so by public transit, 9% by bicycle or by walking, and only 21% by car. These recent data reflect a sharp reduction of automobile use for work trips into the Centrum during the last ten years.

But while the City is spending huge sums of money on its public transit system, it is also participating in a program of highway building that brings thousands of cars in and through the City each day. Because of Oslo's location on the fjord several national highways run through its inner city area. One such thoroughfare brings 50,000 cars a day past Oslo's City Hall.

Several attempts have been made to mitigate the automobile's assault on Oslo's inner city environment. In 1973, the City Council approved a "Gatebruksplan" (a street-use plan) designed to restrict automobile use--especially for work trips-- and give public transit a more favorable status on the streets. Other aspects of the "Gatebruksplan" proposed reducing inner city parking facilities, improving street amenities favorable for bicycling and walking, etc. So far, neither sufficient political will nor adequate organizational authority have provided the support system which this program needs (Prosjektgruppen For Samferdsel 1979, p. 13).

Oslo has also been responsive to impulses from what has been called "The Pedestrian Revolution" (Breines and Dean 1974). As in other Scandinavian countries and indeed many other parts of the world, Norway has promoted a movement aimed at creating what the Scandinavians call "gå-gater" (walking streets). By 1974, 19 cities of Norway had developed car-free streets in their centers. Most of those cities share Oslo's sea-coast and/or fjord-oriented sites (Lerum 1975, pp. 5-7). In Oslo the goal of a car-free centrum has support from such varied groups as The Norwegian Traffic Safety Federation, The National Association of Cyclists, The Norwegian Federation of Bus Owners, Oslo's Association of Trolley Car Operators, The Norwegian Taxi Federation, together with several of the political parties (Jensen 1979, p. 20).

Considerable progress has been made toward a car-free centrum in Oslo in recent years. From only a very few streets in 1973 when the author first lived in Oslo to a whole complex of streets leading to and including much of Karl Johansgate in 1979 have become car-free. As the author experienced during his stay in Oslo that year, the transformation was one of the most visible signs of a city looking to a future with hope. It should also be noted that car-free streets and malls have become increasingly prevalent in the satellite towns of the city.

The Oslo Planning Department continues to study ways and means of solving the traffic problems of Oslo's center. In August 1979, it published a new report on issues and possibilities related to developing an environmentally sound traffic system for the "Oslo Centrum." It brings up to date information about the existing traffic patterns and the environmental problems related to them. It analyzes alternative transportation plans for their possible solution and presents the rationale for the plan

which the study found to be most defensible. While
not going as far as some of the most enthusiastic
advocates of a car-free city, the plan does
recommend steps which would contribute a good deal
toward achieving their goals, including decisive
developments of cycling routes and walking streets
(Oslo Kommune Byplankontoret 1979, pp. 92-98).

However, the traffic congestion of automobiles
in the inner city is as bad as ever in 1984. The
political debate deals with how to improve traffic
efficiency by aid of a tunnel under the city center
at the same time as traffic in the streets should be
reduced by aid of a new local tax, restricting the
access of cars to the inner city.

Developing National-Municipal Cooperation

Transportation planning early became an integral part of Norway's national post-war development
policy. It was particularly important for its
regional development program. In the early 1970s,
its Parliament established a national transportation
plan for the purpose of coordinating national,
county and municipal planning for all of Norway.
The initial thrust--Norsk Vegplan I--was directed to
the rural areas of the country; the second--Norsk
Vegplan II--to cities and small towns. The national
guidelines required that all transportation planning
should be integrated with community planning at all
levels. Every county as well as every municipality
was required to work out a transportation plan to be
submitted to the National Ministry of Transportation
and Communication and thereby integrated with a
developing national plan. Such a plan was prepared
by Oslo in 1975 (Oslo Byplonkontor 1975).

The new document Norsk Veiplan II for Oslo
was the most systematic attempt so far to encompass
the entire transport system into a single plan and
to discuss the related policies of its various
elements as parts of an integrated policy for the
entire system. It served to establish clearer linkages between the municipal transport plans with
those of the national plans. The document contains
a lucid review of the present status of Oslo's
transportation system, of its many problems and

issues, together with proposed recommendations for action. According to the government mandate it became both a report for the national government and the transportation plan of Oslo's new master plan.

But the new plan appeared to have little influence on Oslo's transportation system. The plan was not organizationally articulated with Oslo's planning system. It failed in getting adequate support from the political parties as well as from the organizational structures of the various sectors of the transportation system. As a result decisions continued to be made as before by the highway department, the highway commissioner, and their political organs (Prosjektgruppen For Samferdsel 1979, pp. 14-15).

As an effort to cut across the sectoral segments of Oslo's transportation system, a new plan entitled Oslo Samferdselsplan 1980-1990 was published in 1979. It would constitute the new transportation segment of Oslo's Kommuneplan as well as Oslo's contribution to Norway's National Transportation Plan. It was developed by a project group made up of high officials from such important sectors of the transportation system as Oslo Trolleys, Oslo's Harbor Department, The Highway Department, The National Railroad and Television Systems, The Postal System, and The Air Transport Authorities. It was led by Oslo's top administrative leader, the Chairman of Finance, and directed by leaders from Oslo's Planning Department. The plan was to be submitted for approval by the city council in the summer of 1980. It will hopefully provide the basis for decision-making in the 1980s.

VII. Regional Planning in the Oslo Area

One of the most compelling challenges for all expanding metropolitan areas is the setting up of appropriate boundaries and the establishment of effective political structures for dealing with the most critical problems common to such areas. In other words, creating some kind of regional government for the metropolis.

The merger of Oslo and the large municipality of Aker in 1948 may have made the need for such regional government less urgent than it otherwise would have been. But even as early as 1950, there was established a regional planning committee for the Oslo area to discuss the issues of urbanization in the areas beyond the political boundaries of Oslo. The committee was made up of representatives from Oslo, thirteen municipalities from the Akershus county, and two municipalities from the Buskerud county.

Six years later a Cooperation Committee for the counties of Oslo and Akershus was set up for initiating metro-wide planning. After many months of deliberation, it engaged the services of a prominent national institute for planning and development—the Anderson and Skjånes Firm—to help conduct a comprehensive analysis of the region and provide guidelines for its future development. The outcome was a voluminous set of reports on the prognosis and frames of growth for the region together with guidelines for its future development, including an appropriate transportation system.

These reports and other materials provided a foundation for the work of a new Regional Planning Board of Oslo/Akershus created in 1968 under the provisions of the 1965 Building Act. The responsibility of this new Planning Board was to draft a regional plan. A preliminary draft of such a regional plan entitled "Utkast Til Region Plan for Oslo/Akershus" was published in 1969. (See also Figure 5D.)

The Plan made explicit its attention to the national policy issues concerning the developments of the Oslo region in relation to the rest of the country. It emphasized that a large regional approach could produce a manageable growth of the Oslo metropolis without exceeding its economic and demographic growth in relation to the rest of the nation (Samarbeidskomiteen For Oslo/Akershus 1969, p. 91). It also addressed itself to the problems created by the imbalance between increased concentration of work places in central Oslo and the concentration of the residential population in the outer areas of the region. It attributed the imbalance to unsatisfactory organization within the region itself. Even if the immigration could be

142

reduced considerably, it argued, there would still be a housing shortage, traffic problems, and lack of a satisfactory local services, if the internal, regional problems of distribution were not tackled satisfactorily (Samarbeidskomiteen For Oslo/Akershus 1969, p. 92).

It was to these internal problems of distribution that the New Regional Plan addressed itself. It proposed a three linear development pattern for shaping the metropolis in such a way as to prevent encroachment upon both forest and agricultural lands. Each of the three-pronged areas would have a major growth center. In the western area, Sandvika would be the main center; in the eastern area, Lillestrøm, and in the southern area the Ski new town. All three regional growth centers were centrally placed in the communications network and would serve as locations for a widely varied range of places of work as well as for substantial residential populations. The plan envisaged a rail system improvement which would reduce the traveling time from central Oslo to the three regional subcenter by half, i.e., to somewhere between 15 and 20 minutes.

The plan proposed that the City of Oslo should carry out an urban renewal program for reducing the population movement from the city. At the same time it recommended efforts to reduce the increase in places of work in central Oslo, by assisting industries with no room for expansion in the center to suitable locations in outer regions. The municipal authorities in the outer areas of the region would be urged to secure a supply of industrial areas for suitable location of work places. The plan recommended that authorities in Akershus outside the central region prepare development programs "with a high degree of balance in the growth of housing and places of work."

That the drafters of this regional plan were of a mind to prevent the kind of metropolitan sprawl so typical in the United States, is evident from the following quotation of the document concerning the outer areas of Akershus: "A conscious development of existing local centers will ensure agricultural and recreational areas against spot-development and

143

carving up of larger ownerships which weakens agricultural activities, hampers the running of individual farm units, and makes development in general irrational and uneconomical" (Samarbeidskomiteen For Oslo/Akershus 1969, p. 98).

The activities of the Oslo/Akershus Regional Planning Board came to an abrupt end with changes in the National Planning Law which placed the primary responsibility for regional planning in the hands of the county (fylke) authorities and the local municipalities. Pursuant to those changes the National Ministry of the Environment established in 1976 a new structure for cooperative regional planning involving Oslo and Akershus. In 1979 a regional Contact Committee made of representatives from the Ministries of Municipalities, Transportation, Social Services, Church and Education, and Environment, plus the members of the Oslo/Akershus Cooperative Committee. This "Contact Committee" is chaired by Norway's Minister of Environment. Out of this complex inter-governmental structure, it is hoped that an adequate metropolitan regional planning and development system can develop.

This record of frustrated efforts at establishing such a metropolitan regional authority should, however, not be interpreted to mean that nothing was done about the many complex problems of the expanding Oslo metropolis. In a very insightful and enlightening memorandum with an English subtitle, "The Art of Muddling Through Without Metropolitan Government," Oslo's Finance Chairman, Bernt Lund, reviews these various achievements (Lund 1979, pp. 16-28). They include such regional activities as the production and distribution of electric power, the supply of water resources for the various parts of the region, the establishment of a cooperative sewage and sanitation program, the conduct of transportation planning, and regional approaches to environmental problems. But it is difficult not to conclude with Oslo's Finance Chairman that in spite of these achievements, the Oslo area has as yet not succeeded in developing an adequate all-embracing metropolitan polity for the Oslo area (Lund 1979, p. 30). New efforts during the years 1979-1984, when the national government intervened, have also been unsuccessful.

144

VIII. Developing Environmentalism and Oslo's Future

The most recent documents of Oslo's Department
of Planning reflect a sensitive response to current
developments of Norway's environmental consciousness. Most of the modern problems of energy conservation and environmental protection are addressed.
Virtually all aspects of Oslo's planning and
development are examined in the context of their
solution including the expansion of the metropolis
itself, its developing transport system, and the
protection of the region's environmental resources.

What to do with Oslomarka?

One of the most unique of such environmental
resources is the famous "Oslomarka" (Oslo Forests).
Ever since the Comprehensive Plan of 1950, Oslo had
kept its territory inviolate from urban development.
As has already been indicated, this extensive forest
area of more than 91,000 square miles lies like a
vast greenbelt around Greater Oslo. It reaches out
beyond Oslo's boundaries to involve as many as four
counties and seventeen municipalities. Thus, concern about its future has become both regional and
national. It serves as a major outdoor recreational
area for 20% of all of Norway's population and quite
naturally becomes an area where competing land use
claims make it a special environmental concern
(Miljøverndepartementet 1976, p. 1). Among such
competing claims are those of the historic lumbering
industry, the highway builders, the outdoor recreation enthusiasts, the natural scientists, the environmentalists, and of course those who would like to
open it up for urban development. Thus its inviolate integrity as an "undeveloped" natural resource
has been both challenged and defended for many
years.
Oslo itself has laid claim to and acquired
public ownership of more than a hundred square miles
of the forests around its municipal boundaries. The
most important of these forest areas are "Nordmarka"
in the north, "Lillomarka" in the northeast, and
"Østmarka" in the southeast. Much of Oslo's outdoor
recreational development has been oriented toward

making these forest areas conveniently accessible to all its inhabitants through the famous "Turvei" (hiking trail) system. (See Fig. 5B.) That these forest greenbelts are popular is attested to by the hundreds of thousands using them each year. In a 1972 study it was found that approximately 500,000 used Oslomarka for recreational purposes that year. The largest usages were for hiking, skiing, swimming, and berrypicking (Miljøverndepartementet 1976, p. 18). It is no wonder that when it adopted a new comprehensive municipal plan for Oslo's future in 1975, Oslo's City Council reaffirmed its commitment to the preservation of the boundaries decided upon earlier. In doing this it accepted an extensive study and report by Norway's Ministry of Environment concerning the preservation of Oslomarka for its historic natural usages.

But toward the end of the 1970s the question was raised anew concerning the relationship between Oslomarka and Oslo's urban development. By then space for further development within Oslo's 1948 boundaries had largely come to an end, and Oslo was beginning to experience a distubring population decline. It was losing some of its economically most productive population to its surrounding municipalities in Akershus because of better housing opportunities there. Furthermore, urban renewal in the older parts of Oslo served to reduce the number of housing units by enlarging the old dwelling units being renewed.

If Oslo was to halt the population decline, it was necessary to develop new housing within the city. Hence in preparing a new municipal plan for 1980 to 1990, the Oslo Planning Department presented four alternative strategies for urban development in Oslomarka. It recommended for further consideration the two alternatives that would make the least impact on the Oslomarka and would make possible the greatest continuity with previous policies for its recreational usages (Oslo Byplankontor 1979, pp. 30-33). There can be no doubt but that in the years ahead Oslo's development will continue to bring the issue of Oslomarka into prominent public debate.

Growing Concern For the "Nærmiljø"

Oslo's continuing concern for Oslomarka is a natural expression of a historic Norwegian love of nature. It can be perceived as a specific example of a larger national consciousness which inspires similar concerns for all aspects of Norway's natural environment. But in recent years a new emphasis has been added to this environmental consciousness, a growing concern for what is called "Nærmiljø" (Literally translated as "near-milieu," but perhaps more understandably as "local intimate environment"). As a part of the developing reaction toward the post-war era of rapid growth and development, Norwegians were becoming increasingly concerned about their impact upon the well being of the family and the local neighborhood.

This growing concern is clearly reflected in a Parliamentary Report on long term policy goals for Norway in 1976-1977 (Parliamentary Report No. 75, 1976-1977, pp. 51-60). The Report asserted that Norway's Government had come to the view that an increased emphasis should be placed on strengthening the family and the local community and that every program of development should be assessed in terms of its consequences for the family and the local community as social units.

As a supplement to this report, the Ministry of Environment published another 128-page report entitled "Bedre Nærmiljøer" (Better Local Environments) which dealt with such varied aspects as housing, work places, traffic, noise and pollution, nature and open space, cultural programs, recreational activities for children and youth, schools, health and social service, and other public needs. It emphasized the importance of coordinated local planning and action for improving the quality of the neighborhood milieu, whether in new developments or in the renewing of old neighborhoods. It indicated the responsible roles for each of the levels of government in implementing the national goal of improved local environments, including special financial contributions from the national levels (Stortingsmelding Nr. 16, 1979-1980, pp. 67-76).

Perhaps nowhere in Norway has the concern for the "Nærmiljø" received a stronger emphasis than in Oslo. As an active planner observed at a meeting of the Oslo Chapter of the Norwegian Society for Housing and Urban Planning in 1979, this new environmental emphasis had become a natural reaction to the centralization and institutionalization characteristic of the large-scale mass-produced developments of post-war Oslo (Brevik 1979). He noted that the word "Nærmiljo" was on the lips of nearly everybody, and that the word can be found in all political party programs.

By the end of the 1970s the new emphasis had already begun to modify Oslo's planning and development. In the new housing and community building activities, more low rise housing was taking the place of high-rise towers; and row house terraced housing developments were becoming prevalent. Increased attention was given to the small-scale neighborhood milieu--both in its social relationships and its relationship to nature. At Furuset and Holmlia--the latest satellite town developments--special programs are in place which emphasize the "soft values" of neighborhood and family orientation. Similar innovations are being introduced in the increasingly important urban renewal and rehabilitation programs in the older parts of the city.

"Nærdemokrati"--Local Participatory Democracy

An inseparable part of this new thrust was the emergence of a growing psycho-political interest in increased local participation in planning and community building. As in large urban centers in other parts of the world, there had developed a growing concern about metropolitan trends which tend to militate against the traditional values of historic local sub-communities of the city. The increasing size and scale of urban life had tended to shift public attention away from local community concerns toward the larger metropolitan and national considerations. Related to this had been the expansion of the power and influence of the administrative bureaucracies of both public and private corporate structures, which typically organize problem solutions into bureaucratically managed specialized sectors with little regard for historic community boundaries and local identities. The consequence had been an increasing sense of local impotence and alienation with regard to both the public and private centers of political and economic power.

This growing populist restiveness prompted the city authorities to authorize a major study of how Oslo might be re-organized so as to revitalize local communities and provide a structure for their enhanced participation in public decision-making concerning their future. The prestigious Anderson and Skjånes Institute For Community Planning was engaged to direct the study. Its first task was to develop a rationale and structure for the identification of local sub-communities in Oslo; each of which would have a "Bydelsutvalg" (community council) to represent it in municipal decision-making. The second task was to prepare a system for coordinating the various social services within those sub-communities (Anderson og Skjånes A/S 1972, p. 5).

In pursuit of its first task the Institute prepared a comprehensive description and analysis of the complex web of social organizations and activities of the city relating to schools, churches, census taking, health programs, social services, etc. From that information was developed a map of thirty-three proposed "bydels" (city sub-communities or districts) which approximated the size of the secondary school districts. A two-page description and map of each of the thirty-three proposed "bydels" was presented, indicating some of the distinct characteristics of each. This was complemented by later documents analyzing the structures, functions, and locations of health, education, welfare, and religious activities and their relationships with the proposed sub-communities (Anderson og Skjånes A/S 1973).

Among the important criteria for establishing the boundaries for the new districts were such natural geographic factors as lakes, rivers, the sea, parks, and various topographical features. Another important criterion was the prevailing perception of local communities based on long historical experience. Thus the "bydels" were not to be simply convenient units for administrative or statistical purposes; but were to be perceived as sub-communities of the city. The optimal size of each "bydel" was 14,000 people--much the same as the optimal size of the satellite towns that had been built. In fact, such satellite towns as Lambertseter and Romsøs became "bydels" under this new proposed system. (See Figure 5E).

The proposal was adopted and made operative in January, 1973. Each "bydel" has a "bydelsutvalg"--a council of thirteen members and thirteen alternates appointed by the city council so as to contain the same distribution of political party identities as that of the city council. The activities of the "bydelsutvalg" have increased over the years. It is now charged with the responsibility of preparing a community analysis and report once in every four-year period between municipal elections. All cases of planning and development that impinge on the "bydel" must be submitted to its council for reaction. This includes matters relating to both socio-cultural and physical planning.

A public secretariat has been created for servicing all of the "bydel" councils and for coordinating their common concerns. According to Richard Malinowski, Principal Planner in Oslo's Planning Department, the "bydel" councils have become an important channel of communication between city hall and the local communities. They also are becoming increasingly involved in urban renewal activities. In the new satellite communities that have been built, they help develop community identity and provide a legitimate structure for dealing with their local concerns (Malinowsky, 1979). The concerns of "nærmiljø" have become intrinsically joined with the issues of "nærdemokrati" (neighborhood democracy) and both will likely play an increasingly important role in improving the quality of life in the future Oslo metropolis.

The "Bydel" Councils have become increasingly involved in the urban renewal activities which are becoming more important for Oslo's future. The role of the "bydelsutvalg" in urban renewal is well illustrated by recent renewal activities in the old

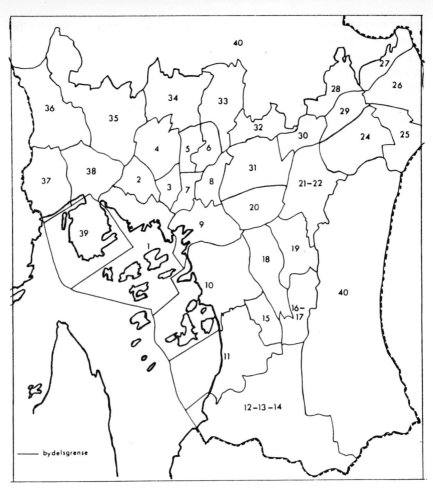

Figure 5E   Boundaries   for   40   political   "bydeler"
             (the   territory   of   local   political
             bodies).

Each   "bydel"   comprises   a   population   of   10,000   –
15,000.

eastern sub-community of Tøyen-Enerhaugen near the center of Oslo. As described in a recent report by the Norwegian Institute for Urban and Regional Research, it functions as an "official mouthpiece" for the local residents' concerns and acts as a coordinating council for the people and organizations of the local community (Norsk Institutt for By-og begionsforskning 1973).

In the new satellite towns that are being built, the "bydel" councils are helping to foster community identity and providing legitimate structures for dealing with local concerns (Malinowsky 1979). There too, the concerns of "nærmiljø" have become joined with the issues of "nærdemokrati" and both seem destined to play an increasingly important role in the quest for an improved quality of life in Oslo's future new-towns.

In addition to the "bydelsutvalg," the quest for an effective "nærdemokrati" has involved attempts to mobilize existing neighborhood social networks for participation in planning and development. One such existing social structure which shows promise of becoming a strategic possibility is the "borettslag" or neighborhood cooperative housing association. There are by now several hundred such associations throughout the city. The associations linked to OBOS alone, number more than 200. These, plus a wide variety of other neighborhood associations, provide the likely networks for increased neighborhood participation in programs for improving the local environments throughout the city (Brevik 1979).

IX.   Concluding Remarks

This chapter's account of planning and community building in metropolitan Oslo has sought to illustrate the dynamics of urban growth and development in modern Norway and provide as clear a picture as possible of how the nation's system of social democracy responded to the many complex issues related to urbanization.

Rejecting the laissez-faire market oriented determination of urban development, the city of Oslo, in cooperation with the national government, has sought to control and direct development through such strategies as the annexation of a large surrounding rural municipality; the public acquisition of land; the planning and development of satellite towns; the promotion of cooperative societies such as OBOS; the building of a metropolitan public transit system coordinated with community development; and the somewhat faltering quest for a planning and development system which could encompass all of the expanding metropolitan areas beyond Oslo's boundaries. All of these strategies assumed the continuance of the historic inner city of Oslo as the central core of the metropolis.

The failure, thus far, of developing an adequate regional structure is perhaps Oslo's most critical problem for the future. Unless some adequate political structure is developed which is congruent with the emerging metropolitan reality which now embraces the county of Akershus and some areas beyond, the logic and strategies of coordinated planning and development that characterized the post-war years, will be considerably thwarted. This problem impinges on virtually every other problem of planning and community building that Oslo faces in the future.

This is clearly reflected in one of the latest planning documents addressing Oslo's development for the decade of the 1980s. It re-emphasizes that Oslo and the neighboring municipalities of Akershus function as a common residential and labor market and that future metropolitan development must be treated as a regional problem. Its discussions of other issues--such as urban renewal of the inner city, increased housing density in other parts of Oslo, expanding the city into parts of Oslomarka, finding a more balanced distribution of housing and work places, and further development of the transportation system--all reflect a pervasive awareness that an effective regional policy would modify the plans for nearly all aspects of Oslo's future development (Oslo Byplankontor 1979).

REFERENCES

Anderson and Skjånes. A/S. Institutt for Samfunns-
planlegging 1972. Bydeler i Oslo. Sandvika.

Anderson and Skjånes. A/S. Institutt for Samfunns-
planlegging 1973. Distriktsinndelinger i
Oslo. Sandvika.

Breines, Simon and William J. Dean. 1974. The
Pedestrian Revolution. New York: Vintage
Books.

Brevik, Ivar. 1979. Bedre Drift Av Lokal Tjenes-
teyting og Fellesanlegg Fordrer Det Nye
Arbeidsmåter og Lokal Organisering. A
mimeographed copy of a lecture for the Oslo
chapter of the Norwegian Society for Housing
and Urban Planning.

Brækhus, Kjeld. 1976. "Oslo: Past, Present, and
Future." Norsk Geografisk Tidskrift 30:
127-138.

Eckhoff, Jan Chr. 1969. Byplan. Oslo: Pax
Forlag.

Greve, John. 1969. Housing, Planning and Change
in Norway. Oslo: Norwegian Building Research
Institute.

Jensen, Pål. 1979. Bilfri By - Hvordan? Oslo:
Vedalia Forlag.

Johnsen Yngvar. 1973. Industri og Samfunn:
Samfunnsmessige Hensyn Ved Utvidelse og
Flytting Av Industri. Oslo: Universitets-
forlaget.

Karevold, John. 1980. "'Borgermester' of the
Capital." The Norseman No. 1. Oslo.

Kjeldstadli, Knut and Vidar Keul. (eds.) 1973. DNA-Fra Folkebevegelse Til Statsstøtte. Oslo: Pax Forlag A/S.

Lerum, V. 1975. Bilfri Gater. Oslo: Transportøkonomisk Institutt.

Lund, Bernt H. 1979. Bykommunen og Dens Omverden. Oslo.

Malinowsky, Richard. 1979. Author's Interview with Malinowsky on December 12, 1979, at the Oslo Planning Office.

Miljøverndepartementet 1976. Utkast til Flerbruksplan for Oslomarka. Oslo.

Mumford, Lewis 1968. The Human Prospect. New York: Harcourt Brace and World, Inc.

Nestor, Per 1979. Boligpolitikken og OBOS Gjennom 50 År. Oslo: Oslo Bolig og Sparelag.

Norges Offentlige Redninger 1979; 5. Bypolitikk: Struktur og Økonomi For De Store Byene. Oslo: Universitetsforlaget.

Norsk Institutt for By-og Regionsforskning. 1973. Har Din Bydel En Framtid?: Bydels Rapport om Tøyen-Enerhaugen. Oslo.

Norway's State Housing Directorate 1968. Housing in Norway. Oslo: Norwegian Joint Committee on International Social Policy.

OBOS bladet 5: 1973. "Boliger og Arbeidsplasser i Oslo Regionen."

Oslo Byplankontor 1975. Norsk Veiplan II for Oslo.

Oslo Byplankontor 1979. Oslo Kommuneplan 1980-1990: Kap. 10.

Oslo Kommune Byplankontoret 1979. Utredning Om Veisysystem for Oslo Sentrum.

Oslo Kommunes Administrasjon 1975. Oslo Kommuneplan 1976-1985.

Oslo Planning Department 1960. Oslo: Planning and Development.

Oslo Town Planning Department 1975. A Summary of the Main Points From Oslo's "Kommuneplan."

Oslo Urban Transport Commission 1971. A Summary of the Report on Urban Transport in the Oslo Region. Oslo: Ministry of Transport.

Owen, Wilfred 1972. The Accessible City. Washington D.C.: The Brookings Institution.

Parliamentary Report (No. 75) 1976-1977. Norwegian Long-Term Programme 1978-1981. Oslo: Royal Norwegian Ministry of Finance.

CHAPTER SIX: CONTROLLING URBAN SPRAWL: SATELLITE TOWNS

I. New Housing in a Controlled Setting

The shaping and control of the "exploding metropolis" has become one of the critical issues of modern society. Barbara Ward alluded to this in her well-known book, The Home of Man, written for the United Nations Habitat Conference in Vancouver in 1976. In describing metropolitan developments throughout the world, she noted that they have almost universally been unplanned. She described the consequences in the following language:

> They have sprawled outward, swamping earlier jurisdictions. The 'giant concrete footsteps' have trampled out the villages and surrounded the small towns. As they stamp about, they create the governmental problem of creating some municipal order, some principles of cooperation, some sense of direction, justice, and environmental control of what is all too often one big muddle of overlapping, competing and even hostile authorities (Ward 1976, p. 234).

Perhaps nowhere are these troublesome attributes of the "accidental metropolis" more manifest than in the United States. One of the severest critics of such "uncontrolled" urban sprawl characteristically found in the U.S.A, is the well-known urbanologist, Lewis Mumford. He laments its assault on the landscape as well as its destructive impact on the human spirit and habitat. "We are creating," he says, "featureless landscapes populated by more and more featureless people" (Mumford 1968, p. 4).

The ultimate logic of this American way of metropolitan growth is perhaps best illustrated by the sprawling, fragmented metropolis of Los Angeles. One scholar describes it as "the fragmented metropolis par excellence, the archetype of the contemporary American metropolis" (Fogelson 1967, p. 2). Nowhere has the automobile culture more decisively shaped the form and character of the human habitat than in this most urbanized region of the American

West. But it is also important to note that much of America's metropolitan development is experiencing a similar metamorphosis.

In Europe, on the other hand, a more sympathetic historic identity with city culture and a longer history of planned urban growth have placed greater constraints on the automobile's impact on the metropolitan habitat. As the historian Frank Coppa has observed, "Europeans have a long history of regulating and subordinating private activity for the welfare of the collectivity, refusing to bow to 'laissez-faire' notions which become virtual dogma in the United States..."(Dolce 1976, pp. 168-171). Out of that tradition most European nations are now developing metropolitan policies and strategies for controlling urban sprawl, including special land use legislation, planned new towns, public transit systems integrated with metropolitan community building and others (Berry 1973, pp. 142-143). These policies and strategies are typically parts of a larger national concern for regional growth and development.

It is in the contexts of such European traditions and developments that Norway's attempts to control urban sprawl can best be understood. An examination of these efforts will shed additional light on Norway's urban and environmental policies and the socio-political contexts out of which they have been developed. Because of its size and predominance, the focus of this chapter is upon the Oslo metropolis, even though similar efforts at controlling urban sprawl are at work in other metropolitan centers.

Although Norway's post-war policies have been aimed at constraining the growth of its capital city, planners and politicians have been pragmatic enough to recognize the inevitability of its substantial expansion. The question was how such an expansion could best accommodate the rapidly growing population in ways compatible with developing urban policies. The most compelling challenge was how, where, and by whom the necessary housing should be built. Some notion of the intensity of that challenge can be seen by the fact that nearly 40% of Oslo's population in 1969 lived in housing built since 1949. During that twenty-year period about 83,000 dwelling units were built. During the next decade another 39,000 dwelling units were built. Out of Oslo's total stock of 230,000 dwelling units in 1984, 140,000 (60%) have been built in the post-war years. Since most of the post-war housing units were built in "satellite towns," an understanding of their role in Oslo's metropolitan development becomes obviously important (Oslo Planning Department 1960, p. 74).

In substance, satellite towns were perceived as comprehensively planned new communities within metropolitan areas which would maintain strong functional ties with the central city. Although they should contain many of the basic elements of a small town, they were not designed as autonomous new towns. On the contrary, they were to be integral parts of the expanding central city. They were to be smaller than the British New Towns and less comprehensive in terms of their economic development. It was assumed that most of their residents would be employed in the greater metropolitan occupational market.

They did, however, share with the British New Town Movement, a fundamental rejection of an essentially market-orientated home building, typical of suburban development in the U.S.A. As architect Jan Christian Eckhoff has noted, they were to represent a departure from the fragmented and functionally segmented perspective that plans housing in one area, cultural centers in another, schools and recreational facilities in still other places, and then builds houses and homes wherever home-builders might decide (Eckhoff 1969, p. 108). This shift to comprehensively planned suburbs in the form of satellite towns was intended to prevent excessive urban sprawl as well as to build more humane communities for the growing population of Oslo. (See Figure 6A)

II. Ullevål Hageby: A Garden City Antecedent

This post-war decision to develop satellite towns, however, was not a product of sudden inspiration. Its concepts and ideals had their roots in

159

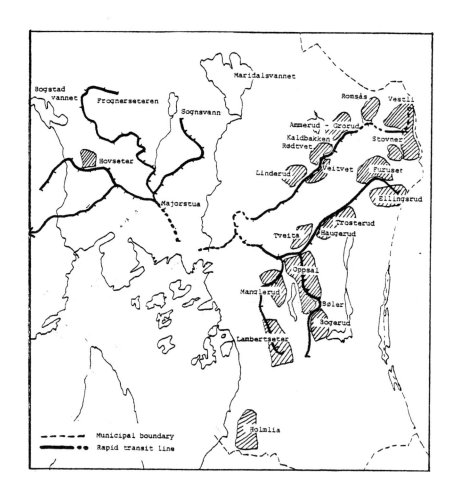

Figure 6A   Location of the larger satellite towns
             built in the years 1952 to 1984.   The
             last one, Holmlia, is still under con-
             struction.   It is located on the south-
             ern branch of the railway.   The other
             satellite towns are located along the
             eastern and southern branches of the
             newly built rapid transit system.   Only
             one satellite town, Hovseter, is located
             on the western branch of the old rail
             transit systems.

earlier thinking and experience. One of the most important influences was the Garden City Movement that evolved out of Ebenezer Howard's ideas and activities in Great Britain. Both his book, <u>Garden Cities of Tomorrow</u> (published in 1898), and his subsequent leadership in developing the first British Garden City of Letchworth in 1903 excited many social reformers and planners in continental Europe as well as in Scandinavia.

The International Town Planning Conferences, usually held in Germany, became an important market place of ideas concerning town planning innovations. Since the majority of Scandinavian architects around the turn of the century received their education and training in Germany, they were fully informed about the garden city developments in England (Peterson 1973, p. 37). Furthermore, a housing reform movement seeking more humane housing and community building for the growing industrial urban areas had become an important part of a larger social reform movement in both England and in Europe. Garden City Associations, patterned after Howard's first such association in England, were started in several European countries, including Scandinavia.

In 1913, an International Garden Cities and Town Planning Association (later named the International Federation of Housing and Planning) was founded, with members from many countries and with Sir Ebenezer Howard as its honored President for its first 15 years (Osborn and Whittich 1963, pp. 150-151). In the same year a Norwegian Association For Housing Reforms was organized, and a bit later, an Oslo Garden City Association. Representatives of these organizations participated in several International Housing Congresses and were positively influenced by the ideals of the Garden City Movement (Li 1942, pp. 52-53).

By the end of the nineteenth century, the housing reform movement had become an integral part of a larger social reform movement in Norway. Professor Eilert Sundt's thorough research and publications concerning the living conditions in Oslo had exposed the deplorable housing situation of the industrial worker and his family. The prominent literary figure, Henrik Wergeland, had identified

161

this bad housing as his leading lament about Oslo; and the growing Norwegian Labor Party had made housing reform an integral part of its crusade for social justice. The solution for the housing problems was increasingly perceived as a public responsibility both nationally and on the municipal political level (Li 1942, pp. 42-46).

As the reform movement gathered more political strength, Oslo's city council became increasingly responsive to its demands for action. In 1909, the council purchased 110 acres of farmland belonging to the historic Ullevål Manor located in the neighboring municipality of Aker. Up to 1900, Aker had been a purely agricultural municipality. But as suburbanization gained momentum, Oslo's expanding population spilled over into the Aker countryside—settling mostly in detached houses on individual lots.

Oslo's purchase of Ullevål Manor was to make possible an alternative pattern for suburban development—a pattern more like that envisioned by the Garden City Movement, and which at the same time would be affordable by the growing working class of Oslo. "To provide the working class with sound and good housing and to make more of them owner-occupied units is a community responsibility of the first order," said Oslo's Mayor Sophus Arctander in his defense of the purchase (Li 1942, p. 38).

Ullevål Hageby was laid out as a "garden suburb" modeled after the English "Hampstead Garden Suburb" built in 1906. That garden suburb had been started as an effort to save a portion of the disappearing landscape around London. It had been planned by Raymond Unwin and Barry Parker, who were the principal architects of Ebenezer Howard's first garden city of Letchworth. Hampstead was an attempt to capture some of the medieval implications of mystery, safety, and enclosure within a new settlement. It was designed to be a community rather than a mere housing development. It contained a central square designed to serve as a center for the community—a place where a "unity of social character" might develop. From this central square, wide avenues were laid out in all directions, giving visual contact with the center from

162

all angles (Peterson 1973, pp. 37-43).

It is instructive to note that Unwin and Parker regarded Hampstead as a "garden suburb" rather than a "true garden city." While clearly favoring the latter, they reasoned that by introducing some of the best features of the garden city into new suburbs they could help prevent the untidy fringe developments created by the haphazard outward rush of rapidly growing cities (Osborn and Whittich 1963, p. 83).

Both the form and the rationale of the Hampstead Garden Suburb seemed particularly appropriate for the Ullevål Hageby situation. The location was precisely at the fringe of Oslo's "outward rush." The choice was perceived as either a continued haphazard and formless suburbanization by allowing the development of individual housing units, or a more comprehensive planned-unit development which would incorporate as many of the virtues of the Garden City as possible. Thus, many of the features of Hampstead came to be reproduced in Ullevål Hageby--including the architecture of its buildings, the establishment of a village center, the layout of its curving streets and its overall environmental design.

Ullevål Hageby was built for a population of about 3,000 people. The first housing units were constructed in 1917 and occupied in 1918. The eastern area of housing, consisting primarily of small single-family housing and intended for the lower classes, was developed first. The western section constructed a bit later, consisted mainly of row house flats designed for more middle class people. Besides a central square surrounded by small shops and other social amenities, Ullevål Hageby contains a community school and is strategically linked to the Oslo Centrum by both public bus and trolley.

Although the City of Oslo acquired the site, the land was leased to and developed by the Ullevål Hageby Cooperative Association. From the very beginning, Ullevål Hageby received considerable attention as a model suburban development. In 1929, an article appearing in the <u>Manchester Guardian</u> commended its esthetic and structural virtues in the following superlative manner:

> The sweetest in Sweden (Norway) was the
> "Garden Town of Ullevål Hageby." We
> walk through the garden city. Large
> rows of stately brick villas and apart-
> ment houses. You should see the houses--
> their elegance. And this is a small
> nation where one would never expect such
> progress (Li 1942, p. 211).

But the community continues to this day to be
regarded as one of Oslo's most charming and cherished residential neighborhoods. There are at present 648 dwelling units, 4 boutique shops, 6
offices, 2 work places, 2 health and welfare
centers, a community assembly hall, a meat market
and two eating places, a school and nursery--all
within walking distance for all the residents. Its
proximity to the new Blindern campus of the
University of Oslo has enhanced its value as a
residential location. The original cooperative
society continues to administer and manage its
affairs, paying increasing attention to such
renovation and upkeep as the more than fifty-year-
old structures naturally require. Åsmund Bringsås,
its current business manager, reports that Ullevål
Hageby continues to be a highly stable community,
where the homes are typically passed down through
family generations.

In 1978, the residents of this garden city
were notified that their community had been placed
on the Oslo City Antiquarian's List as a residential
area that should be preserved because of its historical and cultural worth. The Antiquarian had
pointed out that "this garden city was Oslo's
distinctive response to the garden city movement,
and as such stands as a monument in Norwegian planning history" (Oslo Havebyselskap 1978, p. 10).

Other communities with attributes somewhat
similar to Ullevål Hageby were built in the 1920s.
Their growth and distribution followed the development of Oslo's expanding suburban railway network
(Oslo Planning Department 1960, p. 27). One of the
largest was the Torshov community built between 1918
and 1921. It was designed for about 10,000 people,
most of whom were industrial workers with quite

modest incomes. The German influence contributed to its becoming a more densely populated community with large block units encircling open courtyards. Otherwise, similar garden city influences were at work here as at Ullevål Hageby.

Although these "garden suburbs" never became the predominant pattern for the suburbanization of Oslo, they did play an important role in setting the stage for the later development of the more influential satellite towns built after World War II. In the first place they served as a mediating link between the town planning ideas of the Garden City Movement and the municipal planners in Norway. Furthermore, they provided an occasion for housing reform innovation on the part of the growing labor movement that was destined to become the dominant political force in Norway and in Oslo for the next half century. They established a precedent for municipal acquisition of land for the purpose of developing suburbs within the city. Finally, they played an important role in promoting cooperative ownership of the new housing communities.

It is not unreasonable to assume that the experiences of the political leaders and urban planners with Ullevål Hageby and the other garden city suburbs helped shape the ideas and ideals that were later to be expressed in the post-war satellite town developments. A reading of Einar Li's Oslo Havebyselskap Gjennom 30 År (Oslo Garden City Association Through 30 Years) reveals that many of the attributes and issues of Ullevål Hageby were a portent of those to be later associated with the cooperative satellite towns developed after World War II (Li 1947).

III. The Setting for Satellite Town Developments

When World War II came to an end, the housing shortage in Oslo took on crisis proportions. Since the Nazi invasion of 1940, virtually all home building had come to a halt. Post-war developments prompted an unprecedented growth in Oslo's population. The suburban press upon the fringe areas around Oslo became intense, and led to the very important merger of the large, essentially rural, municipality of Aker with Oslo in 1948. Thus, political leaders and urban planners of Norway's capital city had both the responsibility and opportunity to make major decisions concerning the character and form that Oslo's expanding metropolis should take.

By this time, the Labor Party had become securely established as the dominant political party of Norway as well as of the city of Oslo. As has already been indicated, besides being pro-labor, that party was a champion and architect of the Nation's health and welfare system, a supporter of the cooperative movement, and highly committed to a strong active role of government in both national and municipal affairs. To provide good housing for every citizen at a cost which each could afford, and located in a wholesome community setting became an integral part of the welfare-state ethos. It is in the context of these developments that the decisions to build satellite towns can be properly understood.

The cooperative relationship between the political leaders on the national level with those at the municipal level set the political stage for programs of vigorous municipal direction and control of metropolitan growth. The most important single contribution of the nation's parliament was the establishment of the National Housing Bank (Husbanken) to provide low cost, long-term loans for the people seeking housing. The legislation establishing that bank, as well as other legislation, was clearly supportive of cooperative housing, comprehensive community planning, and the public acquisition and/or control of land resources for urban development. The stage had been set for a large-scale expansion of the ideas and activities that had been initiated at Ullevål Hageby.

The most ardent defenders of the garden city ideas had hoped that the Ullevål Hageby Society could become the chief sponsor for the development of cooperative garden city communities throughout the Oslo region. But neither its structure nor its resources were adequate. A new organization eventually called the "Oslo Bolig-og Sparelag" (Oslo Housing and Savings Society) emerged as the principal vehicle for the development of cooperative housing and residential communities. Both in its cooperative structure and its functional relationship with municipal and national authorities, OBOS (as it became generally known) was patterned after a similar organization in Stockholm, Sweden (Nestor 1979, p. 56). It became the principal city-wide cooperative housing developer in Oslo--the largest such organization in all of Norway. Its commitment to the building of luxury-free but otherwise high quality housing in planned community settings came to be fully shared by Oslo's City Council. So much so, in fact, that it was frequently alleged that OBOS was the "extended arm of the municipality." When the National Housing Bank was created in 1946, OBOS and the other cooperative housing associations throughout the country became the principal organizations through which the national financial support for housing was channeled.

In the early years of its activities, OBOS concentrated principally on meeting the most acute housing problems. Most of its members at that time were renters living in deplorable tenements with little or no security in their tenancy. What they sought through OBOS was better housing without the dread of eviction. They wanted housing with more light and fresh air, and which had the modest modern amenities of indoor toilets, bath and running water. Hence the early OBOS housing was designed to meet such minimum standards for as many as possible at as low a cost as possible.

Most of this early housing consisted of small units in highrise apartment structures (Nestor 1979, pp. 133-134). They lacked the charm and the social amenities of Ullevål Hageby. But as Per Nestor points out, for those who were able to move from the crowded, dark, and primitive tenements to such new but modest cooperative apartments, the move must have seemed like a change from night to day (Nestor 1979, p. 135). And the new security against eviction must have been highly welcome. It is instructive to note that as the OBOS housing developments were organized into cooperative neighborhood associations, each association was designated as a "borettslag," which literally means an association for the right of housing.

In the post-war period, however, an increased economic prosperity and a greater consciousness about social and environmental aspects of housing led to a demand for higher standards of housing than those built in the 1930s. Furthermore, the rapid growth of Oslo's population called for more large-scale developments than had so far been launched. The merger of Oslo with the large rural municipality of Aker in 1948 opened up the possibilities for such large-scale developments. With the addition of more than a hundred thousand acres of land for Oslo's expansion, the question of how that should be done became crucial. It was in response to such a question that the idea of developing satellite towns as a strategy for metropolitan growth emerged. It was this challenge that became the basic concern of Oslo's Comprehensive Plan of 1950 (Nestor 1979, p. 140).

The debates and deliberations associated with that Comprehensive Plan indicate that the ideas of the garden city movement continued to be alive. Oslo's chief planner, Erik Rolfsen, insisted that much of the area (more than 75,000 acres out of a total of 112,000) should be preserved for forests, farms, lakes, and recreation (Nestor 1979, p. 140). He believed that the remaining 35,000 acres could provide enough space for the housing of up to 700,000 people. The Comprehensive Plan projected the building of satellite towns to accommodate between 150,000 and 200,000 people. In his comments about the Plan, Mr. Rolfsen observed that the conception and design of these new towns were based on a modified form of the garden city idea and the neighborhood concept (Oslo Planning Department 1960, p. 10).

To this extent, they would resemble the new towns of Britain. Each would be fairly homogeneous and self-contained, complete with schools, shops, and such other institutions and services one would expect to find in a small town. Within each town, neighborhoods would be developed for approximately 500 families, together with a neighborhood general store and nursery. The towns would be separated from each other by broad acres of parks, fields, or woods. Within each town, the neighborhoods would be separated by green areas which would be linked with each other and connected to the "turvei" (pedestrian pathway) system leading into the surrounding woods, parks, lakes, etc.

Although the size of each town would vary with the topography and other circumstances, each would contain a theoretical minimum between 15,000 and 20,000 people. The population density would also vary from town to town and from neighborhood to neighborhood. The neighborhood closest to the town's center or suburban railway station would be quite densely populated--over 100 persons per acre. The density would decline progressively with the distance from the center. The types of housing would correspondingly vary from apartment buildings to terraced row housing and to low density detached housing as one moves outward from the town's center (Oslo Planning Department 1960, pp. 40-41).

The towns were not to be as large or as self-contained as the British new towns. They were to function more like "satellite suburbs," integrally woven into the fabric of the expanding metropolis, rather than as autonomous municipalities. The towns were to be linked with each other and the Oslo Centrum with a modern public transit system to facilitate their participation in the life and culture of all of Oslo.

Cooperatives would play a major role in the housing developments of the satellite towns. By 1950, the cooperative housing movement had become a very significant force in both national and municipal politics. Its ideals had become an integral part of the welfare state philosophy. Special cooperative housing laws had been enacted and a national housing bank favorable to cooperative housing had been created. In Oslo, OBOS had already become the city's major cooperative housing society with a membership of over 30,000 seeking their kind of housing. It had already built thousands of housing units, and by now enjoyed a highly favored status with the City Council. Thus, OBOS and its kind of cooperative housing activities provided a ready-made alternative to the private, entrepreneurial and market-oriented housing industry which played such a dominant role in suburban U.S.A.

Although the cooperative character of the new housing was similar to that of Ullevål Hageby, the density and architectural designs of the satellite towns would be considerably different. The architectural perspectives of neo-classicism and functionalism which had been taking the place of the more romantic perspectives of the Gothic movement in continental Europe, were also asserting their influence in Scandinavia. The innovations of Walter Gropius of the Bauhaus in Germany and of LeCorbusier in France were well-known. "LeCorbusier's dream of a town consisting of widely spaced tall buildings erected on columns standing in a park reached via Germany the Nordic countries, where it materialized in a moderate Scandinavian form" (The Nordic Housing Exhibition Committee 1978, p. 21). The use of high-rise towers or other high density structures as a means of providing more open space and better utilization of sunlight was not lost to the Scandinavian architects. "Sun, light, and fresh air" had become the new watchwords in urban architecture. Within the built up city, enclosed blocks were ripped apart, and a new housing style—the "lamella" three-story strip housing was born (Åstrom 1967, pp. 34-35). The "lamella" and the highrise tower became the new architectural response to the changing building technology.

The use of this new architecture in the satellite towns was not merely a result of the architects' preferences. The social democrats who had become the dominant political architects of Norway's welfare state system, found such housing especially compatible with their policies for equalizing housing opportunities for everyone (O'Sullivan 1979). They also found such housing expeditious in meeting their goals for large-scale housing developments which would not permit urban sprawl and its devastating assaults on the natural environment. Thus, the housing of the satellite towns came to look more like some of the high density apartment housing found in the inner city of Oslo than like that of Ullevål Hageby. This prevalence of apartment housing in the satellite towns of Oslo, like that in similar developments in the rest of Scandinavia, presents a sharp contrast to the predominance of single family housing found in suburban U.S.A.

170

IV.   Lambertseter: The First Satellite Town

To describe all the satellite towns developed in the Oslo area since 1950 would go beyond the purview of this study. Instead, two have been chosen for illustrative purposes: Lambertseter, which was developed in the decade of the 1950s; and Romsås, which was built in the 1970s. While no claims are made that they are scientifically representative of the two periods, an examination of each will serve to illustrate the central continuities as well as some of the changes of Oslo's postwar satellite town building.

Being the first satellite town in Oslo as well as in all of Norway, Lambertseter generated much public attention as well as high hopes and expectations. While the extremely critical post-war housing shortage itself prompted strong interest in the venture, more than a massive housing production was now envisioned. At Lambertseter the Oslo municipality was to take on the responsibility for the planning and development of an entire new town which should secure an attractive and humane habitat for more than 15,000 people. The preservation of sufficient open space for greenbelts, picnic areas, and playgrounds; the building of sound and attractive housing in a satisfying community milieu for every age group; the provision for kindergartens and day care services within each neighborhood; the development of modern schools and recreational facilities for the young; the establishment of community centers for both young and old; and the building of a town center for the life and culture of sub-city in the nation's capital--all these and more were parts of the dream for Oslo's first satellite town (Oslo Commissioner of Housing 1971, pp. 29-42). (See Figure 6B)

Who Builds the New Town?

As Lewis Mumford has persuasively argued, a prerequisite for implementing such a dream is the public acquisition of the land upon which the new town is to be built (Mumford 1968, p. 157). In 1951, the City of Oslo obtained possession of the

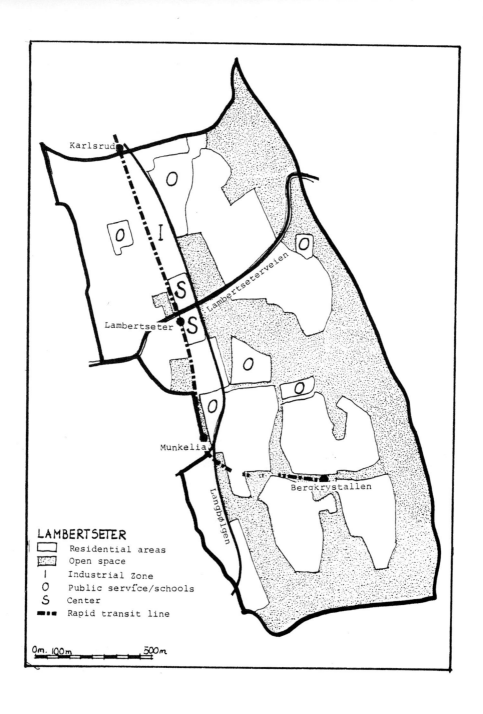

Figure 6B   Lambertseter satellite town.   Land use
           and public services.

172

Lambertseter site for the purpose of developing it into a satellite town. The site had long been a historic farm estate in the Lake Østensjø region of southeastern Oslo. The site contained approximately 500 acres of wooded farmland where some scattered single-family housing had already been built. The city engaged the architects for developing a comprehensive plan for the area according to the satellite town's expectations. The city also assumed the responsibility for building the transportation network and putting in place the public utilities.

OBOS became the principal developer of the housing structures and their related cooperative neighborhood associations. The new National Housing Bank provided the major financial resources needed. Thus was forged the virtual partnership between the National Housing Bank, the City of Oslo, and the Cooperative Society of OBOS which would constitute the principal builders of virtually all of the satellite towns of Oslo.

Land Use Design Features

The land use plan developed was in the main consistent with the satellite town ideals. It provided for a compact settlement, thus taking a relatively small proportion of the area for the development site, and leaving intact much of the wooded area of the historic Lambertseter estate to function as a greenbelt. The town site was divided into six neighborhoods, each having an internal green area and all separated from each other by small greenbelts. The traffic network of roads connecting the neighborhoods with each other and with the town center were laid out along the contours of the terrain rather than on a grid pattern. The town center was located adjacent to the subway rail line and the highway system. An area was also set aside for light industry along this rail and highway system. This is one of the largest such industrial sites in this part of Oslo and accommodates some twenty small industries.

173

The Lambertseter Neighborhoods

Each neighborhood is organized into a local "borettslag" (a housing rights association) which owns the housing of the neighborhood cooperatively. Every member-owner has one vote in that association and through it has an opportunity for participating in the neighborhood's public affairs. The administration and management of the housing cooperative is lodged in OBOS, which serves as the "mother society" of the local neighborhood cooperatives.

Most of the housing was built in three to five story "lamella"-like apartment structures similar to those being built in inner city Oslo at that time. Although the neighborhoods vary in size, they approximate the satellite town ideal of about 500 families in each. In addition to the clustering of the neighborhoods around topographical features of the landscape, neighborhood identity is fostered by having a local "nærbuttik" (a general store), and, as a rule a day nursery and playground for children. The following names of the neighborhoods likely reflect some of the romanticism of the community as well as the distinctive topographical character of each neighborhood: "Blåfjellet" (The Blue Mountain); "Bergkrystallen" (The Mountain Crystal); "Steinspranget" (The Stone's Leap); "Rabben" (The Stony Ridge); "Pynten" (The Point); "Marmorberget" (The Marble Mountain). This kind of place nomenclature is not unlike that found in many other parts of Oslo--both old and new.

Altogether, the neighborhoods contained in 1970 approximately 5,500 apartment units and a population of about 15,500 inhabitants. The population has declined by about 3,000 during the 1970s (Kollandsrud 1978, p. 37). The variations in apartment size is distributed in the following percentages (Sandvik 1979, p. 141):

One room, plus kitchen and bath - 6.1%
Two rooms, plus kitchen and bath - 26.3%
Three rooms, plus kitchen and bath 55.3%
Four rooms, plus kitchen and bath 12.3%

This variety in apartment size was designed to accommodate varied age structures and family size in order that the population of Lambertseter would be as representative as possible of that of the larger metropolitan area. The following table indicates that this objective has been difficult to achieve.

TABLE 6.1   Percentage of Population Categories in Lambertseter From 1955 to 1969

Year	0–14	15–19	20–64	65–69	70 yrs. and Over	Total Population
1955	31.9	3.5	63.2	--	1.4	7,650
1960	30.6	4.5	58.9	2.1	3.0	17,289
1964	26.3	8.8	58.9	2.0	4.4	17,487
1969	21.7	9.2	61.1	3.0	5.0	17,957

Source: Sethre and Kippenes 1970, p. 27.

According to Sethre and Kippenes, the population distribution at the outset was more nearly like that of suburbia than that of the greater metropolitan area as a whole. As the community has matured, however, the population distribution has come closer to that of the general cross-section of the greater Oslo region. By 1975, the percentage of children from 0 to 19 dropped from 35.4% in 1955 to 21.96%, which was close to that of the greater Oslo region. In 1975, the percentage of people in the productive ages from 20 to 69 was 65.6% in Lambertseter compared to 67.3% in the greater Oslo region in 1968. Similarly, the percentage over 70 in Lambertseter in 1975 was almost identical with that of the greater Oslo region (Hassett 1976, p. 20 and Sethre and Kippenes 1970, p. 27).

What is becoming clearer during recent years is that Lambertseter's population is aging. The children of 1958 are grown and have moved away. The population of the elementary school has declined 30% since 1958. The elementary school which was designed for 850 or more children in 1957 had only 438 children in 1978. Only half the building is now used for the elementary school; the other half has

175

been taken over by the secondary school; and the former secondary school has been closed (Kollandsrud 1978, p. 37).

This is a general trend in all the satellite towns, because they are completed over a short span of time. The people who move into the dwellings when they are new belong to the same age group-- young couples with small children and often having an additional child after moving into the new housing. As the majority of them stay in the satellite towns, the distorted age composition lasts over the years. When the children are grown up and move away from home, the age composition becomes particularly distorted. The resulting population decline creates new challenges for urban planning as Rasmussen (1981) has pointed out. One such residential area, for example, had in 1970 an age composition with more than 55% of the population over 50 years of age and 40% over 60 years. By 1984 the oldest have died and a new generation is moving in, taking over the apartments which are fairly inexpensive, but of high quality with attractive locations relative to the city center. (See also Chapter 9:III).

The Lambertseter Center

The builders of Lambertseter had some difficulty in attracting enterprises for its commercial center in the first years of their activity. The area was too new and unknown. Furthermore, the subway was not ready and the population was too sparse at first to encourage small shop entrepreneurs to move in. But after 1955, developments in the center grew rapidly, and soon contained most of the shops and services one would expect in a thriving small town. By 1958, the center contained the following shops and services: a jewelry optical shop, a pharmacy, a laundry, three newspaper offices, a tobacco shop, a restaurant, a bakery, a yarn and crafts shop, a library, a photography shop, a barber shop and hairdresser, a fashionshop, a bookstore, a floral shop, a radio-electric shop, meat and grocery stores, a health center and dentist offices, a doctor's office, a goldsmith, a shoe store, a postoffice and a bank (Rinnan 1958, pp.

176

4-5). By 1980 the Center contained 24 retail shops and 17 service institutions (Røren 1981, p. 13).

When Lambertseter was designated as one of Oslo's district centers for health and social services, such activities became an important function of the Center, providing the services of doctors, nurses, dentists and social workers to the new community. Included in the new public service institutions were a health clinic and a 95-bed hospital (Hassett 1976).

From its beginning, Lambertseter was designed with special provisions for the elderly. Two ten-story high block apartments were built especially for retired pensioners, equipped with hobby crafts activity areas, community kitchens, TV rooms, hair-dressers, foot doctors, etc. One public and three private nursing homes have also been added.

A movie theater, a community youth center, a swimming pool, and a soccer field provide recreational activities for the community. Its school system includes the usual elementary and secondary school programs, as well as an "upper-secondary" school including the historic "realgymnasium" and vocational education. All these, together with a large community church, provide for a fairly comprehensive socio-cultural experience for the community.

Some Concluding Remarks About Lambertseter

Not even its most ardent supporters would insist that Lambertseter had completely fulfilled all the expectations of an ideal satellite town. In the first few years of development, it was criticized for its lack of shops and services, and for the transportation problems associated with an unfinished subway system. Some were critical of its high density housing and expressed doubts about whether people would ever really thrive there and establish roots in the community. Others thought the town was too much like other "bedroom suburbs" and lacked the quality of urban life. Most of these criticisms can in a large measure be counted as parts of the inevitable "new town blues" that all such relatively instant communities experience.

Figure 6C   Air   photo   of   central   parts   of
Lambertseter   satellite   town.   (By   permission   Fjellang   Wideroe   A/S)   Note the
shopping   center   with   private   and   public
services   and   the   crossing   of   two   main
roads   with   a   station   on   the   rapid   rail
system.   Note   also   the   large   open   fields
with   playgrounds   and   the   greenbelt
surrounding   the   town.

But there is good reason to believe that many
of these early criticisms were premature as well as
too harsh. When in 1976, Lambertseter celebrated
its 25th anniversary, Norway's leading newspaper,
Aftenposten, published a generally favorable story
about the festivities and the town's development.
It noted that the early critics of the town had not
been vindicated; that Lambertseter had matured into
a community where the generations live side by side
and can celebrate their history together. Albert
Nordengen, Oslo's mayor from the conservative party,
spoke admiringly of how Lambertseter had demonstrated that a new satellite town can dynamically grow
into a cherished sub-community ("bydel") within an
expanding metropolis (Aftenposten 1976, September
23). A similar assessment is made in a recent study
of Lambertseter by a student at Oslo's "Architekt-
shøyskolen" (Røren 1981, p. 35). Her study provides
an insightful description and analysis of Oslo's
first satellite town during its first quarter-
century history.

Table 6.2   Population and Densities in the Satellite
            Towns in Lake Østensjø Area

Satellite Town	Population	Acres	Persons per acre
Bøler-Bogerud	14,000	340	41.2
Lambertseter	17,000	487	34.8
Manglerud	20,000	750	26.7
Skøyen-Oppsal	17,000	360	46.8
Tveita	10,000	190	52.6

Source: Oslo Planning Department 1967, p. 8

Whatever the judgment of others, the builders
of Lambertseter were sufficiently satisfied with its
development to continue building more satellite
towns. Around Lake Østensjø, four more towns
besides Lambertseter were developed in the late
1950s and early 1960s. Manglerud, like Lambert-

179

seter, was developed on the west side of the lake and linked with Central Oslo by the Lambertseter suburban railway; Bøler-Bogerud and Skøyen-Oppsal were laid out on the east side of the lake and connected to downtown Oslo by the Østensjø subway; and Tveita, northeast of Østensjø, linked with Oslo by the Furuset railway. The size and population of each is shown in Table 6.2. (See also Figure 6A.)

V.   Romsås: A Satellite Town of 1970s

Following these developments in the Lake Østensjø region, extensive community building was launched in the Grorud Valley in Northeastern Oslo along Trondheimsveien and linked with Central Oslo by the Grorud suburban railway. Among well-known satellite towns along this railway are Linderud, Rødtvedt, Ammerud, Grorud, Romsås, and Stovner. As in the earlier developments, the land was typically acquired by the City of Oslo and for the most part OBOS became the principal developer (OBOS bladet: Nr. 6, pp. 6-8, 1968).

The recent development of Romsås provides the best illustration of what comes closest to the "ideal type construct" for satellite town building in modern Norway. Although its basic developmental patterns were similar to those of its predecessors, it has incorporated more completely the whole array of goals and objectives inherent in the satellite settlement policies. Furthermore, it has taken into account some of the criticisms and limitations of the earlier developments. It might be perceived as the "best foot forward" for OBOS and the city of Oslo in suburban design and development during the decade of the 1970s.

The Romsås area is a part of that large north-eastern periphery of Oslo that had been designated for extensive housing development in the City's master plan of 1960. According to that Plan, the area was designated partly as a residential area and partly as an undeveloped recreational area. The surrounding area in the Grorud Valley was otherwise generally designated for residential and industrial expansion (Stahl 1973, p. 10). As in the other developments, the Romsås Estate was acquired by the

City of Oslo and assigned to OBOS for development. Its terrain is very hilly, with precipitous mountain sides towards the west and steep grassy hillsides in the south towards the Grorud Valley. The area is covered with fir and deciduous trees and connected to the larger forest region known as Lillomarka. Its location in the Oslo region is indicated on the map in Figure 6A.

Major Features of the Romsås Design

An examination of the planning map as shown in Figure 6D provides important clues to some of the major ideals and objectives of the town.

In the first place it makes clear the commitment to the importance of providing for sub-neighborhoods within the community. Romsås was designed with six distinctive neighborhoods, each with a name having some significant relationship to a particular characteristic of its immediate natural milieu. While the size of the neighborhoods vary, all six of them together were designed to house approximately 8,000 people in about 2,600 dwelling units, fairly evenly distributed among the neighborhoods.

The planning map also indicates that all of the neighborhoods are linked to each other and to a major community center by a network of pedestrian pathways. All of the pathways (gangveier) are separated from vehicular traffic throughout the whole community. This pedestrian network between neighborhoods is complemented by a "turvei" (hiking trail) system which links all the residents of Romsås with the forests surrounding the community. This is a miniature replication of a "Turvei" system developed long ago in the inner city of Oslo to provide pedestrian pathways into the forests surrounding the city. Along the pedestrian paths are sandboxes, play areas, and other open space amenities such as flower beds, trees, and shrubs to enhance both the human and natural dimensions of the spatial environment. The open space area around which all the neighborhoods are laid out make up approximately fifty acres.

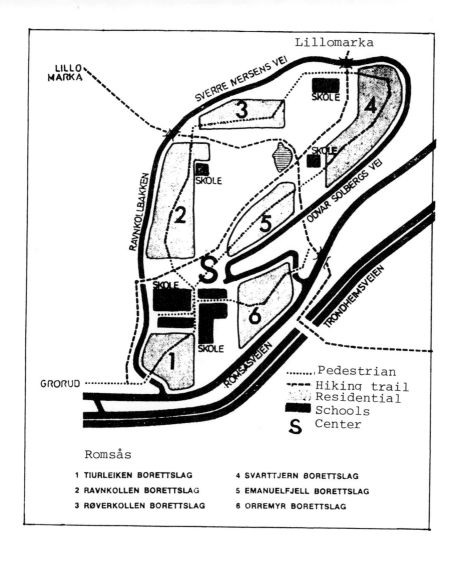

Figure 6D   Romsås satellite town.   Main land-use
with   location   of   residential   areas,
schools, main center and the ringroad.
Automobiles are not allowed inside the
town.   The white area on the map is
green space with trees, a lake, playgrounds and sport fields.

Automobile traffic is restricted to the major
highway and the "ring road" around the community,
leaving the residential areas free from automobile
traffic. Each neighborhood is provided with a
parking garage between the "ring road" and the
housing structures for the residents. Parking lots
are provided for visitors. In order to discourage
the development of an auto-oriented community,
Romsås has been linked with Oslo's downtown by
"Grorudbanen," a major line of the city's public
rail transit system. The subway station is located
in the Romsås Center about 45 meters under ground
level. Three forty-passenger elevators link this
subway station with the pedestrian system of the
community. The station is only 20 minutes away from
the Downtown Oslo subway station. As is true of the
other satellite towns, Romsås was designed as an
integral part of Oslo and not an autonomous, self
contained separate new town. Hence the importance
of articulating the planning of the Romsås community
with the developing mass transit network of the Oslo
region.

Neighborhood Characteristics

Although each neighborhood has distinctive
attributes, each typically contains in addition to
the multi-family three- to eight-story housing
blocks, a neighborhood school; a day care center; a
general store and service center; play areas for
children, larger recreational areas for other age
groups; and parking garages for the residents' automobiles. The plan for the "Svarttjern" neighborhood
in Figure 6E provides a symbolic representation of
the typical elements of each of the neighborhoods.
It will be noted that the housing is arranged in
fairly dense apartment clusters around open play
areas ("leke-plasser") and that a "kiosk" and two
neighborhood stores (nærbutikker") are strategically
located for the residents' daily use. Three parking
garages are located between the apartment clusters
and the ring-road around the town. The neighborhood
is served by an elementary school ("Barneskole"), a
secondary school (Ungdomskole), and a day-care
institution (Daginstitusjon).

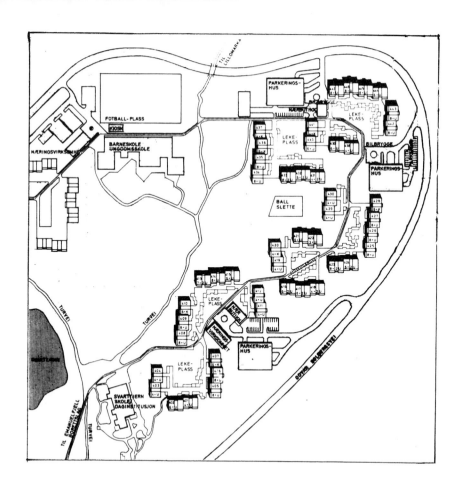

Figure 6E   Svarttjern Neighborhood, (Borettslag)
Romsas, consists of 47 highrise
apartment buildings with 651 dwellings
of which 18 are 5-room apartments, 299
4-room, 234 3-room, and 80 2-room,
completed in 1973-1974. Note the
following translations of the Norwegian
terms on the map: Barneskole = School
7-13 years old, Ungdomskole = 14-16
years old. Næringsvirksomhet = Building
for industries. Lekeplass = playground.
Ballslette = Field for ball games.
Nærbutikk = local shop. turvei = Hiking
trail. Parkeringshus = Parking ramp.

Two small industrial work places (næringsvirk-somheter) are also located in the neighborhood. The residential areas encircle a rather large open space for recreational activities. This neighborhood has the additional recreational amenity of a small lake from which the neighborhood gets its name.

As in Lambertseter, each neighborhood has its own cooperative association called the "borettslag." From that residents' association is elected a neighborhood council which becomes a communications link between the residents and the OBOS administra-tive staff which manages the neighborhood (Oslo Bolig og Sparelag 1968, pp. 16-21).

The Romsås Center

In order that Romsås should not become simply a bedroom suburb, it was clear from the beginning that it should have a town center. Since the Grorud Valley was already developing several such centers, and since Romsås was relatively close to the Grorud Center, a critical planning problem was to design one which would be large enough to provide the basic elements of a community center but one which at the same time would be economically and socially defensible.

Two important planning strategies for providing such an optimal community center were used; the strategy of coordinated inter-sectoral planning, and the mixed land-use strategy. A Romsås Center coor-dinating secretariat was established in the Oslo Planning Department to coordinate the planning and developments of each of the various municipal departments responsible for developing the Center. This included such varied sectors of municipal planning as education, health, social welfare, recreation and open space planning, postal service, public utilities, transportation, sewage and sanitation, and architectural design.

Figure 6F   Air   photo   of   Romsås   satellite   town.
Note the schools and local center in the
center   of   the   photo,   as   well   as   the
large open spaces and the road system.

The outcome was a plan for a very compact center providing the following major elements (Romsås Senter, 1975, pp. 1-14):

1. A covered walkway, vehicular street with underground parking spaces, a subway rail station together with a reception center and administrative offices. The amount of space allocated to these was 4,900 square meters.

2. Educational facilities for a secondary school including a large assembly, a youth center, athletic facilities and library designed to serve both the school population and the larger Romsås community. 5,800 square meters were used for these facilities.

3. A health center and hospital with a cafeteria, several meeting rooms, and a community kitchen. The hospital was designed for a capacity of 120 patients. The health center includes both a medical and dental clinic as well as social security offices and a hospital chapel. The health facilities occupy 7,900 square meters of space.

4. The commercial center and related rental spaces take up 3,500 square meters of space. In addition to the major shopping center, this space is rented for a postal service, a kiosk, a market, warehouses, and offices for various entrepreneurs. Most of the major services found in fairly large villages are available to the inhabitants of Romsås.

5. The Center also contains 201 housing units. Forty-five of those are designed with special features for the physically handicapped; 80 are planned for housing the retired elderly; and the remaining 76 residential units are designed for the staff servicing the health center and other aspects of the Romsås Center.

Both the Center and the neighborhoods of Romsås have been designed to allow for changing functions, activities, and spatial needs as the community

187

changes.

This rather detailed account of the recently developed satellite town of Romsås will hopefully illumine some of the major orientations and motifs of one of modern Oslo's principal strategies for managing the expansion of an historic city into a modern metropolis. Students enrolled in the Scandinavian Urban Studies Term at the University of Oslo who had also seen similar developments in Denmark, Finland and Sweden, observed that Romsås had some of the environmental and esthetic charm of both Tapiola of Helsinki, and Vällingby of Stockholm even if built on a smaller scale.

As everyone knows, the future of Romsås lies essentially in how its residents will transform this "urban container" into a living human community. It is reasonable to assume that like Ullevål Hageby, developed more than sixty years ago and the first satellite town of Lambertseter developed in the 1950s, Romsås too, will mature into a community which will link its inhabitants to a sense of history and nurture an appreciation of Romsås as a distinctive place in the Oslo metropolis where they will participate in the ongoing drama of Norway's capital city.

VI.   Satellite Towns and Metropolitan Development: Some Assessments

It is in the context of such a perspective that the satellite towns can be most meaningfully tested. The crucial test will be their contribution to a humane transformation of the historic city of Oslo into a socially satisfying and politically manageable modern metropolis. As has been indicated earlier, there is considerable division of opinion concerning this question. Many are criticial of the housing densities, and the tendency toward their standardization. Some fault them for not providing enough new employment opportunities in the new towns, necessitating long daily trips to and from work. Perhaps the largest dissatisfaction comes from those who still have in their minds an image of the ideal single family ancestral home along a fjord, on a mountain, or in some romantic valley where they would live closer to nature.

In recent years, architects, sociologists and other professional scholars have initiated more systematic assessments of the satellite towns. One of the most comprehensive of these is a two-volume case study of Ammerud. The first volume by architects Anne Sæterdal and Thorbjørn Hansen published in 1969 provides a detailed and intimate account of how and by whom Ammerud was planned and developed, including critical comments by the authors.

Although the report does provide very helpful description of how and by whom the community was planned and built, it is essentially a critical survey of what happened rather than a consistent analysis of how the process deviates from an ideal model (Sæterdal and Hansen 1969, p. 165). It emphasizes that the National Housing Bank, OBOS, and the City Council failed to provide for user input into the planning and building process; and that they persisted in processes and patterns which they considered financially sound and which would produce the size and pattern for urban development that they had decided upon in the beginning of their new-town building. The second volume, written by architects Grete Bull, Thorbjørn Hansen and Ragnhild Haug for the Norwegian Building Research Institute was published in 1971 (Bull, Hansen, and Haug 1971). This volume provides a sociological profile of the inhabitants of Ammerud; why they moved there, and the general nature of their living conditions. A special section is devoted to an evaluation of the housing and neighborhood amenities. The last part of the book examines how such community structures as the residential cooperative associations function in the life of the community.

The study reveals that the population contains a preponderance of young families with children which previously had lived in rather poor and insecure conditions in other parts of Oslo. Many were incomplete nuclear families. A few were singles. There were many children but few elderly. A few were affluent and a few were very poor, but most would be considered middle class. The survey indicates that the escalating costs of home and community building translated into troublesome

189

housing costs. It also sharply accented the fact of Ammerud being a "purely residential" area lacking in work opportunities as well as community services.

In one of its summary statements it observed that Ammerud, like other settlements in Oslo's peripheral areas, had become places where people live and sleep and that have more and more become dependent on the Oslo Center. Even as the places of work were becoming centralized, so too daily consumer goods, trade, health services and schools tended to be concentrated in large shopping centers, centralized hospitals, etc." (Bull, Hansen, and Haug 1971, p. 145). It is noteworthy that some of the innovations in the Romsås development took into account these and other criticisms of Ammerud and other earlier satellite towns.

Although the Ammerud study was quite critical, it did not reject the essential concepts and objectives of satellite town development as a strategy for controlling urban sprawl. The principal thrust of the criticism was rather that the goals and concepts of the satellite town ideals were too often compromised for economic reasons, or because of unwillingness to adapt developmental strategies to new perceptions and realities.

In recent years, more subtle and complex critiques are appearing. Gullik Kollandsrud notes that the building of satellite towns has been too statically conceived and has not adequately taken into account the dynamics of a modern urban community. The housing structures of most of the towns lack the flexibility needed. They cannot readily be altered to fit the changing lifestyles and family folkways of a post-industrial society. Instant community building does not make adequate room for the adaptations needed for a changing population or changing lifestyles and expectations. Kollandsrud thinks that all of the satellite towns were "over-dimensioned" in the light of the declining birth rates and changing population structures (Kollandsrud 1978, pp. 35-36). Implicit in this criticism is the notion that a more organic and crescive community growth would be preferable to the totally planned relatively instantly enacted satellite town.

Another criticism focuses upon issues related

to the bureaucratization and standardization associated with mass-produced satellite towns. The very scale of their development, it is argued, has led to an ever-increasing size and bureaucratization of such organizations as OBOS, the National Housing Bank, and the administrative structures of municipal government. As their power and authority have become increasingly centralized, the sense of powerlessness among the people concerning their opportunity for shaping their own habitat diminishes (Kollandsrud 1978, pp. 27-30).

Much of the new criticism also reflects a reaction against the architectural legacy of functionalism and neoclassicism. Werner Christie Mathisen articulates this in a recent article in Miljø Magasinet. Admitting to being strongly influenced by Lewis Mumford, he expresses great apprehension about the "functional city" where all the luxuries are cut out. He doesn't want a city milieu dominated by uniformity and colorless effectiveness. The city must be more than a "homemaking-machine." It should also be "a fountain for dreams and fantasies." It seems apparent that this poetic and romantic reaction to the rationalism implicit in the functional city was addressed to the satellite towns and similar housing developments in Oslo (Mathisen 1979, pp. 23-25).

Perhaps the most threatening critique of the satellite town developments is the suggestion that the ideology out of which they were born has lost much of its appeal. The very success of modern Norway's socioeconomic development has led to an affluence that the pioneers of cooperative community building could not have anticipated. With this affluence has come renewed interest in individual as over against cooperative ownership of housing. The needs for self-expression and control through shaping one's own environment has become more important. The insights of anthropology and psychology that housing is concerned with more than "light, fresh air, and secure roof over one's head" has become more popular. The symbolic status value of housing and its potential for self-expression has become increasingly important and made mass-produced, standardized housing less attractive

(Butenschøn 1979, pp. 10-12).

Whether or not this new consciousness of a more affluent society is one of the harbingers of a "post welfare state ethos" is not the concern of this study. What needs to be noted, is that the basic goals of controlling urban sprawl by building comprehensively planned nucleated sub-cities integrally linked with the central city has not been fundamentally challenged. The essential concepts and objectives of the satellite towns as a strategy for controlling urban sprawl; as a means for articulating public transit development with planned urban growth; as an appropriate involvement of the public sector in urban development; as a means of protecting land resources and the natural milieu from undue metropolitan plunder have not been rejected.

In a sense, satellite town building is nearly finished. The essential multi-nucleated form of Oslo's expanding metropolis has been established. The challenge now is shifting from launching more new towns to improving and building upon those already built, and renewing or rehabilitating older sections of Oslo's inner city. It is in these activities, as well as those taking place in the completion of the latest satellite towns such as Furuset and Holmlia, that the criticisms of the older satellite towns will have their greatest impact. Already apparent, are an increasing concern for what the Norwegians call the "nærmiljø" (The intimate milieu of one's residence); a greater variety of housing types with more emphasis upon low-rise high density-housing; more opportunities for resident participation in community planning; and other adaptions to changing expectations of a more affluent society (Thorp et al, 1973).

REFERENCES

Berry, Brian J. L. 1973. The Human Consequences of Urbanization. New York: St. Martin's Press.

Bull, Grete; Thorbjorn Hansen and Ragnhild Haug 1971. Å Bo i Drabantby. Oslo: Norges Byggforsknings-institutt (Norwegian Institute for Building Research).

Butenschøn, Peter. 1979. "Fra boligkamp til Villakosmetikk" in Miljo Magasinet No. 4.

Dolce, Philip C., ed. 1976. Suburbia: The American Dream and Dilemma. Garden City, N.J.: Anchor Press/Doubleday.

Eckhoff, Jan Christian. 1969. Byplan: Norske By Samfunn i Vekst-Mot Hva? Oslo: Pax Forlag.

Fogelson, Robert M. 1967. The Fragmented Metropolis. Cambridge, Massachusetts: Harvard University Press.

Hassett, Holly M. 1976. Lambertseter Today and Tomorrow. Oslo: A Research Monograph For the Scandinavian Urban Studies Term at the University of Oslo's International Summer School.

Kollandsrud, Gullik. 1978. Trehusbyen: Kan den Gjenskapes. Oslo: Treopplysningsrådet.

Li, Einar. 1942. Ullevål Hageby. Oslo: Kirstes Boktrykkeri.

Li, Einar. 1947. Oslo Havebyselskap Gjennom 30 År. Oslo: Arbeidernes Aktietrykkeri.

Mathisen, Werner Christie. 1979. "Drømmen om Byen" in Miljø Magasinet, No. 4.

Mumford, Lewis. 1968. The Urban Prospect. New York: Harcourt, Brace and World, Inc.

Nestor, Per. 1979. Boligpolitikken og OBOS Gjennom 50 År. Oslo Bolig-og Sparelag.

Nordic Housing Exhibition Committee. 1978. Nordic Housing 1945-1980. Nordic Association of Architecture at the UIA Congress in Mexico.

OBOS bladet Nr. 6. 1968, "Hvor og Hva Skal Bygges" (Where and What Shall be Built?).

Osborn, Frederic J. and Arnold Whittick. 1963. The New Towns: The Answer to Megalopolis. Cambridge, Massachusetts: M.I.T. Press.

Oslo Bolig og Sparelag. 1968. "OBOS Skal Bygge Boliger for 8000 Menesker Pa Romsås" in OBOS bladet Nr. 6.

Oslo's Commissioner of Housing. 1971. Housing in Oslo. Oslo: The Oslo Office of the Commission of Housing.

Oslo Havebyselskap. 1979. Årsmelding og Regnskap 1978. Oslo: Aktietrykkeri.

Oslo Planning Department. 1960. Oslo Planning and Development. Oslo: Oslo Planning Office.

O'Sullivan, John. 1979. December 12th Interview with architect O'Sullivan at Arkitekthøgskole of Oslo.

Popenoe, David. 1977. The Suburban Environment of Sweden and the United States. Chicago: The University of Chicago Press.

Rasmussen, Tor. Fr. 1981. "Byutvikling og planlegging i et fordelingspolitisk perspektiv" Svensk geograpfisk Årsbok, pp. 185-199.

Rinnan, Frode. 1958. Lambertseter 1958. Oslo: Oslo Bolig-og Sparelag.

Romsås Senter. 1975. A brochure prepared by the Planning and Building Committee coordinating the development of the Center.

Røren, Kari. 1981. Lambertseter: Beskrivelse og analyse av bolig-, befolknings-og arealutvikling i en drabantby i forandring. Oslo byplan - konteret.

Sandvik, Einar. 1979. OBOS: 50 År For Tryggere Hjem. Oslo: Oslo Bolig Sparelag.

Sethre, Dag Ingar and Viggo Kippenes. 1970. Drabantby Problematikk i Generalt og Lambertseter Spesielt. Oslo: Diplom Arkitekthøgskole av Oslo.

Stahl, Wendy. 1973. People, Planners and Politicians: A Case Study of the Romsås Satellite Town. Oslo: A Research Monograph for the Scandinavian Urban Studies Term at the University of Oslo's International Summer School.

Sæterdal, Anne and Thorbjørn Hansen. 1969. Ammerud 1: Planlegging Av En Bydel. Oslo: Norges Byggforskningsinstitutt.

Thorp, Kari, (Red) 1973. Småhus For Alle. Oslo: Treopplysningsrådet.

Ward, Barbara. 1976. The Home of Man. New York: W. W. Norton and Co.

Åstrom, Kell. 1967. City Planning in Sweden. Stockholm: The Swedish Institute.

CHAPTER SEVEN: REGIONAL CITIES AND NORWAY'S URBAN DEVELOPMENT

I.   Outlines of an Urban System

While there is no question about Oslo's dominance as Norway's major metropolis, it is important that attention be directed to the other leading cities of the country and to their role in Norway's urban development. As Tor Rasmussen has suggested, these cities function as nerve centers for Norway's emerging post-industrial economy and culture (Norges Offentlige Utredninger 1979:5, pp. 134-135).

Shortly after Norway's enactment of the national planning act of 1965, its Ministry of Municipalities and Labor published an elaborate monograph on planning and development pursuant to the provisions of that Act. Chapter Ten of that document focuses upon the planning and development of the leading urban centers of the country. It suggested a hierarchy of urban centers around which planning policies and developmental strategies might be organized. Oslo was of course identified as the center for discharging the functions appropriate to Norway's capital city. The next rung of city centers was identified as "landsdelssentra"--or leading city centers in each of the five major regions of Norway. Without presuming to officially designate which cities should function as such centers, it suggested that Tromsø might do so in northern Norway, Trondheim in central Norway, Bergen in western Norway, Stavanger in the southwest and Kristiansand in the south.

The third rung of centers was identified as smaller regional urban centers of the country with 30,000 or more people which were typically surrounded by smaller centers or settlements related to them. The smallest settlements of the hierarchy were identified as "bygde" centers, in the more rural areas of the country (Johnsen 1970, pp. 125-133).

In view of Norway's national commitment to regional development, it is appropriate that a book such as this should focus attention on such regional

196

cities. To adequately deal with all such regional
cities would require a book by itself. In this
chapter, we have chosen to examine the planning and
development of the leading city center of each of
the five regions other than that of Oslo. An analysis of the planning efforts in the city regions and
centers is crucial for an understanding of the urban
and regional developments in Norway. The directions
for future developments were laid in the 1970s when
the fundaments for the municipal and county plans
were assigned. The main points of these plans are
reviewed in this chapter. For the location of these
cities, see map in Figure 3A.

As has already been noted, a basic premise of
Norway's commitment to regionalism involves increasing the resources of regions and municipalities of
low or declining economic growth. While at first
such an orientation tended to reflect an anti-city
bias based on the nation's concern about what was
perceived to be an over-concentration of people and
socioeconomic resources in Oslo, there also emerged
an awareness of the important role that the leading
urban center in each of Norway's major regions had
to play in promoting each region's economic and
social well-being. It became apparent that an
increasingly large number of Norwegians preferred a
life style and socioeconomic milieu that would be
difficult to secure in the various parts of the
country apart from the existence of relatively large
regional urban centers. Out of such a perspective,
it became increasingly acceptable to perceive of
each region's leading city as a pivotal focal point
for regional development. From this perspective the
city became identified as an important national
resource (Anker et al. 1972, pp. 11-12).

This is especially true in relation to their
role in helping to implement the general goals of
Norway's regional policies, which can be briefly
summarized as follows:
1. An equalization of community well-
   being throughout the nation.
2. The promotion of equal opportunity for
   persons and groups in all parts of the
   country.
3. Increased economic productivity and

197

work opportunities in parts of the country with low economic growth.
4. The development and expansion of local communities that can be economically viable, provide socially satisfying community services, nurture cultural interests, and promote a sense of general well-being.

II. Tromsø and Norway's Commitment to its North Country

Perhaps in no city of Norway has its recent growth and development been more directly related to Norway's regional policies than in Tromsø. Having been designated as the leading city of North Norway, it became an important participant in the regional development of that part of the country. An examination of its development therefore provides an insightful illustration of what might happen to a regional city when it is treated as an important national resource for a country's socioeconomic and cultural development.

Like many of Norway's coastal cities, Tromsø has a long history as a trading and cultural center. Håkon Håkonson of Norway built the first Norwegian church there in 1250. In 1794, it received from the King of Denmark the official status of a "kjøpstad," a self-governing city, with all the trading privileges associated with such a status in Denmark's eighteenth century mercantilism. (See Chapter 2.V.). Since that time the city experienced a fairly steady growth. From 1890 to 1950, its population grew from 10,390 to 22,537. Although this is a small-sized city, it needs to be remembered that it lies about 250 miles north of the Arctic Circle and is the largest city of the world so far north.

But Tromsø's most striking growth has occurred since 1950. By 1984 its population had more than doubled to 47,500 inhabitants, making it one of Norway's most rapidly growing municipalities. Much of this growth can be attributed to Norway's post-war urban and regional policies and their special focus upon northern Norway's reconstruction and development. Of special significance for Tromsø, these policies included programs for industrial growth and modernization, new and improved transportation systems by land, sea, and air, expanding health, education and cultural programs, and the application of all the planning and community building policies and strategies of the country.

Planning and Community Building in Tromsø

Tromsø's official planning documents describe the impact of these policies upon its growth and development. They document the public efforts at directing and controlling the city's growth. By annexing surrounding areas in 1964, Tromsø became one of Norway's largest geographical municipalities, thus enabling the city to both plan and control its metro-urban growth.

Tromsø's 1976 developmental plan for the central city delineates three principal areas with six related centers. On the island of Tromsøy--from which the city gets its name--there are two principal city centers: Tromsø center and Bredvik; on the mainland in the east there are the two centers of Tromsdalen and Kroken. On the large island west of Tromsø, there are also two centers, Kvaløysletta and Storelva. (See Figure 7A.) The sounds on both sides of the Tromsø island are bridged.

This plan is very typical for the tendencies and wishes in urban planning in the 1970s. Decentralization was the key word. Even in smaller urban regions in Tromsø, growth and new housing were spread over large areas and local centers were established. As far as possible, each of the centers are to be compact, multi-functional and vital living environments, with a balance between residential and occupational sites. However, as new jobs are mainly in the service sector, they are located in the urban core and it becomes a necessity, therefore, to travel fairly long distances to jobs.

Similar efforts are being initiated to control the developments in the outer areas of the Tromsø region. One objective is to stabilize the primary industries by protecting tillable land from urban development, securing the fishing activities, and prioritizing harbor facilities. Another objec-

Geographisches Institut der Universität Kiel

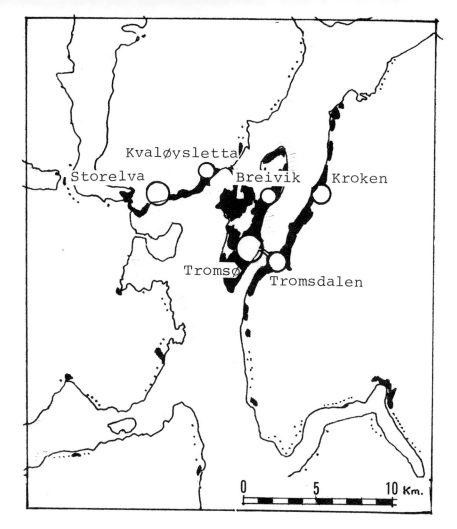

Figure 7A   Tromsø City Region

The old city of Tromsø was located on the southern
part of the small island (22 sq. km.) in the middle
of the sound.   Gradually the built land spread out
over the whole island, that also got an airport.
The sound to the mainland in the east was bridged in
1960, linking Tromsø to the national road net.   The
sound in the west was bridged in 1973, linking the
city to the large island of Kvaløy.   The size of the
municipal land area today is 2,520 sq. km., of which
34 sq. km. is cultivated.   Population is spread
along the coastline, below 50 meters above sea
level.   Most of the land is above that altitude.
Local sea transportation is still of vital importance.

200

tive is to locate strategic industrial and service-
oriented enterprises in designated centers of its
peripheral areas.

Special emphasis is placed upon the
strengthening of the "bygde" centers in the outer
areas of the city-region; providing them with public
schools, daycare centers, recreational facilities,
community centers, post offices, health and social
service institutions, housing for the elderly,
general merchandise stores, pharmacies, and service
centers for boats and automobiles, etc. Fourteen
"bygdesentra" were recommended in Tromsø's
Generalplan for 1975 (Tromsø Kommune Generalplan
1979: Nr. 5, pp. 3339). Each center would be linked
to the Tromsø Center with a planned transportation
network. It is apparent that the nurturing of the
planned neighborhood and community centers are an
integral part of Tromsø's overall regional
development design, not unlike the basic aspects of
Oslo's developmental pattern.

Economic Planning and Development

Tromsø's emphasis upon the promotion of the
local community centers in its outer areas is
related to its recognition of the critical importance of its historic primary industries of farming,
forestry, fishing and hunting. An aggressive implementation of Norway's extensive conservation policies relative to such industries is considered vital
for Tromsø's economy (Tromsø Kommune Byplankontoret
1976, pp. 3-3 to 3-7). Such environmental concerns
also apply to such related issues as the protection
of the region's special outdoor landscapes for
recreational purposes as well as scientific research
in the fields of botany, zoology, and geology.

Although there has been a sharp decline in
the number of workers engaged in these primary
industries, such decline cannot be interpreted as a
measure of declining importance of these industries
for Tromsø's economy. In the first place, much of
the decline in the number of workers and establishments in farming, forestry, fishing and hunting is
attributable to modernization and rationalization of
these activites. Furthermore, the related develop-

201

ments of fish-processing and marketing enterprises in Tromsø are of great importance to Tromsø's economy.

Because of its strategic location, Tromsø is the leading fishing center of the county of Troms. There are nine fish-processing industries in the center city of Tromsø as well as several small plants in its surrounding areas. The 1977 production of Tromsø's fish industries totaled more than 217 million Norwegian kroner or approximately 40 million dollars (Tromsø Kommune Byplankontoret 1978: Nr. 2, pp. 19-20). The marine activities associated with the fishing industry also contribute substantially to the city's economy. The modernization and expansion of the fishing fleet is considered important for the future. There continues to be a close affinity between fishing activities and the other primary occupations of farming, forestry and hunting, since many are engaged in two or more of such activities. Altogether their productivity provides important resources for the region's economy.

The percentage of workers engaged in the secondary industries in Tromsø is considerably lower than that for the nation as a whole. In 1970 Tromsø's percentage was only 16.5% compared with 27.5% for the nation. But they continue to be important, nonetheless. The importance of the fish-processing industry has already been noted. In recent years, the building and construction industries have become increasingly important.

The establishment of a university and medical school, the building of a major hospital, as well as a large county government building are examples of how Norway's public sector contributions to Tromsø have increased construction work in the city. Similar construction of new office buildings for the expanding private services in the fields of banking and insurance together with the rapidly growing housing industry have contributed much to the vitality of the building industry.

But by far the most impressive economic developments in recent years have taken place in the tertiary industries. As northern Norway's leading regional center and the county seat of Troms, the city has experienced dramatic growth in the number of public employees. It is estimated that the number of employees in the tertiary industries increased by 450 to 500 each year during the decade of the 1970s.

The establishment of a national university and medical school at Tromsø is of great significance for the city and its region. It is perhaps the most significant symbol of Norway's commitment to its regional policies. The following objectives, among others, were listed for locating the university in Tromsø:

1. To contribute significantly to solving the problem of the lack of an educated work force in northern Norway.
2. To provide the youth of northern Norway better access to university education.
3. To foster an enrichment of northern Norway's social and economic development.
4. To provide a setting for research activities specially appropriate in northern Norway.

The development of its medical school and the related central hospital is of obvious importance for the strengthening of the health services in the region. The university is also important for its contribution to the political, social and cultural environment of the city and its region. It helps make Tromsø a more attractive place for establishing enterprises not hitherto typical in northern Norway (Tromsø Kommune Plankontoret 1976, pp. 3.56-3.58).

The first students entered the University in 1972. By 1977-78 it had an enrollment of 1,500 students and 550 employees, half of which were of the teaching staff. From 1971 to 1977 there were approximately 170 new work places added each year to the university and the central hospital. It is estimated that by 1990 there will be added somewhere between 700 and 1,000 additional employees.

Other important public sector innovations have been the establishment of a national theater, a regional center for the Norwegian Broadcasting Corporation, and an airport; all of which have added to the variety of service-oriented work opportunities.

Within the private sector there has been substantial growth of service-oriented occupations in the fields of banking and finance, in hotel, restaurant, and tourist-related activities; and in retail sales, etc. There was an increase in saleswork alone of approximately 170 positions a year from 1970 to 1976 (Tromsø Kommune Plankontoret 1978: Nr. 2, pp. 34-36).

An overall view of the changing occupational structure of Tromsø is presented in Table 7.1. The total number of employees increased by more than 4,000 between 1960 and 1970. By far the greatest increase took place within the service industries sector, increasing by 61.9%. Within this sector the public-private personal services increased the most with an increase of 77.6%. The increase in saleswork and finance came next, with a 60% increase. The growth in the secondary industries was also substantial, with an increase of 46.7%. The largest increase within this sector was found in the mining-industrial activities, where 1,067 employees were added to the labor force. As could be expected, the number of employees in the primary industries declined substantially, losing 530 employees--a decline of 22.6%.

It is appropiate to note that the general occupational structure of Tromsø has become similar to that which prevails in the other urban regions of Norway, with a predominance of employment in the tertiary services, a fairly stable employment in the secondary industries, and sharp decline in the primary industries. Like the other city regions of Norway, its planning and development activities are guided by Norway's national policies related to social welfare, land use planning, environmental conservation, managed settlement patterns, and the nurture of culture and community in every part of the country.

The shape and character of Tromsø's development gives a clear illustration of the principle of decentralized urbanization, with urban concentration taking place in the context of a relatively small metro-urban region containing a central city core and a series of satellite sub-communities around its

Table 7.1 Occupational Distribution of Tromsø
          Work Force 1960 -1970

| Occupation | Number Employed | | | | Change | |
| | 1960 | | 1970 | | 1960 | 1970 |
	Number	%	Number	%	Numbers	%
Farming & Foresting	511	4.7	323	2.1	-188	-38.8
Hunting & Fishing	1,834	16.9	1,492	10.1	-343	-18.6
Primary Industries	2,345	21.6	1,815	12.1	-530	-22.6
Construction	1,563	14.5	1,887	12.5	+324	20.7
Mining & Industry	1,417	13.1	2,484	16.5	+1,067	75.3
Secondary Industries	2,980	26.7	4,371	29.0	+1,391	46.7
Commerce & Finance	2,003	18.3	3,164	21.0	+1,161	60.0
Communications & Transport	1,061	9.9	1,416	9.5	+355	33.5
Public & Private Services	2,410	22.3	4,281	28.4	+1,871	77.6
Tertiary Services	5,474	50.8	8,864	58.9	+3,390	61.9
Total	10,799	100.0	15,050	100.0	+4,251	39.4

Source: Tromsø Kommune Byplankontoret 1978. nr. 2,
         pp. 2-3.

periphery linked to the center with transport systems coordinated with community planning.

While Tromsø is the leading urban center in northern Norway, it should be remembered that other city centers are also important to that region; such as Harstad--also located in the county of Troms; Bodø, in Nordland County, and Alta in Norway's northernmost county of Finnmark. Each performs similar urban functions within the contexts of its distinctive regional setting.

III. Trondheim and Middle Norway

Middle Norway, called Trøndelag, consists of two separate counties simply differentiated as North Trøndelag and South Trøndelag. The largest and most prominent city of this part of Norway is Trondheim. Besides being the county seat of South Trøndelag, it has also been identified as the regional center of the Trøndelag region in Norway's "distrikt-politikken." (See Figure 3A).

The Historic City

Perhaps in none of the major regional cities of Norway, does the impact of its long historic past more significantly influence present planning and development than in Trondheim. Founded as early as 997 A.D. by the Viking king Olav Tryggvason, the city became the capital of Norway and its chief ecclesiastical seat during the Middle Ages. In many ways the history of Trondheim was center stage for the history of Norway itself, and for many centuries the city was a real or potential rival of Bergen and Oslo as Norway's most important city. Thus virtually every period of Norway's history left its mark upon this city's culture and imagery. Its nature-given setting at the junction of the double-looped mouth of the Nidelven River and the ice-free Trondheim Fjord provided a good sheltered harbor for an active coastal trading center, with convenient linkages to the rich inland regions of central Norway.

Much of the present-day imagery of Trondheim mirrors influences that go back to the Middle Ages. The famous Nidaros Cathedral, the King's Court and residence, the guild halls, the early school and hospital, the cloisters and the craft shops-- together with the street pattern connecting them-- became the nucleus of the emerging city. As every discerning visitor knows, the legacies of this medieval period of city-building are still visible in Trondheim's city scape. Similarly, legacies of the renaissance and the age of the enlightenment are also visible. Kjøpmannsgata reminds us of the grow- ing dominance of the merchant class; the wooden warehouses on the pier along the river Nidelven stand as reminders of the importance of shipping; and extant residential and other community buildings say much about the life and culture of this patri- cian led pre-industrial period of Trondheim.

The images left from the industrial period are even more manifest. The city engineer Carl Adolf Dahl prepared the city for its industrial development. He planned and had built new bridges and city water works, modernized the fire fighting system, secured the water reservoirs system, and initiated the development of electricity and a light-rail transit system.

Along with these improvements in the city's technical infrastructure, new industrial develop- ments dramatically transformed the city's character. A large and rapidly expanding tannery, a machine parts factory which expanded to produce steam engines and locomotives, a textile factory, a brick and tile factory, a brewery and sugar processing plant, a large bakery, and more became the new shapers of the cityscape. The transportation system was also transformed. A steamboat began operating in earnest. By 1880 the Oslo to Trondheim railroad connection was completed.

With industrial development came important socio-cultural changes as well. The city's popula- tion grew rapidly, public education expanded, a public library was opened in 1862, and Trondheim's Technical School was organized in 1870. New archi- tectural styles emerged as the building industry shifted from crafts production to mass production. Mass-produced facades began to ornament shops, offices and housing to accomodate the tastes of the emerging class of new industrial and commercial entrepreneurs. Their impact upon Trondheim's present city imagery is clearly documented in a remarkable recent publication entitled Trondheims Bybilde (Fasting 1978, pp. 76-144).

This long history of Trondheim--containing elements of civilization from the Viking period, the Middle Ages, the Renaissance, and the Industrial Era--has not only left a legacy of highly varied visual city imageries. It has also quite naturally contributed to the notions that people of Trondheim have of what the city means to them and what it should be like in the future. This is reflected in their response to the many compelling challenges that are accompanying the transformation of Trondheim from a relatively small compact and un-specialized urban community to the greatly expanded metro-urban region which it has now become.

Trondheim as a Regional City

As the chief commercial, administrative, and communications center of middle Norway, Trondheim as a city region nearly doubled its population from 1900 to 1950. It grew from a population of 54,790 to 102,784. The process of urbanization continued at an accelerated pace after 1950, reaching a population of 157,181 by 1981. Its population increased by nearly 53% from 1950 to 1981. The fact that dur-ing this same period the rest of the Sør Trøndelag county actually declined from 95,903 to 87,579--a decline of 8.7%--indicates the impact that urbaniza-tion was making in Middle Norway. By 1960 the Trondheim city region contained 52% of Sør Trønde-lag's population. Twenty years later that propor-tion had grown to 64.4%.

In terms of Norway's national policy of trying to maintain a balanced population growth in every part of the country, it was clearly evident that it was the Trondheim City Region that provided the crucial magnet for keeping people in Middle Norway. But from the perspective of the same policies, Trondheim's rapid growth represented a troublesome thinning out of population in Middle Norway's hinterland and exacerbated the "press" problems in Trondheim.

208

Trondheim's growth also involved an extensive expansion of its municipal boundaries, until at the present time the Trondheim City Region contains more than 120 square miles. Of that vast territory, approximately 70% is comprised of forests, mountains and agricultural land. Thus like Oslo, Trondheim has important responsibilities for the management of both scarce agricultural land and natural open areas for forestry and recreation. It should also be noted that the expansion of Trondheim's borders brought several smaller municipalities into the city's territory. Not only did they contribute to the city's population growth, but they also became sub-community centers for absorbing Trondheim's population growth. The data in Table 7.2 reflect some aspects of these demographic dynamics.

Table 7.2 Towns in Trondheim City Region and their population in 1960 and rate of increase from 1950 to 1960.

Town	1960 Population	% Increase 1950-1960
Trondheim	58,638	3.5
Melhus	3,836	13.8
Leinstrand	3,671	28.1
Byneset	2,009	6.0
Buvik	1,283	4.8
Strinda	38,047	130.9
Tiller	2,829	77.9
Klobu	1,635	16.5
Malvik	5,486	16.5
Total Trondheim City Region	117,434	14.3

Source: Rasmussen 1969, p. 182

Every one of the peripheral towns experienced a higher population growth than the Trondheim center city. By 1960 the combined population of those sub-communities had reached 58,796, thus exceeding that of the center city of Trondheim. This developmental pattern continued in the 1960s and 1970s. In 1984 the total population of Trondheim city region was 157,182. (See Table 3.3.) For futher explanation of this growth pattern, see Chapter 9.3.

Trondheim as a Post-Industrial City

An examination of the economic changes taking place in Trondheim provides perhaps the most helpful clue to the socio-cultural meaning of its dramatic growth. Changes in Trondheim's occupational structure clearly indicate that the major employment increase has come in the tertiary occupations. Table 7.3 provides an overall picture of the developing employment trends.

Table 7.3   Employment By Occupation in Trondheim in 1970 and 1976

OCCUPATION	1970	1976	CHANGE	% CHANGE
Agriculture and Forestry	890	710	−180	20.2
Industry	12,600	12,190	−410	−3.2
Power Generation, etc.	5,810	5,900	90	1.5
Sales-Commerce	12,390	12,800	410	3.3
Communication and Transport	5,730	6,750	1,020	17.8
Banking, Insurance, Restaurants & Office Services	6,810	7,300	490	7.2
Public Administration, Health Services Education & Research	9,560	12,360	2,800	29.3
TOTAL	53,790	58,010	4,220	7.8

Source: Trondheim Kommune 1979. Kommuneplan 1979; Radmannens Forslag

210

Of the total increase in employment of 4,220, nearly 2/3 were accounted for by the 2,800 added to the work force in the public sector. If one adds to that sector all the categories typically associated with the tertiary occupations, all of the increased employment is accounted for in that sector. The primary industries of agriculture and forestry declined by 20.2%. Even the employment in the secondary industries declined by more than 3%. As of 1976, the distribution of Trondheim's employment by the three classic occupational sectors was as follows:

Primary Industries	1.2%
Secondary Industries	31.2%
Tertiary Industries	67.6%

Thus more than two-thirds of Trondheim's workers are engaged in the service industries, typically requiring the most advanced education. The fact that by far the largest increase takes place in public administration, health services, education, and research helps explain this development. Many of those workers are engaged in teaching and research at Trondheim's Technical University. Many others are employed at the large Central Hospital of the Sør Trøndelag County. This hospital now also serves as a University Hospital.

The expanding services of the county government of Sør Trøndelag have added considerably to the number of professional people employed in that area of the public sector. In other words, Trondheim has become increasingly important as a government center as well as a health and higher education center.

Its continued importance as a religious center together with the extensive growth of the banking and insurance industries also contribute substantially to the number of employees with advanced education. As a result of these and other developments, such as expanding tourism and commerce, contemporary Trondheim can quite properly be perceived as becoming predominantly a post-industrial city related to an increasingly information-oriented "knowledge society."

Planning and Community Building in Trondheim

All of these changes led to profoundly new and challenging problems concerning the appropriate shape and character of Trondheim's structure as a city. Up until the end of the nineteenth century, most of Trondheim was contained within borders relatively congruent with the natural boundaries established by the river Nidelven and the Trondheim Fjord. But now, this historic city has become the center for a greatly expanded metropolitan area. A whole series of complex questions arose concerning how this expanded city might best be planned and developed. The enactment of the National Planning Act of 1965 provided the stimulus for Trondheim's first systematic quest for a comprehensive plan suitable for the new realities.

Three alternative scenarios were examined concerning the fate of the city center. One scenario envisioned a large, compact centralized city with all the major city functions concentrated within boundaries of the historic city. It was defended by some as the most appropriate development for one of Norway's major regional centers. A second alternative accented a decentralized approach, spreading the city functions outward in the surrounding areas, a pattern of suburbanization more typical in urban America. The third scenario was dubbed the "moderate city alternative" which affirmed the essential continuity of the historic center as the Trondheim region's central city (Eckhoff 1969, pp. 58-65).

It was this "moderate city" alternative that prevailed. It was agreed that those parts of "mitbyen"--i.e., the historic center city--which are highly valued for their distinctive historic and architectural qualities should be preserved as much as possible; that such historic structures as the Nidaros Cathedral and the Archbishop's Palace, etc. must be provided surroundings appropriate for their place in the city's imagery. It was also agreed that not only should the central city provide the greatest possible variety of shops and services and work opportunities, but it should also provide a milieu friendly to the pedestrian, i.e., the streets

212

should be as auto-free as possible. Much attention should also be paid to the architectural form and character of new construction such that it would be compatible with the exisitng city imagery.

Because of the problems of limited space in the central city, it was recommended that an over-flow city subcenter be established at Heimdal--a few miles south of the center city. In this, as well as other sub-communities in the expanded city region, housing construction and related neighborhood developments would continue. (See Figure 7B.)

Transportation planning and development to provide convenient linkages between these sub-communities and the center city were also tackled. Special emphasis upon protecting the inner city from troublesome thru-city traffic led to a plan for developing a ring-road around the core of the city in order to make it as pedestrian oriented and auto-free as possible.

These and other plans of the 1960s were a prelude to more systematic and comprehensive plans to follow. Pursuant to the National Building Act of 1965, Trondheim's city council structure was reor-ganized so as to faciliate greater coordination in planning and decision-making. The objective was that virtually every department of the city's gov-ernment should become involved in the comprehensive planning and development of the City.

From an examination of the Trondheim Kommune-plan of 1979, the character and directions of this comprehensive planning and development becomes discernible. In the first place, the original commitment to the preservation and continued nurture of a moderately compact but environmentally pleasing inner city is evident. In 1970, the City's execu-tive council created an office for registering the older buildings and structures that should be preserved, and appointed a Committee of Antiquarians for conducting a thorough inventory of them and preparing a report of its findings and recommenda-tions. Since Trondheim was one of Norway's cities affiliated with the European Historic Towns Forum, the Committee participated in its 1975 Congress on Historic City Preservation.

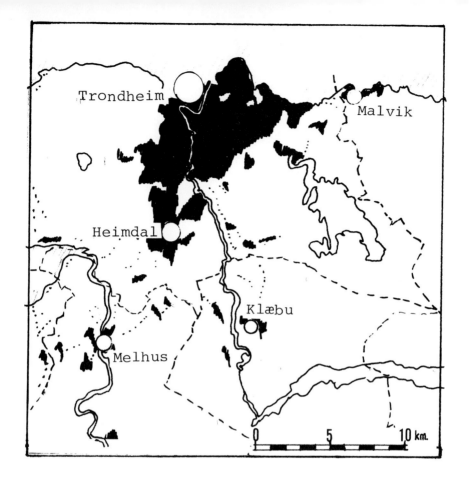

Figure 7B   Trondheim City Region

The historic city center with the cathedral is located between the river and the fjord. The new center of Heimdal satellite town is located 9-10 km. south of the old center along the railway line and along the highway leading to Oslo. There are also many other small sub+centers within the built-up area.

After the amalgamation with surrounding municipalities, the land area of Trondheim is 327 square km. with a population of 134,000 in 1984. Surrounding municipalities beyond this area also participate in the urban expansion with commuters to Trondheim bringing the population of the city region up to 163,000 in 1984.

The Committee's report came in the form of a remarkable document entitled <u>Trondheim's Bybilde</u> or Trondheim's City Image. Its central premise was that that which gave Trondheim a place with significant identity was a combination of landscape, city plan and distinctive buildings--a combination that has emerged from a long historic process unique to that City. The document developed a rationale for a program of preserving both historic buildings and distinctive urban settings. It emphasized the importance of people having identity with places and surroundings with historic symbolism. It stressed the value of the varied "visual information" provided by a city that preserves visual images from the past even as it necessarily builds for the present and the future. It noted that such images from the past are important aids to the teaching and appreciation of history. Furthermore, it argued that some of the attributes of the past city milieu were socially sound; noting especially the advantage of the multifunctional attributes of the older city where work, residence and public life were intermingled. It concluded that a viable local community must have the greatest possible balance between residential neighborhoods and workplaces.

That this document has made an impact on the city's planning is clear from one of the inner city maps of 1976 indicating the many areas where special preservation strategies are designated. These areas appear in virtually every part of the inner city; and there is evidence of activities already under way toward implementing some of the recommendations indicated in this planning map.

Such planning and developments, in the interest of preserving significant historic cultural and architectural images from the past, provide a clear illustration of how a sense of history plays an important role in city-building in places like Trondheim.

Other plans for the care and nurture of Trondheim's inner city involve transportation plans for pedestrian and bicycle paths, as well as an auto-free pedestrian-oriented street at the city's center and public transit designed to reduce the impact of disturbing automobile congestion and

pollution. Efforts are underway to renew and reha-
bilitate older residential neighborhoods and to
build new housing compatible with the historic inner
city milieu and which might meet the needs of
special groups such as the elderly who make up an
increasing part of the present population.

For the purpose of planning the greater
metro-urban area of Trondheim, the city region has
been divided into six areas. Comprehensive analysis
and plans are prepared for each prior to their
inclusion in the general plan for the entire city.
These analyses include information about the natural
landscape and resources, the population trends and
occupational structures, the housing conditions and
possibilities, the existing schools and school
needs, and such other service resources and needs as
day care programs, health and social programs,
recreational facilities, etc. (Trondheim Kommune
1979, pp. 216-236).

As was true of Oslo, Trondheim's planning and
community development builds upon the premise that
the city is a community of many sub-communities and
that each sub-community should be provided such
basic resources and services that are appropriate
for a relatively large village, but at the same time
be linked to the center city with adequate public
transit services. While much remains to be done,
the structures and processes for planning and community building are in place, and programs are
proceeding for plan implementation.

As can be expected, there are a number of
persistent vexing problems and conflicts that
complicate such implementation. One of the most
basic problems is the land-use conflict in the
undeveloped areas of the city. The national policy
rigorously restricting the use of tillable land from
urban development continues to place powerful constraints on housing and neighborhood developments in
the outer regions of the city. The 1979 "Kommuneplan" envisions the greatest development in the
eastern part of the city as well as in the expansion
of the satellite town of Heimdal.

Other large areas must be preserved for agriculture and forest use. There are also conflicts
between the automobile-oriented interests and those

that are more deeply concerned about preserving the
city's serenity and conserving energy and clean air.
That Trondheim is the smallest city in the world to
operate a public light-rail system indicates it has
not given up its general commitment to conservation
of both energy and environment. The struggle to
provide a balance between housing and jobs within
each of the sub-communities of the city continues to
be a challenge.

Furthermore, many of the goals of Trondheim's
best plans are costly and involve financial obligations and commitments of both county and national
governmental authorities. The extent of such commitments in turn revolve around their appropriate
role in the nation's regional policies. As has been
indicated by a Parliamentary Committee report on the
structure and economy of the large cities of Norway,
there appears to be a need for greater national
recognition of their importance for the well-being
of each of the major regional areas of the country
and that this should be reflected in greater
financial supports for implementing plans such as
have been developed by Trondheim (Norges Offentlige
Utredninger 1979: 5).

IV.   Stavanger: Historic City and Emerging Oil
       Capital of Norway

A similar transformation is occurring in
Southwest Norway's major city of Stavanger. Like
Trondheim, it is one of Norway's oldest cities, with
a history that dates back to the middle ages.
(Chapter 2.III). It shares with Trondheim a special
identity with Norway's early beginnings as a unified
nation. It has accumulated through its long history
similar symbolic socio-cultural identifying imageries. As a religious center it hosts what has been
said to be Norway's most beautiful cathedral. Like
Trondheim, its city form is shaped around a fjord-
oriented seacoast harbor. Its central city architecture of panelled, white-painted timber houses and
shops has become a national project for historic
preservation. After centuries of relatively slow
growth as a fishing and trading center, it has
become, like Trondheim, a county seat as well as the

217

officially designated capital city for one of Norway's major regions. Like Trondheim, the city is located in one of Norway's most productive agricultural regions, greatly constraining its options for expansion.

These similarities aside, Stavanger has the distinction of having become the "oil capital" of Norway. The discovery and development of the North Sea oil resources and Norway's decision to make Stavanger the national center of its petroleum activities, catapulted the city into both national and international attention. They have also greatly accelerated Stavanger's expansion as a metro-urban center. Perhaps in no other regional center of Norway, have the tensions between Norway's long historic past and the compelling forces of urban change been more sharply drawn and more acutely felt than in Stavanger. In a sense its development has become both a symbol of modern Norway's response to urbanization as well as an important object for special national concern as a testing ground for Norway's urban and environmental policies.

To understand Stavanger's response to the challenges of the developing oil culture, however, it is important to examine it in the context of the city's distinctive history and its socioeconomic developments prior to its introduction. Reference has already been made to its identity as an old city that has served as a container of culture and civilization derived from the many periods of its historic past.

Its culture, architecture and city-form continue to reflect the diverse symbolic representations of such a varied history. Representing the past are the twelfth century cathedral, narrow vehicle-free cobbled streets, wooden houses and picturesque open-air markets. The new is reflected in modern hotels, high-rise office and apartment buildings, new banks and specialty shops, together with modern hydrofoils and other means of marine travel to accomodate both tourists and other travelers.

As the southern-most gateway to Norway's fjord country, Stavanger has added the role of tourist center to its fishing, shipping and trading industries. As a busy seaport together with a modern airport and railroad station it has become a communications center for Rogaland County in Southwestern Norway.

The Changing Economy of Rogaland and Stavanger

Located at the southern part of the fjord country, Rogaland County is interlaced with a whole series of fjords and valleys which through the centuries have linked Stavanger's hinterland with the trading and shipping activities of its seacoast setting. Its economy has become highly diversified.

While only 15% of Rogaland's land area is tillable--with 7% for farming and 8% for forestry-- it is still one of the most important farming regions of Norway. The "Jæren" region of which Stavanger is a part has one of Norway's largest level plains. Its stony soil has been converted to a modern "Goshen." Together with other tillable land areas on the islands and in the valleys of the countryside, these valuable lands produce a wide variety of agricultural products, including fruits and vegetables, meat, poultry, and a wide variety of dairy products. Although Rogaland has the least forest areas of all the counties of Norway, it is nevertheless of some importance to the economy.

As would be expected, fishing constitutes another important primary economic industry, including the production of salmon, trout, shrimp, cod, lobster and herring. While all these primary industries continue to be important for the area's general economy, their contribution to the labor market has declined sharply in recent years. The number employed in such industries declined from 15,697 in 1960 to 11,796 in 1970--a decline of 24.9% in ten years (Fylkesplan For Rogaland 1975, pp. 8-9 and p. 257.)

Industrial employment in Rogaland increased during that same period from 34,574 workers to 39,941--an increase of 15.1%. Among the manufacturing industries registering growth during the 1960s were the iron and metal industries, lumbering, furniture and furnishings, graphics and publishing, machine products, and oil refining.

219

Industries with little growth or decline were producers of textiles, wood products, leather works, and electronics. Declining employment in these industries as well as in the primary industries is largely attributable to mechanization, rationalization, and an extensive development of hydroelectric power. Such industries as the manufacture of farm tools and machinery in Jæren, Europe's largest aluminum industry at Karmøy, the modern fish canning industry in Stavanger are illustrative of such developments. As of 1970, approximately 42% of Rogaland's workers were engaged in industrial work-- i.e., the secondary industries--this compared with 38% for the nation as a whole. This sector of employment in Rogaland increased by 15% from 1960 to 1975.

The greatest increase in employment has taken place in the tertiary industries, which grew from a total of 36,291 workers in 1960 to 43,968 in 1970--an increase of 21.2%. The most impressive growth took place within the public and private services sector which increased by 71.8% during the decade. By 1970 some 50.9% of the workers in Rogaland were engaged in the tertiary industries. This compares with 53% for the nation as a whole (Fylkesplan for Rogaland 1975, pp. 9-10, and p. 269).

As one would expect, the employment distribution of Stavanger is more heavily weighted in the direction of the tertiary industries. Table 7.4 presents a summary of the employment situation in Stavanger in 1976.

It is clear that Stavanger has developed a rather highly diverse economic structure with 37.4% of its workers engaged in the secondary industries and 61.8% in the tertiary industries. The number engaged in the primary industries has declined to less than 1%. Between 1960 and 1976 there was a steady overall growth of approximately 200 jobs a year with an accelerating rate of growth in the late 1960s and in the decade of the 1970s. From 1970 to 1976 the number of jobs increased by 950 a year. The greatest growth occurred in the tertiary industries, where the annual rate of growth was 2.9% between 1960 and 1970 and 4.1% between 1970 and 1976.

Table 7.4   Employment in Various Industries in
            Stavanger 1976

Industries	Number Employed	%
PRIMARY	305	0.8
Oil and Gas Production	1,275	3.4
Food Production	1,982	5.3
Graphics, Printing & Publishing	1,479	4.0
Metals, Machine Tools & Instruments	3,617	9.8
Other Industries: textiles, wood products, chemicals, minerals, etc.	1,491	4.0
Construction, Power & Water, etc.	4,036	16.9
SECONDARY	13,880	37.4
Wholesale, retail hotels and restaurants	7,355	19.9
Transportation, Postal and Telecommunications	3,319	8.9
Banking, finance, insurance & clerical	2,185	5.9
Public services, etc.	10,051	27.1
TERTIARY	22,910	61.8
Total Employment	37,095	100

Source: Stavanger Generalplankontoret 1978, p. 54

The secondary industries declined during the
1960s but experienced an increase of 1.9% a year
from 1970-1976. This increase was largely attributable to the introduction and development of the oil
industries, where the number employed grew from 925
in 1973 to 8,706 by 1978. Of this number 4,008 were

employed on land and 4,698 on the sea. By 1984, Stavanger anticipates the total number of employees in the city will grow to 45,000 (Fossan 1978). Since the workers engaged on the sea are not registered as Stavanger employees, the 1,275 workers identified as oil production workers in Table 7.4 constitutes only a small part of the oil industries' employment impact. Furthermore, some of the oil-related activities are listed under other employment categories in the table. It is estimated that some 2,700 were employed in oil-related work in Stavanger in 1976. By 1984 it has increased to more than 10,000.

The impact of the oil industry on the economy and culture of Stavanger is becoming one of its most consuming concerns. That the industry has been a boon to its economy is self evident. The number of oil employees in all of Norway increased from 6,000 in 1973 to 37,500 by 1980. In Stavanger itself, the number grew from a mere 386 in 1973 to about 9,000 seven years later. In all of Rogaland County the number grew from 2,084 to 19,298. Some 40% of those employees in Rogaland County worked in the primary oil activities in oil companies and drilling operations. About 35% worked in such secondary oil activities as transit services, catering, oil base activities and maintenance. Most of the others were engaged in construction work related to the building of oil-drilling platforms and other structures and facilities (Fossan 1982, pp. 1-19).

As headquarter city for such major oil companies as Esso, Phillips, Mobil, Amoco and Gulf, together with the increasingly important Norwegian Statoil, Stavanger has taken on a dramatically renewed industrial vitality. They have provided vigorous stimuli to the growth and development of Stavanger's high technology and service industries both within and beyond the oil sector of its economy. In a sense, Stavanger has become Norway's major workshop of the North Sea, with more than 250 companies providing goods and services for the off-shore oil industry.

The high technology legacies of Stavanger's ship building industry have been adapted to the needs of the oil industry. The historic Rosenberg shipbuilding firm, for example, has become a major builder of complex condeep oil drilling platforms for the North Sea (Stavanger Information Department 1983). A recent publication of Norway Exports provides an impressive list of the diverse offshore-related companies and their widely varied technological products and services. They cover fields of engineering, construction, electronics, machinery and equipment, supplies and services as well as environmental programs for safety and anti-pollution (Gooderham 1980).

The expansion of Stavanger's tertiary industries deserve further comment. In the first place, it is noteworthy that by 1960, more than half of Stavanger's employees were engaged in them, and that the proportion increased steadily afterwards, reaching 61.8% by 1976. By far the greatest portion of the employment is contributed by the expanding public services in the fields of health, education, research, social concerns, and cultural programs. As of 1976, they accounted for 27.1% of Stavanger's employment. Next came the commercial services of the city's jobs. Transportation and communications are next in importance, followed by banking, finance, and insurance.

As in the other cities of Norway, these tertiary industries play an important part in making Stavanger a regional center of an increasingly knowledge-intensive society. Since close to 50% of the work force in the tertiary industries are women, their role in Stavanger's economy has greatly increased. These developments are in large measure attributable to Stavanger's role as the county seat of Rogaland as well as Southwest Norway's capital city. The County and the Norwegian State have become the biggest employers in the city. They count in their employ the staffs of such diverse public institutions as a regional college, a technical institute, a regional hospital and health center, a nursing school, psychiatric institutions, and central governmental offices for public administration and planning for both national and county programs.

Human Growth and Development of Stavanger

As Stavanger's labor market expanded after World War II, it became a magnet for an ever-increasing population. From a population of 67,121 in 1950 the city grew to 90,000 and the Stavanger City Region had become Norway's third largest with a population of more than 175,000 inhabitants. With such a growth, its population spilled over its municipal boundaries into neighboring towns in the Jæren region of Rogaland. Table 7.5 tells the story of the population growth of Stavanger and these other towns.

Table 7.5 Population Growth in the Stavanger Region
1950-1977

Municipality	1950		1960		1970		1977	%	Increase 1950-1977	%
Stavanger	67121	58.2	75798	55.8	83292	51.8	88200	49.6	21079	31.4
Sandnes	19511	16.9	25430	18.7	30705	19.1	35146	19.8	15635	80.1
Hå	7640	6.6	8564	6.3	10607	6.6	11967	6.7	4327	56.6
Klepp	4985	4.3	5981	4.4	8878	5.5	10391	5.8	5406	108.4
Time	5201	4.5	6212	4.6	8124	5.1	9424	5.3	4223	81.2
Gjesdal	3729	3.2	3878	2.9	4446	2.8	5133	2.9	1404	38.0
Sola	5030	4.4	7056	5.2	9898	6.2	11820	6.7	6790	135.0
Randaberg	2111	1.8	2872	2.2	4709	3.0	5770	3.2	3659	173.0
Stavanger Metro Region	115328	100	135791	100	160659	100	177851	100	62523	54.2

Source: Stavanger Generalplankontoret 1978, p. 34

While Stavanger itself showed a continuous growth during the decade following 1950, its proportion of the urban population of the entire metro-urban region steadily declined from 58.2% in 1950 to 49.6% in 1977. Sandnes, the largest other municipality in the region, grew from 19,511 to 35,146 during that same period. This represents an increase of 80.1% compared with Stavanger's increase

224

of 31.4%. All the other municipalities also experienced a higher rate of growth than Stavanger during this period.

Planning and Community Building in Stavanger

Stavanger's population growth and expanding socioeconomic functions precipitated many complex problems and challenges. Perhaps the overall challenge can best be stated as developing an adequate and appropriate urban container for an exploding city region. This general task included such major problems as (1) housing the growing population, (2) finding suitable sites for and developing the new work places needed, (3) protecting and securing the historic charm and vibrancy of the city's center, (4) nurturing the vitality of the sub-communities of the city, (5) finding an adequate metro-urban regional structure for the greater Stavanger area, and (6) developing a transportation system congruent with those goals. What was needed was the kind of comprehensive planning called for by Norway's Building Act of 1965.

An examination of Stavanger's comprehensive planning documents indicates that all these issues were addressed. A few comments about how each issue was attacked will indicate the directions of Stavanger's approach to fashioning its future urban container. Perhaps none of the problems was more pressing than developing housing for the growing population. It was determined that the city would need to build about a thousand housing units a year. The questions concerning where they should be located, who should build them, and what kinds of units should be built also became important policy issues.

As in other cities of Norway, all these questions were related to the assumption that housing and community building are inseparably linked to each other. The distribution of the housing developments reflect the City's decision to develop new housing in virtually every existing sub-community ("bydel") of the City, rather than relying on the strategy of assembling vast areas for building new satellite towns.

An exception to this might be the new community of Tjensvoll, designed as a satellite town similar to those developed in Oslo. Like them it included a large number of housing units around a compact village center with shops, offices, schools, health and social centers, and other typical small town amenities (Stavanger Kommune 1978, pp. 164-68). As the space for housing within the city became exhausted, Stavanger pursued inter-municipal planning and development with the other cities of the Jæren region.

The city itself has played an active role in site acquisitions and relied extensively on a quasi-official cooperative housing society--the "Stavanger Bolig-Byggelag" which is similar to that of OBOS in Oslo for the development and construction of the new housing. The decision concerning types of housing to be built reflects the tension between the acute need for housing on very limited area resources on the one hand and the traditional housing patterns of Stavanger's past. The single family housing structures characteristic of Stavanger's past has strong popular appeal. But the need for higher density housing is also compelling. The following distribution of the varieties of housing types became the official policy guide for resolving the tension:

Single family housing	20%
Low-rise high density housing	60%
High-rise--high density housing	20%

The distribution of housing types actually built from 1970-1976 was as follows:

Single family housing	32.4%
Low rise--high density housing	31.1%
High-rise--high density housing	36.5%

These and other data indicate a steady trend toward increasing high density, including a much greater use of high-rise structures (Stavanger Kommune 1978, pp. 32-33). Even in developments beyond Stavanger's city limits, the pressure for high density housing is great because of Norway's strong national policy constraint on the use of productive agricultural land for urban purposes.

The city government also plays an active role in site development and location for the new industries, businesses, and public institutions that are needed. Efforts are made to establish a balance between residential developments and the location of work places, both at the city center as well as in the sub-communities, in order to reduce vehicular traffic as well as to contribute to the vibrancy of life within both the city's center and its sub-communities.

Stavanger's special concern for preserving the historic charm of its city center has already been alluded to. One of its first responses to post-war expansion was to demolish the white-painted wooden houses and shops of the city's old-town in order to make room for the new. In 1956, however, the city council decided to conserve 35 houses. In 1967 this was extended to 79 houses and during the 1970s the number was increased to 180 houses.

These efforts toward preserving and revitalizing Stavanger's old town, were given a new boost in 1975 when it was selected as one of Norway's pilot projects in connection with the European Architectural Heritage Year. It was chosen because the preservation and cultivation of the old part of the town had become a central task for Stavanger and for Norwegian conservation work generally. It was also chosen because this part of Stavanger represents the panelled and white painted timber architecture typical of Norwegian coastal towns.

The final outcome of these conservation efforts has been to create a distinctive center city "Gamleby" which is to Stavanger what "Gamlestan" is to Stockholm, Sweden. It has become a tourist's delight and an urban treasure for the native Norwegian (Madsen and Holm 1975). It is symbolic of Stavanger's commitment to the preservation and nurture of an attractive and vital city center.

Toward a Regional Metropolis

Beyond the quest for an attractive and effective urban container for Stavanger's city center, it has become necessary for the City to participate in the planning and development of an inter-municipal metropolitan region. Stavanger was one of the first of Norway's cities to initiate such efforts. Its

227

first venture was the creation of an inter-municipal committee from the four municipalities of Stavanger, Sandnes, Randaberg and Sola to secure a suitable urban growth which would bring the forces of expansion under control and at the same time protect the important agricultural land from urbanization. After an analysis of the trends of urban expansion in the area the Committee proposed a linear form of urban development between Stavanger and Sandnes, taking advantage of the existing national railroad and highway connection between these two points (Eckhoff 1969, pp. 31-32).

An added impetus toward establishing a metropolitan region came with the enactment of the National Building Act of 1965, giving legal sanction and encouragement for such developments. A regional council of Jæren municipalities was established which fostered cooperative planning and joint action in such matters as water supply and drainage and developing industrial sites. Other joint efforts were launched to seek out non-tillable land sites for housing and urban development.

The Jæren urban region has taken on new significance in the light of the developing oil activities in the Stavanger area. It is no longer possible to contemplate Stavanger's development as Norway's oil capital without including the entire Jæren region. The impact of the oil activities on the region is already extensive. By the end of the 1970s, its population growth was three to four times that of the national average. But, as has already been noted, Jæren continues to occupy a strong position in Norway's agricultural program. Thus it becomes a locus for one of Norway's most acute conflicts between its policies of farm land conservation and its current efforts to accomodate the urban developments related to the expanding oil activities (Bekkeheien 1978, pp. 235-240. See also Stavanger Kommuneplan 1978, pp. 59-70).

In response to such tensions, Rogaland's chief administrator set in motion a strategy for regional planning and development of Jæren. A new Jæren Regional Council was created in 1977 for inter-municipal cooperative development of the region. Plans were initiated for joint planning and

228

development of (1) housing, (2) site locations for urban development which would not encroach on agricultural land, and (3) guidelines for urban expansion in areas identified as acceptable. The map of the Jæren Region in Figure 7C indicates the areas that are prioritized for agricultural uses and the eight rather small areas initially identified as suitable sites for urban development.

Should all these areas be developed, it would significantly alter Stavanger's urban form and present new challenges for planning and community building. Transit planning and development will become an essential part of such activities. Like other urban centers of Norway, Stavanger has launched a comprehensive transit planning system coordinated with Norway's national transportation planning system. It has developed a long-term tranportation plan designed to facilitate access to the city center while at the same time protecting it from untoward traffic congestion and pollution.

The plan involves among other things the building of a ring-road with separate lanes for bicycles and walking paths around the center city in order to preserve its auto-free pedestrian char- acter. Similarly, the traffic plan is designed to protect such other inner city serenities as Lake Breiavatnet, the city park, the fruit, fish and vegetable markets, and historic buildings. The plan also anticipates the building of a harbor road with separate lanes for bicycles and pedestrian trails. The main thoroughfares leading into the city shall include separate lanes for cyclists and pedestrians. The principal vehicles for Stavanger's public transit are buses, ferries, and some use of the national railroad. Efforts are being made to consolidate the bus system in order to increase its effectiveness in achieving the city's goal of making public transit its major transportation system (Nork Vegplan II: Stavanger Kommune 1975 pp. 6-24).

Even though this account of planning and community building in Stavanger is far from exhaustive, enough has been described to indicate that it has become one of Norway's very important regional urban centers where the nation's

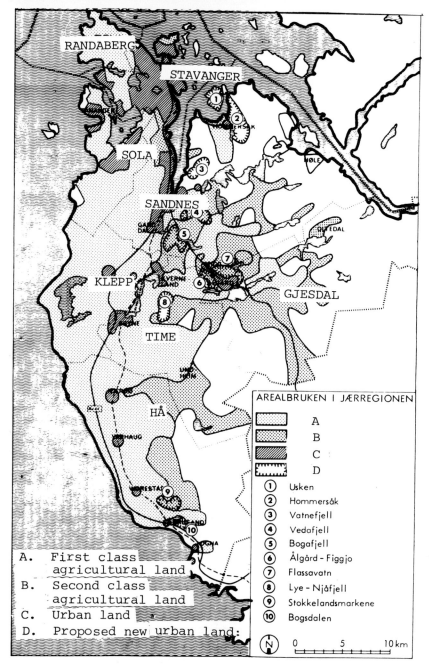

Figure 7C Stavanger City Region

The region extends far south into the area of agricultural Jæren region. The main planning problem is
the conflict between agricultural land and the need
for land for urban expansion. This has resulted in
a dotted location of many small built-up dwelling
areas.

environmental, urban and regional policies are being both implemented and tested.

V.   Kristiansand: Capital of Southern Norway

The predominant city along Norway's southern coast is Kristiansand. It is the largest city of the Vest-Agder County and serves as its capital. Its strategic location on an excellent harbor and fjord had contributed to its continued growth and development as this area's principal city region containing more than 60% of Vest-Agder's population. The three other smaller municipalities included in the Kristiansand urban region are Vennesla with a population in 1984 of 11,100, Sogne with 6,900 inhabitants, and Songdalen with 4,600 inhabitants.

Historical Backdrop

Kristiansand began as a renaissance "new town" established by King Christian IV of Denmark in 1641. The new town was to serve as a trading center for an extensive lumber industry that had been developing in southern Norway, as well as a naval base for Denmark's expanding merchant fleet. The king's plans for the town envisioned a city of 15-20,000 people. The streets were laid out along a grid pattern typical of so many European new town plans of that era. Within a few years of growth as a commercial center, the city became both a military garrison for the Danish Crown as well as a diocesan center for the established church of the kingdom.

Meanwhile, the city continued to develop along the plans initiated by Christian IV for 200 years or so. It has the distinction of being the only Norwegian city that bears the distinctive impression of a renaissance city. It continued to serve as an administrative center for the Danish Crown as well as a center for commerce and the handicraft industries for some 200 years. According to the census reports of 1801 its population of 4,816 were identified with the following occupational groupings (Dyrvik 1976, pp. 207-213):

Merchants	10.7%
Civil Servants	9.0%
Shippers	13.7%
Craftsmen	21.6%
Laborers	45.0%

It took another hundred years for the city to approximate the size King Christian IV had originally envisioned. By that time (1900) its population numbered 14,666. During this period several new industries were developed, notably in lumbering and shipbuilding. By 1855, it listed some forty mills and five shipbuilding establishments. By 1875 its merchant fleet had increased to 126 vessels with approximately 1,200 employees. These in turn expanded the commercial activities of the city which precipitated the building of railroads in the 1890s and new roads and bridges to accomodate the automobile in the second decade of the twentieth century (Byplankontoret i Kristiansand 1978, pp. 3-1 to 5-10).

By the end of the first world war, the bases had been laid for the emergence of Kristiansand as the leading urban center of Southern Norway. Its harbor had been expanded and modernized, hydroelectric power had become the new source for light and power, and its boundaries had been expanded to provide a more adequate container for its expanding urban functions.

By 1946, the Kristiansand urban region, including the neighboring municipalities of Vennesla, Songdalen, and Sogne had a population of 42,556 inhabitants. From 1950 to 1970 its population increased by about 2.5% a year. The growth continued after 1970 at a slower rate, but reached a population of 80,717 by 1976 (Rasmussen 1979, p. 408). By 1984 the population had increased to 85,000 (Statistical yearbook). The Kristiansand urban region's share of the total population of the county of Vest-Agder increased from 37% in 1900 to 61% in 1977. From 1970 to 1977 approximately 95% of the county population growth took place within the Kristiansand urban region (Vest-Agder Fylkes kommune 1979, pp. 41-42.

The impact of such growth upon the city's development can be perhaps best illustrated by the

fact that by 1970 about three-fourths of Kristiansand's population lived in homes built after World
War II. About 24% of the new houses were in moderate
high-rise apartment structures, 49% in low-rise,
high-density housing such as row or atrium-type
structures, and 27% in separate single family housing (Kristiansand Byplankontoret 1978, pp. 44-45).

The Changing Economy

As in the other city regions, the changing
occupational structure of Kristiansand helps explain
its growth. Table 7.6 provides a summary of these
changes.

Public functions of government and planning
of both Kristiansand and the Vest-Agder County have
also added considerably to Kristiansand's public
sector activities. All in all, Kristiansand is
taking on the socioeconomic and cultural characteristics similar to the other major urban centers of
Norway.

Planning and Community Building in Kristiansand

The rapid growth of the city and its surrounding region as well as the national legislative
mandate of the 1965 Planning Act precipitated
increased attention to planning and publicly-
directed community building in Kristiansand. Its
first "generalplan" was completed in the latter part
of the 1960s and approved by Norway's Ministry of
the Environment in 1973.

Its planning was based on the assumption that
Kristiansand's population would increase by approximately 1,200 each year during the decade of the
1970s. It called for the preparation of developmental areas for housing, economic activities, and
other services which would support such a growth.
Because of its strategic location in Norway's
southern coast, its favorable natural setting, and
the existing economic growth impulses, it assumed
that the city was destined to become one of Norway's
most rapidly developing cities. It assumed further
that its expansion should be guided by goals particularly congruent with its role as an officially

Table 7.6 Economically Active Population in the
          Kristiansand Region by Industry
          1950-1970, numbers and percent 1950-1970

	Number		Percent	
	1950	1970	1950	1970
Farming & Foresting	1,930	676	9.1	2.5
Fishing & Hunting	520	189	2.5	0.7
PRIMARY INDUSTRIES	2,450	865	11.6	3.2
Building & Construction	2,105	2,632	10.0	9.7
Iron & Metal Industries	2,874	4,602	13.6	16.9
Other Industries	4,177	4,436	19.8	16.3
SECONDARY INDUSTRIES	9,156	11,670	43.3	42.9
Office Work	2,579	4,433	12.2	16.3
Public Administration & Defense	1,008	1,922	4.8	7.0
Public & Private Service	1,717	2,353	8.1	4.2
Sea Transportation	1,407	1,708	6.7	6.3
Other Communications	1,434	1,581	6.6	5.8
Personal Services	1,257	1,168	5.9	4.3
TERTIARY SERVICES	9,402	14,688	44.5	53.9
Undeclared	120	30	0.6	0.1
Total Workforce	21,128	27,253	100	100

Source: Myklebost, Hallstein 1978. Bosetningsut-
         viklingen i Norge 1950 1975, p. 122

designated major regional center for Southern Norway, and as a county capital of Vest-Agder. (See Figure 7D).

But by the middle of the decade of the 1970s the assumptions about the city's growth needed modification. Both its natural population growth and its growth by immigration from other municipalities of Southern Norway declined. While during the 1960s people from the entire region of Southern Norway moved to Kristiansand, and more people moved from Kristiansand to Oslo than vice versa, this mobility pattern was reversed in the 1970s. For these and other reasons the city developed a revised "Generalplan for the Kristiansand City Region" for the decade of the 1980s. The new plan envisioned a more moderate growth.

The plan's attention to the problems and possibilities for the city's center is particularly noteworthy. It addresses the critical question regarding the future functions and character of that part of Kristiansand originally laid out by Christian IV's first plan for the city. It rejects the notion of a city center as merely a place for the buying and selling of goods and services. It insists that it is more than a commercial center; that its social and cultural functions are just as important. It emphasizes that the center should be a nurturing place for cultural growth, development and renewal; and that its physical development should mirror the city's culture and give symbolic expression of its historic past as well as its present day social realities (Plankontoret i Kristiansand 1978, p. 2-5).

Out of this general orientation the planning document outlines what must be done to transform Kristiansand's historic center with its more limited functions of the past to a dynamic city center which must also serve as a metro-urban center, a county seat, and a major regional center for Southern Norway. It suggests, among others, the following guidelines for determining the center's future:

> 1. The needs of the growing public and private services should be given high priority; including services to the residents in the center, the public

Figure 7D Air Photo of Kristiansand

Kristiansand is known as the city with the best
planning achievements in Norway. Already in the
1950s the municipality bought up new land for its
urban expansion. Since then sufficient building
land has been available, with the result that
sufficient dwellings have been built with the
results that prices have been kept low. The city's
conservation of the renaissance street pattern in
the center and its ability to regulate traffic and
keep a vital center with large areas reserved for
pedestrians only is noteworthy. Kristiansand is a
city with the charm of ocean, skerries, sunshine and
mild winds, that make the city and its region a
popular summer resort.

institutions related to municipal and
county governance, office structures for
financial institutions and professional
activities such as legal, medical,
architectural and counselling services.

2. Similar priority should be given to
   accomodate the space needs for such
   socio-cultural activities and institutions
   as cinemas, musical concerts, theaters,
   museums, churches, libraries, recreation
   centers, hotels, restaurants, etc.
3. A successive moving out of functions that
   are less appropriate for the center, such
   as warehouses, construction industries,
   transport offices, and auto-repair shops
   to neighboring community centers.
4. A vigorous housing program to arrest the
   decline of residents in the center.
5. A more systematic development of the
   city's harbor environment; eliminating
   activities not related to it and making
   room for a joint terminal for ships, rail
   and auto transport.
6. An expansion of the auto-free pedestrian
   area at the heart of the center, where
   specialty shops and craft activities can
   flourish.
7. Preservation of parks and open spaces.
8. Transportation planning favoring public
   transit and limiting automobile use in the
   center.
9. Conservation of historically significant
   buildings and neighborhood environments.

Enough has been said about the city's plans
for its center to indicate Kristiansand's perception
of its importance for the life and culture of the
city itself as well as of its surrounding regions.
Similarities with perceptions noted in the other
major cities are too obvious to need further
elaboration.

As was noted in the other major cities that
have been described, planning and community building
in Kristiansand reflect a strong commitment to the
importance of its sub-communities. The planning and
development for the city's future involves a compre-

hensive approach to development in each of its sub-communities; involving housing, economic development, schools, health and social services, churches, parks and playgrounds, and transporation planning. Being surrounded by extensive forests in its background and fronting on a pleasant southern seacoast harbor and fjord, its plans involve efforts at protecting them from untoward developments and preserving them for outdoor recreational activities as well as for their other productive and communications functions.

The Plan for Kristiansand's future includes an extensive chapter on churches, culture and recreational activities. It calls for new churches as new communities are developed. It discusses the possibilities of developing a regional theater in addition to continued support for the present Kristiansand theater and children's theater. It recommends continued support for Kristiansand's city orchestra, the cathedral church's "Motettkor" and "Schola Cantorum" and other musical groups. Possibilities of a new building for the city museum, and the development of additional branches to supplement its new library are discussed. Plans are suggested for neighborhood houses in every sub-community of 3,000 or more inhabitants to serve all age groups, together with a wide variety of recreational programs throughout the city.

That the planners of Kristiansand are deeply concerned about the city's esthetic milieu and structural form as well as its socioeconomic and technical development is made evident in the two chapters of the city's Comprehensive Plan entitled "Miljø" and "Byggeform." They urge a city center renewal that preserves the human scale of its historic past even while accomodating the socio-economic and cultural needs of the present (Plankontoret i Kristiansand 1978, pp. 10-1 to 11-4). It is clearly evident that there is no intention of developing a mere "economic city" for the 100,000 or so inhabitants of Kristiansand's twenty-first century.

VI.   Bergen: Capital City of "Vestland"

The largest regional urban center--next to
Oslo--is Bergen; which for centuries has been
Norway's "western window to the world." Because of
its naturally protected harbor and favorable
location for international trade, it early became
Norway's leading shipping and commercial center.
During its first two centuries--the twelfth and
thirteenth--it prospered as the political capital of
all of Norway, leaving important symbolic memories
of that medieval period.

The following two hundred years it was one of
the Hanseatic cities that controlled much of the
commerce of northern Europe. It was the mercantile
trade of those centuries that contributed much to
its wealth, reputation, and distinctive identity as
a major seaport and center for international trade
and commerce.

But it was also part of Bergen's destiny to
become the leading trading center for all the rest
of western Norway for centuries. Because of
Norway's mountainous topography, most of its west
coast commerce was carried on by seafaring transport. Thus until as late as 1909, when the Oslo-to-
Bergen railway surmounted the vast Hardanger mountain plateau making possible east-west travel,
Bergen combined its hegemony over Norway's international trade with its role as the nation's commercial capital of western Norway.

During the nineteenth century, Bergen's
economic activities were expanded by industrial
development. Census reports for the last half of
that century show a rapid growth of both industry
and handicrafts. By 1900 they employed approximately 40% of the City's workforce compared with
only 25% in 1850. These developments in turn gave
added impetus to Bergen's commercial activities so
that by the end of the nineteenth century, commerce
and industry had become the two dominant pillars of
Bergen's economic life (Helvig og Hageberg 1977, p.
13-20).

Although its hegemony as western Norway's
leading commercial center became increasingly
challenged by other coastal cities in the first half

of the twentieth century, it experienced a steady and healthy growth from a population of 83,638 in 1890 to 213,015 by 1960--a 155% growth. From 1910 to 1960 it experienced an average growth per decade of 12.7% (Rasmussen 1969, pp. 184-185).

Anyone even dimly aware of the City's history, will know that its economic prominence as a commercial and industrial center are far from the only explanation of its importance in this part of the world. During its long history of steady growth, it also became an important cultural, educational, and religious center of Norway and "Vestland." Its art galleries and museums, its national theater and symphony orchestra, its university and other institutions of higher learning, its churches and health institutions have all played an important part in making this one of Norway's most vibrant and stimulating cities.

If one adds to that its distinctive charm that derives from its blending of the old and new so characteristic of so many of Norway's cities it is easy to understand the Bergensians' fondness for their urban community. Figure 7E is an air photo of the city.

Bergen's Changing Status in Contemporary Norway

While Bergen continues to rival Oslo as one of Norway's major urban centers, it is important to take note of contemporary forces of change that are altering its role and status. When Norway developed its regional policies it quite naturally designated Bergen as the "landsdelsenter" for "Vestland" Norway. This region was comprised of the three counties of Hordaland, Sogn and Fjordane, and Møre and Romsdal--with a total population in 1975 of 718,695 inhabitants. Bergen also continued as the capital of Hordaland County. Thus Bergen has continued to play an important role as a political, cultural, and educational center of the nation as well as of the "Vestland" region.

But Norway's regional policies also gave impetus to a changing allocation of socioeconomic and cultural functions among the various urban communities of both "Vestland" and the entire

Figure 7E Air Photo of of Bergen's Central Parts

Bergen's charm derives from its location, between
the sea and its seven surrounding mountains, as well
as from its blending of old and new urban landscape
and its changing weather between sun and rain. The
urban expansion has partly taken place on islands
and on land on the "other" side of the mountains
that have been opened up for new housing because of
tunnels. Seawards communications to the nearest
hinterland is gradually complemented by roads,
bridges, tunnels and cars.

western coast of Norway. The national commitment to the strengthening and promotion of strategic urban centers in each of Norway's major regional parts has served to reduce Bergen's historic hegemony in western Norway. The developments in Tromsø in the north, Trondheim in middle Norway, Stavanger in the Southwest and Kristiandsand along the southern coast, that have already been described, have quite naturally weakened Bergen's historic position.

Furthermore, Norway's post-war policies of encouraging decentralized urbanization around the many smaller centers of the country have also weakened Bergen's competitive commercial and industrial position within the "Vestland" region itself. In the Møre and Romsdal County, for example, the rapidly growing city of Ålesund has become a leading competitor as a commercial center as well as an urban magnet for people in the area migrating to the city. Even in such matters as the circulation of its daily newspapers, Bergen's press is losing out to Ålesund's expanding daily press. Similarly Bergen is losing some of its commercial status to many other smaller centers in the region which under Norway's regional policies have taken on expanding functions as small-scale urban centers.

The building of new roads and bridges, together with the promotion of new economic and socio-cultural activities, both public and private, have played an important part in such changing allocation of functions among the various centers of the area (Helvig and Hageberg 1977, pp. 13-3 to 13-8). Table 7.7 presents some statistical evidence of Bergen's declining share of the region's economy.

It is clear that trade and industry, the two pillars of Bergen's historic economic hegemony, have shown the greatest decline. According to Professor Helvig of the University of Bergen this decline has continued into the decade of the 1970s.

An examination of Bergen's employment trends in the various occupations from 1955 to 1975 provides a helpful indication of its changing socioeconomic role in contemporary Norway. Table 7.8 provides the relevant data for such an analysis.

Table 7.7 Bergen's Changing Percentage Share of
"Vestlandets" Employment in Various
Occupations from 1960 to 1970

	Percent of Vestlandet Employment	
Industries	1960	1970
Farming, Fishing & Forestry	2.0	1.8
Manufacturing Industries	27.1	23.5
Building, Construction & Waterworks	23.9	22.0
Trade, Finance, etc.	44.0	37.6
Sea Transport	38.7	27.0
Other Communications	28.2	29.1
Public & Private Service	36.4	35.0
Personal Services	32.2	26.3

Source: Helvig and Hageberg 1977, p. 13-9.

The data indicate that in spite of Bergen's declining economic and socio-cultural hegemony in western Norway, its overall employment has grown steadily during the post-war years. Even in the industrial sector there was steady if modest growth up to 1970, when it began to decline.

According to Bergen's most recent comprehensive plan this decline in industrial employment continued throughout the decade of the 1970s. The major decline occurred in the textile-leather goods and ready-wear industries, which experienced a reduction of 3,300 workers. This decline was due to the closing of many establishments plus the reduction of workers in others due to the restructuring and rationalizing of the industry.

Even though the number employed in Bergen's primary industries is very small and steadily declining, they still play an important role in Bergen's life and economy. Its agriculture supplies about 20% of Bergen's dairy products consumption and 7% of its meat. While Bergen's forestry employs few

Table 7.8   Changing Employment Trends in Various
Occupations in Bergen 1955-1975

Occupations	Number Employed			Percent		
	1955	1970	1975	1955	1970	1975
Primary Industries	1,269	804	650	1.7	0.9	0.7
Secondary Industries	30,657	33,072	31,400	42.7	48.6	35.1
Tertiary Industries	39,925	51,983	57,450	55.6	60.5	64.2
Total Employment	71,851	75,859	89,500	100	100	100

Source: Helvig and Hageberg 1977, p. 13-9.

workers, its related wood products industry and
marketing as well as related vocational training and
research are important parts of Bergen's life. So
far as fishing is concerned, Bergen continues to be
an important center for the production and marketing
of fish products (Kommuneplan For Bergen 1982-1989
pp. 108-111).

The chief explanation of Bergen's continued
economic growth, however, is attributable to the
rapid expansion of its service industries, where the
number employed grew from 39,925 in 1955 to 57,450
by 1975. By 1975 more than 64% of Bergen's workers
were engaged in those industries.

As in the other cities of Norway, the largest
number were engaged in public and private services
related to the growing importance of public sector
employment, and private service work in Bergen's
post-industrial economy. The number employed in
this employment sector increased from 11,959 in 1955
to 25,200 by 1975--an increase of approximately
111%. By 1980 it is estimated the number employed

244

in this sector will increase to some 27,000 workers. The other sector of most significant growth is in the private fields of tourism, sales, banking, finance, and insurance.

It seems apparent that for Bergen's future the continued nurture of these two sectors of the tertiary industries will be crucial. Bergen's latest comprehensive plan projects a substantial increase in public sector employment for the decade of the 1980s, and a relatively stable employment in the private service fields of sales, banking and insurance (Kommuneplan For Bergen 1982-1989 pp. 113-118). The same document anticipates that the secondary industries will continue to maintain their relatively weak position in the coming decades.

There is, however, one encouraging development that shows promise of helping Bergen maintain its position as an industrial center-namely the developing oil activities in its area. Its geographic proximity to some of the most promising oil and gas fields directly west of Bergen makes Bergen a natural location for oil company central offices, for related research and development activities and for the supportive commercial, financial, and transportation services accompanying such developments. In 1976, Bergen's city council committed itself to promote its possibilities in this industry and in 1981, the government of Norway approved new guidelines for the oil development designating Bergen as a second oil center of the country.

Already, such leading petroleum companies as Norway Statoil, Norsk Hydro, Gulf and Getty Oil, along with several oil-related firms have established operations offices in Bergen. New research centers and special technical training schools have emerged. Supply ships and tug boats are replacing the traditional steamships in Bergen's historic harbor. New hotels and restaurants are opening to accomodate the new activities. Of special interest for all its architectural efforts to reconcile the old and the new is the recently opened SAS Royal Hotel on Bergen's historic wharf (The Norseman No. 2, 1983, pp. 56-57). By 1981 some 67 establishments with 3,163 workers in oil activities had been brought to the city. It is estimated that the numbers will increase substantially in the decade of the 1980s.

Planning and Community Building in Bergen

As in the other cities we've examined in this chapter, Bergen's growth brought in its wake new challenges for the city's planning and community building activities. Perhaps the most pervasive challenge was how to develop a new and adequate urban container for the city's increased population and expanded functions. The historic boundaries of Bergen became too limited, making necessary their expansion. In 1972 Norway's parliament expanded its boundaries to include the surrounding municipalities of Åsane to the north, Arna to the east, Fana to the south, and Laksevåg to the west. These municipalities at that time contained the following populations:

Fana	45,081
Laksevåg	26,135
Åsane	20,448
Arna	11,955

While the new area for the city would normally provide more than adequate space for Bergen's transition to an enlarged metropolis, such a transition involves overcoming some striking difficulties. In the first place historic Bergen is encircled on its landward side by a series of seven mountain ranges which separate it from most of its new subcommunities. Furthermore, the areas amenable for urban development are widely scattered in relatively narrow stretches. Such conditions inevitably complicate and increase the cost of developing the adequate community structures as well as the needed technical infrastructure for Bergen's expanded metropolis.

The planning and community-building structures and processes for responding to these challenges were essentially similar to those of the other cities already described. Operating under Norway's national planning legislation, the City Council was the dominant force in guiding the developments. Its comprehensive plans prepared the groundwork for decision-making relative to the distribution and areal location of the various urban functions throughout the enlarged city.

Perhaps the most significant change that has accompanied Bergen's expansion has been the outward movement of its population from Bergen's inner city core to its periphery and to the surrounding communities joined with it in 1972 and other communities further out such as Os and Askøy. As Table 7.9 indicates, this outward movement had begun decades before the post-war period.

Table 7.9   Changing Areal Distribution of the Population in the Bergen Urban Region 1910-1975

Year	Population	Percent in		
		Center City Core	Rest of Bergen	Surrounding Communities
1910	102,000	63	19	18
1939	153,000	35	35	30
1950	177,000	29	35	36
1960	204,000	20	36	44
1970	232,000	13	29	58
1975	238,000	11	25	64

Source: Helvig and Hageberg 1977, p. 5-1.

The phenomenal decline of the inner city core from 63% of Bergen's population in 1910 to 11% in 1975 provides an impressive index of Bergen's transformation. In 1910, some 65,000 people lived within walking distance from the city center. By 1975 this number had been reduced to appoximately 26,000. After 1960 even the peripheral areas of Bergen began to yield its prominence as a residential area to the surrounding communities.

This changing areal distribution of the population was of course related to the rapid growth of the automobile culture and to expansion of economic and social institutions in the city center. But it was also related to housing rehabilitation and urban renewal in the inner city that reduced the historic high density of the central Bergen, as well as to planned housing developments in new satellite towns and in the surrounding communities that became part of Bergen in 1972.

These changes left a legacy of familiar vexing problems. In the first place, it led to an imbalance between workplaces and places of residence. As indicated in Table 7.10, this imbalance has increased steadily since 1950.

Table 7.10 Relationship between Residence and Workplaces - 1950-1980 in Bergen City Center

			% of Total in Bergen Region		
Year	Residences	Workplaces	Residences	Workplaces	Job Ratio
1950	23,500	37,000	33.0	52.0	157
1960	18,800	39,500	22.6	49.4	210
1970	13,600	42,000	14.3	46.0	309
1975	10,600	43,000	11.0	46.0	406
1980	9,000	44,000	?	?	489

Source "Sentrumsproblemer i Stagnerende Norske Storbyer--Samtale Med Professor Magne Helvig." Bedriftsøkonomen nr. 4, 1979, p. 183

While the number and percentage of residences in Bergen's center have sharply declined, the number of workplaces has continued to increase. The fact that the percentage of all of Bergen's workplaces is gradually declining reflects a trend of increased location of workplaces in the surrounding communities of Bergen--a trend which is being positively promoted by the city.

Another vexing problem associated with the outward population movement is its resulting demographic imbalance, with a concentration of the elderly, the single, and young adults in the center of the city and out migration of young families to the surrounding areas. Bergen's Comprehensive Plan for 1982-1989 indicates that a whole series of efforts are at work to address these and other problems related to developing an adequate urban container for its expanded city.

These efforts involve improved housing opportunities in the inner city and planned housing and community-building in outer areas; relocation of economic activities not needed for its center city to appropriate sites closer to outer residential communities; industrial and harbor plans for directing the heavy traffic between harbor and industrial areas outside the city center; improved public transit for reducing auto use to and from work; cooperative planning with county and national authorities in developing a highway network which reduces thru-city auto traffic; and improvements and new developments in the city's technical infrastructure.

The Plan also reflects the City's concern for continued nurture of Bergen as leading Norwegian center for higher education and research; a regional center for the fine arts and health care and such other activities as play an important role in making Bergen one of Norway's most dynamic post-industrial cities (Kommuneplan For Bergen 1982-1989).

But in implementing such extensive and complex goals, Bergen, like the other major cities of Norway, is becoming increasingly aware of its need for increased financial support and cooperation from both the county and national authorities. In many ways, Bergen's problems are much like those of Oslo and to some extent Trondheim in that while the national government does not wish their demise, its urban and regional policies have concentrated primarily on support for the smaller urban and community centers, assuming that the local resources of the larger centers are more adequate for dealing with the special problems of the larger cities.

In recent years, there has been growing national recognition that some of these problems need national attention and concern. In 1972, the government published a study of living conditions in the large cities--focusing especially upon Oslo,

Bergen and Trondheim. Much attention was given to Bergen in that study, illustrating the persistent problems of social inequality between the various sectors of the city, the special problems of both the inner city and its surrounding communities. The study emphasized that the big city problems must be seen as both national and local concerns (Norges Offentlige Utredninger 1978:52).

This study was complemented by another government publication in 1979 assessing the pressing structural and economic problems of Oslo, Bergen and Trondheim, and their implications for possible new urban policies. This study, too, emphasized the importance of the large cities for Norway's well-being: their importance as industrial and commercial centers in the modern economy; as "landelsenters" for Norway's major regional areas; as centers for higher education and research as well as the nurture of the arts and the humanities. It also accented their special problems and concluded with a chapter on developing a national urban policy for Norway's large cities (Norges Offentlige Utredninger 1979:5).

These government supported studies of the special problems of Norway's major cities have precipitated increased concern and debate about the country's national urban policies. A recent publication entitled Bypolitikk i Norge recapitulates many of the issues dealt with in the earlier studies and builds upon them a wide-ranging critical re-examination of Norway's large city policies. One of its authors goes so far as to argue that Norway has not really developed any large city policies at all; that its main concern has been to preserve the nation's traditional settlement patterns, leaving the fate of the cities in the hands of their munici-pal authorities and their socioeconomic resources. He faults populism for contributing to the national government's neglect of the large cities, arguing that its orientation provides a poor foundation for urban politics (Baldersheim (ed.) 1983, pp. 22-36). He argues for a much more aggressive and creative national policy which explicity affirms the national importance of the larger cities, and acknowledges their dependence upon national resources for performing their role adequately. He applauds recent government decisions to increase the funding of the National Housing Bank in order to increase its urban renewal loans, and to provide national financial support for the development and operation of metro-urban transit systems.

Other writers in this publication are critical of Norway's progress in developing adequate metrourban regional structures for the comprehensive planning and development of the larger urban areas and describe the political roadblocks preventing such progress. They point up the persistent conflicts troubling large cities, such as the national interests and concerns versus the needs and interests of the cities, the conflict between the larger urban municipalities and their suburban communities, and the tensions between sector planning preoccupations and the more holistic orientation.

From these and other studies it has become apparent that the fate and future of such urban centers as have been described in this chapter will play an increasingly important role in the future shaping of Norway's urban and regional policies.

REFERENCES

Anker, Erik et al. (eds.). 1972. Planlegging i Byer og Tettsteder. Oslo: Norsk Forening For Bolig-og Byplanlegging.

Baldersheim, Harold. (ed.) 1983. Bypolitikk i Norge. Oslo: Gyldendal Norsk Forlag.

Bedriftsokonomen. Nr. 4, 1979.

Bekkeheien, Jan. 1978. "Jærregionen-jordvern og interkommunalt samarbeid om utbygging." Plan og Arbeid No. 5 pp. 235-240.

Byplankontoret i Kristiansand 1978. Forslag Til Sentrumsplan For Kristiansand.

Dyrvik, Ståle. 1976. Den Lange Fredstiden 1729-1782. Volume 8 of Knut Mykland, Norges Historie. Oslo: J. W. Cappelans Forlag.

Eckhoff, Jan Chr. 1969. Byplan: Norske Samfunn i vekst--Mot Hva? Oslo: Pax Forlag.

Fasting, Lars. 1978. Trondheims Bybilde: Instilling Om Verneverdige Bygninger og Bygnings Miljøer i Trondheims Sentrale Områder. Trondheim Kommune.

Fossan, Bjørn. 1978. "Endringer i Arbeidsmarkedet i 70 - Årenes Stavanger, "Plan og Arbeid" Nr. 5, pp. 220-225.

Fossan, Bjørn. 1982. Offshore Activities--Impacts on the Stavanger Region. Stavanger: Department of Strategic Planning.

Gooderham, Rolf. (ed.) 1980. "Offshore Products and Services," Norway Exports. Oslo: The Export Council of Norway.

Helvig, Magne and Michael Hageberg. 1977. Søkelys Pa Bergen Sentrum. Bergen: Geografisk Institutt, Norges Handendelshøgskole og Universitetet i Bergen.

Johnsen, Yngvar. 1970. Plannlegging: Hvordan Planlegger vi Arealbruk og Utbygging. Oslo: Kommunal og Arbeidsdepartementet.

Kommuneplan For Bergen 1982–1989.

Kristiansand Byplankonteret. 1978. 1979–90 Generalplan for Kristiansand.

Madsen, Stephan Tschudi and Yngvar Holm. 1975. 3 Places in Norway. Oslo: Farverådet.

Myklebost, Hallstein. 1978. Bosetningsutviklingen i Norge 1950–1975. Bergen: Universitets-forlaget.

Norges Offenlige Utredninger. 1978: 52. Levekår i Storby. Oslo: Universitetsforlaget.

Norges Offentlige Utredninger. 1979: 5. Bypolitikk: Struktur og Økonomi for de Store Byene. Oslo: Universitetsforlaget.

Norsk Vegplan II: Stavanger Kommune 1975.

Plankontoret i Kristiansand. 1978. Forslag til Sentrumsplan For Kristiansand.

Rasmussen, T. Fr. 1979. "The Distribution of Population in Norway, Regional Changes and Regional Policies" in Antoni Kuklinski et al., Regional Dynamics and Socioeconomic Change. Tampere: Finnpublishers.

Rasmussen, Tor. Fr. 1969. Byregioner i Norge. Oslo: Norsk Institutt For By og Regionforskning.

Stavanger Genenalplankontoret. 1978. Sysselsettings-og Næringsanalyse av Stavanger.

253

Stavanger Information Department. 1983. Stavanger: Quay to the North Sea.

Stavanger Kommune. 1978. Utbyggingsplan 1978-1981: Boligutbygging.

The Norseman. No. 2, 1983. Oslo: Nordmanns- forbundet.

Tromsø Kommune Byplankontoret. 1976. Tromsø Generalplan 1975.

Tromsø Kommune Byplankontoret. 1978. Nr. 2. Generalplan 1979: Næringsliv og sysselsetting.

Tromsø Kommune Byplankontoret. 1978. Generalplan 1979: Utbyggingsmønster.

Trondheim Kommune. 1976. Kommuneplan 1979.

Vest-Agder Fylkeskommune. 1979. Utkast til Fylkes- plan 1979. Kristiansand.

CHAPTER EIGHT: CONTEMPORARY NORWAY: ITS ECONOMY AND POLITICS

I.   Introduction

Concerning the years immediately following the first world war 1914-1918, the contemporary historian Chr. A. R. Christensen wrote the following in 1961:

> A four-year nightmare was over. The mass murder and enormous material destruction had come to an end, and the world could catch its breath after one of history's greatest catastrophes. But that did not mean a return to what is commonly called "normalcy," that conditions would remain as they had been before. Everything had changed. It was as though a world-enveloping earthquake had shaken its very foundations politically, socially, economically, and morally. The old order had collapsed and could not be put together again. Those that thought they could turn back to the past and calm down in it, soon discovered that what was required was an adaptation to new and constantly changing circumstances. And so it has been ever since. New elements had entered into history, a new unrest, new problems, and new forces. Where these new elements would lead, no one knew. (End of quotation as translated)

II.   Between the Wars: Conflicts, Growth, and Values

In many ways, the period between the two great wars was a difficult time for Norway's social development. Crisis followed crisis. Some crises had their roots in the unstable world conditions beyond Norway's borders. Others were created by powerful domestic conflicts. Unemployment was high and labor strikes were many and long drawn out. Farmers were hit hard by the crisis in the money

255

market, and many farms were forced into bankruptcy. Tensions between the industrial workers and the bourgeoisie were great.

Nevertheless, this period between the wars was also a time of socioeconomic growth and rapid industrialization. Emigration to the USA had stopped. Cities grew, and in spite of high unemployment, the number of jobs increased. There was also a steady growth in the gross national product.

The period was also characterized by dynamic political conflicts set in motion by the struggles of the labor movement and the organization of the industrial workers. The Labor Party became the dominant political party, with 31% of the popular vote in 1930 and 40% in 1933. During this period, this party abandoned its revolutionary posture in favor of a more conventional parliamentary politics. In 1935 it formed an alliance with the Farmer Party and succeeded in attaining a parliamentary governing majority committed to solving the problems of both the unemployed worker and the debt-ridden small farmer. This new farmer-labor thrust contributed to the Party's getting 43% of the popular vote in the parliamentary election of 1936. The "whole nation at work" became the dominant slogan of that campaign, and the working foundation of the Norwegian government the last year prior to the outbreak of World War II.

Strong cultural and religious conflicts between liberal, conservative, and fundamentalist perspectives also became increasingly strident during the period between the two wars. Controversies and tensions over religious issues have long traditions in Norway. Debates concerning theological dogmas and doctrines as well as about the role of the church, the clergy, and the laity in the religious life of the country were pursued with great passion. Even today, strong controversies arise periodically over fundamental philosophies of life.

Language-policy conflicts between "landsmål" and "riksmål" and within the two language-policy camps have also often been raised to the point of fanaticism and irreconcilable intolerance. The same can be said concerning questions regarding secular humanism and sexual morality. The areas of community life which preoccupied wider circles of Norway's population than most other societal concerns were questions relating to religious orthodoxy, alcohol consumption, sexual morality, and language policy. They dominated the cultural debates of the 1920s and the 1930s. Even during the period following 1945, these questions have provided a latent undercurrent for the more recent cultural and political debates. There are few Norsemen that are not willing to participate in debates over value questions, both national and international. Such debates often evoke strong feelings and passions.

The dark clouds in the European heavens during the period between the two wars also cast their shadows over the political life of Norway. The stock market crash of 1929 made a deep impression in the early 1930s. Hitler's expansionist adventures in Germany contributed to nationalistic sentiments with fascistic overtones also in Norway. New political parties emerged and conflicts between the politics of the right and the left were sharpened. Calls for peace and order emerged in the hopes of stemming the well-organized forward march from the political left.

Fear of the consequences of Hitler's policies was great within the political left, which included both bourgeois liberals and social democrats. Little Norway, however, could only be a passive spectator of the awesome events taking place in Europe. There were, however, sentiments in favor of strengthening the country's defenses in all of Norway's political parties but from differing points of view between the parties of the left and the right. That Norway's defenses were not strengthened significantly was largely due to political disagreement as to how the accompanying increased tax burdens should be divided.

III. Regions and Homogeneity

But historic forces of regional and national homogeneity were also at work during this period. Because of its distinctive natural topography, Norway has always been a greatly cut-up country.

257

The sea has been its most important communications artery. Its mountainous terrain has made difficult the building of good roads, and travel time between its major regions have been long. This has also been true within the municipalities and counties where the network of roads had been poorly developed before World War II. These conditions have given the Norsemen a strong sense of regional identity.

Even though there have been great population movements within the country between the two wars and since, there are few Norsemen who are not absorbed in their personal or ancestral regional identity. This is often combined with a romantic attitude toward life in the rural community as a farmer and woodsman or as a fisherman/farmer with attachment to the sea and a small plot of land. The rural past is not far removed from most Norwegians. This often finds expression in a positive attitude toward outdoor life in both summer and winter and on both land and sea.

In spite of this regional consciousness and identity, and in spite of the passionate controversies over cultural values, Norway remains an unusually homogeneous nation. In political and economic matters, there has always been a strong demand for equality and justice. As the nation's railroads, motorways, and airports were built, and the ubiquitous automobile became everyman's possession, the demands for equal regional transportation services grew steadily. Similar pressures for regional equality in the fields of public education also arose. It has always been demanded that teachers should have the same qualifications and the same salaries no matter where in the country they work. Gradually the educational offerings to children have become the same in all regions of the country.

Since 1969, all Norwegian children up to the age of fifteen have nine years of required education. For higher education and university training, public stipends and loans are available for everyone. Children from people with higher education, however, are more inclined than others to pursue advanced studies.

Radio and TV, too, have contributed greatly

to equalization and to the nurture of a homogeneous culture throughout the country. There is only one channel for its TV programs, such that all Norsemen have precisely the same offering. This contributes to both an internationalization and homogenization of the population.

IV. Common Program in 1945: Consensus and Harmony

World War II gave Norway and its political and cultural leaders many new experiences. The German attack on Norway on April 9, 1940 came as a great shock for most Norwegians. Such a misuse of power was alien to most Norsemen. The German occupation from 1940 to 1945 welded people together for a united front against the enemy. To be sure, the nation suffered a military defeat and all conventional political activity was forbidden. But the pre-occupation political leaders, as well as people from all other groups of Norway's society participated in a resistance movement that involved cooperation.

The extent of the illegal activities carried out during the war has perhaps been exaggerated. When the war was over, all seemed eager to call attention to what patriots they were and what important contributions they had made in the resistance movement. What is certain, however, is that all groups of the population had taken part in the resistance work. Prominent persons from all groups of society worked together, whether they had participated in politics before or not. Persons from both the right and the left landed in German concentration camps where they learned to know each other as persons. They learned that their political and human differences were smaller than they had thought before. They found that they could agree on the most important questions concerning the kind of society they wanted when the war was over. After the war, new persons entered into politics, making constructive contributions toward the shaping of the nation's postwar order.

The new coalition government (seven bourgeois, six social democrats, and two communists)

259

that was named shortly after the conclusion of the
peace, with Einar Gerhardsen (Labor Party) as prime
minister, had no other program declaration other
than a mutually agreed upon joint program called
"Fellesprogrammet." The contents of this Program
had been prepared through political negotiations
during the last year of the war, and put into a
final document after the liberation by leading
persons who had confidence in the emerging political
leadership. All political parties concurred in the
Program; although the Communist party did so with
minor reservations.

When the call for a new Parliamentary election was set for October 8, 1945, all parties had
developed their own platforms. But even if they
differed from each other in particulars, they were
all animated by the spirit of the Joint Program.
That spirit continued to influence the political
activities of Norway far into the 1960s, and perhaps
up to 1970. Although there had been strong disagreements on many issues along the way, it can
nevertheless be said that even in the 1980s the main
outlines of that Program provided the essential
features of Norway's emerging policies.

The "Joint Program" became the cornerstone of
Norway's emerging welfare state structure. In the
course of nearly forty years, that structure has
been increased greatly, and even now is not finished. That which is being debated in the 1980s is
neither the cornerstone nor the basic dimensions of
that welfare state structure. Rather, the main
concerns are whether or not the country can afford
to pursue policies which increase the welfare system, or if some parts of the programs should be
reduced in order to improve other parts of it. The
nature of the welfare policy issues have, however,
tended to change during the past forty years.

It can, of course, be debated whether or not
the source of the social developments of the last
30-40 years should be primarily attributed to the
contents of "Fellesprogrammet." Historians are
pondering what other factors have been at work.
They note that already in the 1930s there were signs
pointing to the direction of the welfare state. It
has also been rightly noted that the present welfare

state has in many areas gone beyond that anticipated in the Joint Program of 1945. This discussion, however, is not of major importance for this treatise.

What **is** of great importance is that "Fellesprogrammet" established the goal of a holistic view of society as a guideline for practical politics. It was a statement of concensus concerning the most important questions which contributed to a harmonious social development. Hence for an understanding of modern Norwegian society, one might well begin with some chosen excerpts of "Fellesprogrammet" of 1945 under the subtitle of "The Joint Program of the Political Parties for Reconstruction:

I. The Program

The day our country and our freedom, our historic socio-political order and our entire cultural foundations were in deadly peril, we experienced that we were one people in spite of our differing views of life and social conditions, and in spite of old struggles. We wish to preserve this experience as a living impulse for our people's life and work in Norway's future.

In the shadows of prisons, concentration camps, and places of execution a sense of comradeship was created which we had never known before, an ability to withstand and cooperate which we did not know we possessed, so that at last we could experience victory with our honor and our self respect intact.

In the light of the tasks lying before us, we will call upon the same willingness to sacrifice, the same comradeship, and the same capacity to withstand and hold together.

To transform the defeat of dictatorship and brutality to a triumph of democracy and cooperation shall be our thanks to those who gave their lives in the struggle. Together we won the war--together we will win the peace.

Out of this vision we exhort our people to rally around the following principles:

Norway shall be governed according to its democratic principles as set forth in the Eidsvoll Constitution and democracy's developments up to 1940. No form of dictatorship can be tolerated.

The personal and political rights that the Constitution guarantees all citizens of our country, must remain inviolable, and Norwegians must once again be able to live securely under the protection of the law after having suffered the violence, terror, and denial of legal rights during the occupation. Everyone shall be free to express his opinions and champion them, and no one shall with either violence or threat of violence exert pressures over the opinions of others.

All who are able to work shall have the right and obligation to employment. Our regained freedom and independence shall be defended and protected.

For the immediate transition period, we present the following guidelines:

1)-----------------------
2)-----------------------
3)-----------------------
4) Carrying out the necessary initiatives for securing the nation's basic resources, and rebuilding the destroyed districts and our damaged production facilities. No unemployment must be tolerated. All public and private enterprise shall be put to work in the restoration of our economy. Extraordinary attempts will be made to restore the technical training that was neglected during the war and develop an adequate skilled labor force. Currency

regulation and price control, rationing and control over the distribution of raw materials, will continue until the new Parliament can draw up guidelines for these matters. The former welfare benefits will be maintained.

5)------------------------

6)------------------------

II. Economic Policy

1. The essential tasks for our economy and all economic activities in the country are to provide jobs for everyone and increased production in such a way as to create a just and fair distribution of the results and provide good living conditions for everyone.

In order that our society might carry out an effective and deliberate economic policy with such purposes in mind and fully take advantage of all private and public energy, initiatives and enterprise in a trusting and planned cooperation between the state and the private interests, there will be organized a central administration equipped with the necessary structures for carrying out such tasks.

Our financial policies must seek to create stability, confidence, and stimulate the economy and must be organized in concert with social needs.

Prices, finances and credit systems must be regulated in accordance with guidelines which shall be established for our country's economic policies and which will be consistent with the objectives of this Program.

Scientific research in the fields of production must be further developed and efficiently organized with a central institute for applying the research findings in the service of production. More effective economic statistics will be gathered.

Employment services will be further developed so as to better pursue the goal of full employment. Where necessary, programs for transfer and re-training of surplus labor for new production will be developed.

All wage-labor conditions will be regulated by negotiations between employer and employee organizations and their functionaries in such a way that all conflicts will be resolved without strike, lockout, or boycott.

2. Tax policies shall accomplish a just division of the burdens among the various income and owner groups with special emphasis upon lightening the tax burdens of families with children.

----

3. Our farm policies must give agriculture an equal status with the other industries and aim at evening out the living conditions in the country. The farm must be secured as the family's possession and the foundation of the farmer's work. Increased efforts must be made to bring new land into cultivation and keep our tillable land in good condition.

The forests must be restored, first and foremost along the coast and in the north where they were badly treated during the occupation. Efficient cultivation, the development of practical methods of production and types of equipment must be encouraged as well as effective utilization of all forest products. Better relationship between forestry and pasturing must be promoted.

4. Our fishing ports must be further developed, and planned work toward a rapid renewal of the fishermen's equipment and our fishing fleet done in such a way that they will continue to be owned by the fishermen. The production potentials of Norwegian workshops and factories must be fully utilized in these efforts.

----

5. Industrial constuction must aim at the development of activities that are naturally suited for our country. Above all, there must be a significant increase of large ship-building factories that can build and repair the major part of our merchant fleet. The iron and steel problem must be solved. Our natural raw products, i.e., wood, ore, fish, fruit, etc., must be put to the highest possible use by our own industrial plants.

Our hydro-electric power system must be developed to meet both the needs of industry and the general public, coordinating the electrical power stations in such a way that the whole country can as quickly as possible receive electric power, and the railroads be electrified.

A national plan must be developed for cooperation among our various means of communication: boats, automobiles, trains, and airplanes, to meet the transportation needs of our industries and the tourist traffic. The road system must be developed to deal with the increased auto traffic and to meet the needs of inaccessible rural communities.

III. Social Policies

1. Social legislation must be developed which will make the archaic poor-relief system superfluous. The social insurance systems must work together so as to create an insurance arrangement covering the hazards of sickness, disability, unemployment, and old age. The question of children's protection must be taken up for new consideration.

Housing, which has been catastrophically neglected during the war, must play a prominent role in the post-war reconstruction. The war-ravaged regions must be given the first attention, and plans must be worked out for securing attractive and suitable developments which will provide sound and adequate housing for everyone.

A deliberate temperance work must be pursued for the proteciton of the youth and the promotion of greater popular temperance.

IV. Church and Culture Policies

1. The Norwegian Church shall continue as the state church and within that framework be provided the appropriate structures for carrying out its work.

2. The entire school system must be coordinated so that all levels of education, from the elementary to the most advanced, will proceed naturally into each other, whether in vocational training or in the more academic fields of learning. There shall be established an advisory organizational structure for the entire school system which shall be administered from a single ministry of education. Everyone, without considera-

tion of economic condition or place of residence, must be given opportunity for an orderly education adapted to one's talents and abilities. The small and poor neighborhood schools must be given special help to raise their standards to acceptable levels.

To educate citizens for a free and democratic society must be a leading principle for the work of the schools. The schools must therefore be character-forming, evoke in children and young people feelings of responsibility, respect for others, human worth, tolerance, and the capacity for cooperation. They must orient them to the building up of the community in which they will live as citizens and make them familiar with our national culture, our history, and our traditions.

----

5. Our scientfic, scholarly, and other cultural institutions must be provided the conditions that correspond to their high value for the cultural level of the entire nation and must be given the widest possible autonomy. No economic or political or other types of pressures must be exerted. Students at the university and other institutions of higher learning must be provided reasonable living conditions; and scholars and students must be provided stipends for keeping them in touch with the life and culture of other lands. (End of excerpts from "Fellesprogrammet" as translated.)

When one in 1984 looks back upon the developments after World War II, one can say that with regard to all its essential points, this "Joint Program" has been fully carried out in the course of the last forty years. In the political consciousness of the country, the Program has been put on an almost equal footing with the Constitution. One notes, for example, that in three places of the Joint Program document, it is asserted that unemployment will not be tolerated or that full employment shall be required. In 1954, this was incorporated as a new paragraph in Norway's constitution.

Some parts of the Program had already been accomplished by 1945, such as the establishment of the basic principles of personal and political rights. Other parts were accomplished later, such as provisions for equal elementary schooling for all children of the country. The adequate meeting of the critical housing needs throughout the country was not realized until the 1980s, but each year saw improvements.

Economic equalization between farmers and industrial workers was not achieved until 1978. That year the farmers made up about about 9% of the population compared to about 30% in 1945.

In the social arena, the social insurance system has been extended far beyond what had been thought possible in 1945, when the social conditions generally were significantly different from those of today.

Tax policies have been a source of a constantly recurring controversy. What constitutes a just distribution of the tax burden is quite naturally a question that is debated every year. The gross taxes and fees to the state which made up 31% of the gross national product in 1950 increased to 50% by 1980. During the 1980s the tax take has been reduced slightly to somewhere between 47% and 48% by 1983.

The most significant question of "Fellesprogrammet," however, was what kind of economic policy should be pursued for ensuring economic growth, increased prosperity, and full employment. This is naturally an area where one cannot arrive at an economic goal that can be reached once and for all. As a small country with a relatively large

268

export trade, Norway's economy is greatly dependent upon international economic conditions. Nevertheless, it has been possible to maintain that which was defined as full employment, i.e., 1.5% to 2.0% unemployment, during the entire period from 1945 to 1981.

After 1981, the rate of unemployment has increased slightly to 4.0% in 1984. This will certainly be the most significant political issue in the parliamentary election of 1985, together with the questions concerning the level of taxation and how much and what kinds of public welfare shall be provided.

V.   From Poor to Rich

During the forty years from 1945 to 1985, Norway has been transformed from being a poor country to a rich country. This economic growth is attributable to several factors, one not to be forgotten factor being that the whole western world has become richer. The newly-won affluence of Norway is quite likely to a large degree a result of the interplay between the Norwegian and the international economy.

But it can also be affirmed that "Fellesprogrammet" and its consensus policies provided an important driving force for economic growth, partly through large investments and increased productivity in industry, and partly through promoting the transfer of the labor force from occupations of low economic productivity to high productivity occupations.

Up until World War II, Norway could be characterized as a poor rural country. Not until 1950 did more Norsemen earn their living from industry and mining (367,000) than from agriculture, fishing, and shipping (356,000). After 1950, as already indicated in Table 3.4, the occupational shift from primary industries to secondary and tertiary occupations has increased by leaps and bounds. By 1980, the population engaged in the primary occupations had declined to 8.0%, while those engaged in the secondary occupations had grown to 29.3% and those in the tertiary industries to 62.7%.

Within the tertiary sector, it has been the

public services in the fields of health, education, and welfare that have shown the sharpest increase. These occupational shifts reflect dramatic changes in a country's history. The changes were most keenly felt in the 1960s but also strongly felt throughout the 25 years after the war.

While it is not possible to describe in detail the economic growth statistics in this brief chapter, it is instructive to note that the GNP has more than quadrupled. The production per inhabitant has more than tripled. Other OECD-countries have experienced approximately the same rate of growth. What has particularly characterized Norway's development is that the public authorities have fortunately succeeded in conducting a policy which has given the country a steady growth.

Furthermore, Norway's development has been characterized not only by higher taxing levels than most other countries but nearly half of those public revenues are returned to private households in the form of social benefits, public assistances, and subsidies. Additionally, a large part of the public revenues are distributed as support for industries with low earning potentials and industries in crisis, in order to maintain wholesome employment levels in every region of the country. Such support is mainly aimed at the remote areas of the country and not given to industries in the larger cities. This gives Norway an unusually equal distribution of income among workers and recipients of social security in all parts of the country.

The industrial economy experienced a steady growth up to the beginning of the 1970s. The traditional industries were developed the most, as desribed in "Fellesprogrammet." The dramatic expansion of Norway's hydro-electric energy system and the consequent abundance of cheap electricity for the electro-chemical and electro-metallurgical industries played an important role in shoring up the nation's exports. Because of rising price levels, the production of Norwegian consumer goods, however, has declined. The textile industries in particular have experienced a sharp decline because of competition from cheap imports. As in other modern economies, Norwegian industries have also experienced internal structural changes.

The oil crisis of 1972, with its consequent sharp increase in energy costs, made a strong impact on Norway's economy not unlike that of other countries. The shipping industry was particularly hurt because of the declining demand for oil tankers. Many ships had to go into storage.

But Norway has not only been negatively impacted by the oil crisis. During the summer of 1966, oil explorations had begun in the Norwegian continental shelf of the North Sea with promising results. By the spring of 1970, it was confirmed that the Ekofisk field had good productive possibilities. Oil production began the following year.

In 1979 the large Statfjord field was opened. In less than ten years, Norway became an oil nation where most of the leadership in both exploration and production is carried out in Norway itself. The production of platforms and other oil industry-related equipment are produced in Norwegian factories. The sharp increase in oil prices following the crisis of 1972 had made it economically possible to extract oil from the bottom of the sea, even in such troubled waters as the North Sea.

The management of the national economy in the 1970s has, however, been difficult, partly because of the international economic crises, and partly because the oil economy created cost pressures on other sectors of Norway's economy and thereby reducing their international competitive capability. The annual rate of inflation reached the high of 13% in 1981. Even though this has been reduced to somewhere between 5% and 6% in 1984, it is still higher than in countries we like to compare ourselves with. Before 1975, Norway's rate of inflation was about the same or lower than that of other western nations.

VI.   Conflicts Within the Harmony

Even though the basic trends of economic and social developments of Norway's welfare state have been strong and steady, all have not developed without some conflict. In our discussion of some of the more important emerging controversies, we shall

271

largely disregard the traditional controversies concerning temperance, language, religion, and ethics that persist as continually recurring issues. For more than a century, these have been a part of the Norsemen's everyday experience to which they have become accustomed to live with. There has been a slow but balanced development regarding these controversies in the direction of liberality and tolerance on the part of most partisans. The fundamentalists, however, perceive this itself as a sign of decadence.

One fundamental disagreement between the Labor Party (partly supported by the center parties) and the Conservative Party has involved the questions concerning price control and the state's interference in economic affairs by way of public supports or regulations. In 1945, because of the special post-war situation, Norway enacted its first price control legislation with the support of all political parties. Within two years the conflict between the political right and the left surfaced over a debate concerning a more encompassing price control legislation which was adopted by Parliament against opposition from the right.

In 1953, Parliament adopted a permanent law concerning control and regulation of prices, profits, and competitive conduct. The law gave the state authorities broad powers for initiating programs for full employment, effective development of production potentials, preventing factory shut downs, and a reasonable distribution of the national income. The debates over this legislation unveiled the principal dividing lines between the parties of the right and the left in Norwegian politics. The Conservative Party, which has been a minority party, has been a defender of the least possible state intervention in economic affairs. The Labor Party, which has had the support of the center parties in these matters, has championed a strong and active state involvement in directing the nation's economy. Due to the opposition from the right, however, the Labor Party has shown considerable moderation in its positions. In fact, the desire for harmony from both sides has served to moderate the debates as well as their political resolutions. One important

272

aspect of this debate has been the desire for strong economic growth. On this, both the Labor Party and the parties of the right have been in agreement. On the means for achieving this objective, however, there has been less agreement. But as long as the Labor Party policies were successful, these disagreements over means tended for the most part to be pursued only in discussions.

An important aspect of the politics of economic growth has been the development of hydro-electric power. Here the parties of the right have agreed that this is a state responsibility. When opposition to waterpower expansion became an important issue of political debate in the 1970s, such protests came from the leftist segments of the socialist parties as well as from bourgeois liberals. As in other parts of the world, these protests were grounded on ecological perspectives and a general perception that economic growth had gone too far. It was argued that more humane considerations should influence community and societal development.

These desires to preserve Norway as a society in ecological balance as far as possible independent of international economic forces, led to a deep cleavage in political life in the early 1970s, when the question of joining the European Common market became the dominant issue. This debate split Norwegian society into two camps with nearly the same number supporting each. The cleavage penetrated the major political parties. It also split region against region, with the east central region and the large cities having a majority support for joining the Common Market and the rest of the country having majorities opposed.

The ecological sensitivities associated with the Common Market debate, were further aroused by the discovery of oil in the North Sea. The drilling for oil in Norway's part of the North Sea began in 1965. By then the question of how Norway should regulate the research and development of the natural resources in the continental shelf had been cleared up. In 1963 it was decided by a royal decree (decision made by the king's cabinet) that Norway had hegemony over the Continental Shelf. Two years later, Norway entered into an agreement with Denmark

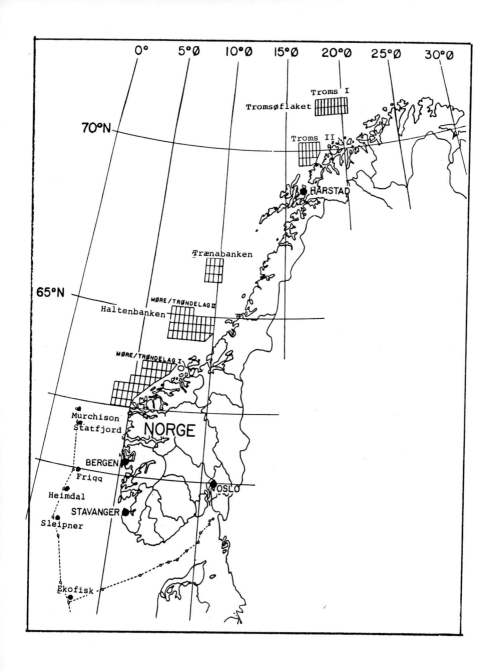

Figure 8A Oil Fields in Production and under
Exploration in Norway's Economic Zone.

and England concerning the dividing line between those nation's claims in the Continental Shelf.

The production of oil and gas in the Ekofisk field began in 1971 in the southernmost area of Norway's part of the North Sea. Later a series of other oil and gas finds were put into production farther north.

For a long time there was strong opposition to these developments from the same groups that had opposed hydro-electric power developments. Particularly strong was the opposition to starting exploratory drilling north of the 62nd parallel. The most usual argument against oil development was the fear of accidents which could lead to pollution of the sea and to conflict with the fishing interests. This was a frequently-used argument by those who opposed Norway's entry into the European Common Market. Gradually, as the income from the North Sea oil increased without any serious problems of pollution, the opposition subsided.

Since the end of the 1970s, one of the greatest political problems has been the matter of controlling the impact of the oil income upon the rest of the nation's economy. From 1975 to 1981, Norway's rate of inflation was significantly greater than was considered acceptable. After 1981, with a government dominated by the conservatives, the rate of inflation has reduced somewhat. But it is still higher than in other countries with which Norway is naturally compared.

All in all, except for the years during the debates concerning Norway's entry into the Common Market, Norway's political life has been characteristically stable. The Labor Party's large majority was gradually reduced until 1965 when the bourgeois parties captured the majority and formed a coalition government. But this bourgeois coalition was led by a prime minister from the Center Party and the influence of the Conservative Party was minimal. The new government pursued policies which were essentially similar to those pursued by the Labor Party. Its economic policies were led by the same kinds of Keynesion economics that had been used by the Labor Party. A new university was established in Tromsø, and the development of a welfare state was continued.

With the 1969 election, the Labor Party nearly recaptued a parliamentary majority, winning 74 of 150 seats. The tenuous bourgeois government continued the Keynsian economic politics and liberal attitudes with regard to the welfare state and tax policies. During this bourgeois government, gross taxes increased from 34.9% of the GNP in 1965 to 44.6% in 1971. The net taxes, however, only increased from 21.4% to 26.4% during this same period. The differentials between the gross taxes and the net taxes were used for transferring resources between the various sectors of the industry and between various population groups. Among other things, the social security system was made to cover everybody in 1967. While this resulted in a much improved social security system, it also greatly increased the nation's expenses.

In 1971, however, there developed such strong frictions within the government that the coalition broke up. The most important source of friction was the controversy over the European Common Market. The Conservative Party (Høyre) and half of the Liberal (Venstre) party favored joining, while the Center Party (formerly called the "Bondeparti") and the Christian Peoples Party were opposed.

The leadership of the Labor Party favored joining the Common Market and formed a minority government in 1971. In the plebiscite of September 1972, only 46.4% voted in favor of joining the Common Market while 53.5% voted against. This result shook up the political life, but only for a few years.

In the parliamentary election of 1973, the Labor Party suffered s sharp setback. It elected only 62 of the 155 memers of the parliament, a loss of 10 members. At the same time, a coalition government with the Socialist Left Party could not be formed either. That party had taken an opposite stand on the Common Market and differed with the Labor Party leadership on other matters as well.

The bourgeois parties, too, were so split up that they were unable to form a majority government. The Labor Party formed a minority government under the leadership of Trygve Bratteli. This party con-

Table 8.1: Development of Total Taxes
Percent of Gross Domestic Product.

Year	Gross taxes total	Subsidies and other transfers to private households, total	Net taxes total
1950	30.8	11.9	18.9
1960	32.4	12.2	20.2
1695	34.9	13.5	21.4
1967	38.7	14.2	24.5
1970	41.2	17.4	23.8
1971	44.6	18.3	26.4
1972	46.3	19.1	27.2
1975	47.1	19.8	27.4
1977	48.4	21.5	26.9
1980	50.7	21.4	29.3
1981	48.8	21.2	27.4
1982	48.3	21.5	26.8
1983	48.0	21.6	26.4

tinued the further development of the welfare state,
and gradually reestablished a new consensus and
harmony. By the election of 1977, the worst sores
had been healed. The Labor Party elected 76 out of
the 155 members of parliament and formed a new
minority government. This government was supported
by four representatives from the Socialist Left
whose numbers had declined sharply. But cooperation
between these parties was made difficult both
because of ideological differences and personality
conflicts. The gross taxes during the period of
this government increased from 46.3% of the GNP in
1972 to 50.7% in 1980.

At the same time, a new disturbance entered
into political life. The Conservative Party emerged
more and more as a party that wanted to reduce the
public sector of community life, and to remove many
of the public regulations and services. An added
pressure in this direction came with the formation
of a new conservative party championing a drastic

reduction of taxes, duties, and public interventions.

This political opposition more and more focused the searchlight upon the high tax rates and upon what was perceived to be the superfluity of detailed regulations of the individual's relationship to the community. Particularly among homeowners did these arguments, paradoxically enough, find support. The paradox consists of the fact that it was the regulatory policies of the Labor Party that made it possible for the majority of Norwegians to own their own homes.

As these homeowners became well established in their homes, their debts beginning to be paid up, and their personal incomes increased because of the public policies promoting economic growth and distribution, they became the same homeowners to raise their opposition to those very same policies.

By the election of 1981, the Conservative Party became the biggest bourgeois party, with 53 of the 155 parliamentary representatives. The number of Labor Party representatives dropped to 66. With the support of the other bourgeois parties, the Conservative Party formed the new government. This government has a far more conservative profile than that of the former conservative coalition governments.

Hence, Norwegian politics is back again to the same types of conflicts that prevailed during the period between the two wars--conflicts that were buried by the "Fellesprogrammet" of 1945. To be sure, these conflicts have rippled the surface waters of political life throughout the post-war years, but in the 1980s these ripples have grown to billowy waves. In 1984, one year before the next parliamentary election, one must be cautious about trying to predict how those waves will behave in the future. But some things can be said about the dilemmas that lie ahead.

On the one hand, the Conservative Party has promised big tax reductions. This has been a strong contributing factor for giving this party its greatest support since 1924. Its new power position is a reflection of its having won support from all groups of the population.

278

On the other hand, tax cuts involve a necessary reduction in public resources. This involves a reduction in monies for the welfare benefits to which the public has become accustomed, and the supporters of the Conservative Party continue to want. Reduced support for the public service sector has also led to increased unemployment from a normal rate between 1.5% and 2.0% to ca. 4.0%.

The organizational pattern for disbursing the welfare benefits is to a large degree based on the role of the local municipalities as the principal distribution channels. The revenues of the municipalities are partly derived from their taxes and partly from revenue transfers from the state. The tax reductions that the government has carried out has, however, sharply reduced the municipalities' revenues. As a result, the municipalities need increased contributions from the state if they are to carry out the tasks assigned them under Norwegian law.

The national finances have steadily improved as the oil incomes have increased. If it were simply a matter of money, it would then be feasible to satisfy the demand for the welfare services. It is, however, not as simple as that. Increased use of oil incomes increases the dangers of higher inflation. This in turn threatens to weaken competitiveness of other industries as over against foreign competitors.

From this writer's point of view, these conflicts can only be resolved by a stronger political leadership than has emerged so far. The Conservative Party has come to power in an epoch of the nation's economic development when it seems more imperative than ever before to pursue a comprehensive regulatory policy. This is particularly true if the Constitutional paragraph number 110 concerning full employment shall be honored.

The oil profits, together with the economic recessions in the world market, have created new problems for a country that wishes to maintain both its welfare state benefits and full employment in all regions of the country. It is uncertain which political party will recieve the majority necessary to solve this problem in the 1980s and the rest of the twentieth century. It will certainly not be an easy task, and it is impossible to know which of the leading political parties possesses the strength and the talents needed for such a task.

Perhaps the problem can be solved only if the same discipline and sense of solidarity that "Fellesprogrammet" was built upon forty years ago can be recaptured. It is highly likely that a solid majority supports the maintenance of the current welfare benefits. But then the new generations must learn the old lesson that "one cannot have one's cake and eat it, too."

There are many grounds for pessimism concerning the Norsemen's willingness to learn from these new economic realities. For nearly forty years, a steady economic growth has made it possible to solve the financial problems by way of the principle of "a little for everyone." Norway could continue to do this in the 1970s, based on its oil incomes--even as the economy stagnated and unemployment increased in other western nations.

The economic situation emerging in the 1980s continues to promise a high national income based on its petroleum production. But unwise use of the oil monies can create serious imbalances in the rest of the economy. During the course of the last twenty to thirty years, Norway has become a corporate state where organized groups have gotten more power than ever before. Not only have labor unions and employer organizations increased their influence, but so too have idealistic and humanistic organizations and other pressure groups. These make demands that are mainly valid for their own special interests. They demonstrate little responsibility for the totality. Furthermore, politicians often ally themselves with the special interests. This contributes to a situation where the tendency is to turn away from prioritizing and instead responding to special pressures, and thereby straining the entire economy. The politicians who defend a holistic perspective tend to lose out in this struggle.

The necessity of turning back to old values and virtues is therefore apparent. One must live according to one's means and demonstrate discipline

280

and solidarity if society is to be kept in balance and welfare benefits maintained. Time will tell whether people can manage that.

REFERENCES

Bjerve, P.J. Trends in Norwegian Planning 1945–1975. Statistisk Sentralbyrå, Artikler nr. 84, Oslo 1976.

Christensen, Chr. A.R. Vårt folks historie, Vol. 8, Aschehoug, Oslo 1961. p. 113.

DÆDALUS, Winter 1984. The Nordic Enigma.

DÆDALUS, Spring, 1984. Nordic Voices.

Enzenberger, H.M. Norsk utakt. Universitetsforlaget. Oslo 1984.

Hernes, Gudmund. Forhandlingsøkonomi og Blandingsadministrasjon (Negotiating Economy and Mixed Administration) Universitetsforlaget, Oslo 1978.

Mykland, Knut (ed.). Norges histoire. 12 volumes. Cappelen, oslo 1979.

OECD. Historical Statistics. 1983.

OECD. Economic Outlook. 35. July 1984.

Sejersted, Francis. Norsk økonomi etter krigen (stensil). Historisk institutt, Oslo Universitet. 1978.

Sejersted, Francis. Demokrati og rettsstat. Universitetsforlaget, Oslo 1984.

Statistisk Sentralbyra: Aktuelle skattetall 1982 (Current Tax Data) Oslo 1982.

Statistisk Sentralbyra: Historisk statistikk 1978. Oslo 1978.

Statistisk Sentralbyra: Kojunkturbølger fra utlandet i norsk okonomi. (International Cycles in Norwegian Economy) Oslo 1979.

Statistisk Sentralbyra: Norges okonomi etter krigen. (The Norwegian Post-War Economy). Oslo 1965.

Statistisk Sentralbyra: Økonomisk utsyn 1900-1950. (Economic Survey) Oslo 1955.

Torgersen, Ulf. Norwegian Political Institutions. In Natalie Rogoff Ramsøy (ed.). Norwegian Society. Universitetsforlaget. Oslo 1974.

Ustvedt, Yngvar. Det Skjedde i Norge, 1945-1972. 3 volumes. Gyldendal, Oslo, 1978, 1979, 1981.

CHAPTER NINE: NORWAY'S URBAN FUTURE

I. Contemporary Urbanization: Macro-level

Two Levels of Urban Expansion

"The rapid growth of cities is always a twin
process of internal transformation and readjustment
combined with outward expansion, since the urban
community is a dynamic organism constantly changing
in a variety of ways to meet new needs and conditions," wrote the Estonian geographer Edgar Kant,
who after 1945, as a refugee in Sweden, became an
inspirer for Scandinavian geography. (E. Kant:
"Suburbanization, Urban Sprawl and Communication" in
Migration in Sweden, p. 245, Lund Studies in
Geography, 1957).

The description in the preceding chapters of
the Norwegian urban developments in the post-war
period, is a confirmation of the accuracy of this
statement. The statement can be used to advantage
as a point of departure for an assessment of future
urbanization in Norway.

The outward expansion of the cities stems
from the strong economic growth and restructuring of
industry as briefly described in Chapter Three. This
outward expansion has occurred on two geographical
levels: the macro-level and the meso-level. The
meso-level comprises transformation and expansion
within each of the individual urban areas and will
be discussed in a later section of this chapter.

The Macro-level of Regional and Urban Change

On the macro-geographical level, there has
developed an urban system with growth poles and
power centers for economic activity which is
constantly developing and changing. Oslo is the
main center of this Norwegian urban system, whether
it is a question of capital formation and technology
or of administration, services, and culture. Even
though the urban system is not strictly hierarchi-
cal, it is Oslo that, to a substantially greater
degree than the other urban areas in Norway, belongs
to a superordinate international urban system.

New innovations first take root in Oslo and thereafter in those larger urban centers which are in close contact with each other through good communications and close-knit networks of personal contacts. These larger city regions, where the population base is large by Norwegian standards, are also places where the centers of higher public administration, service, and education have been located. The administrative functions of major private businesses, especially in trade and services, have also to a large extent been located in the largest city region within each of the major regions and each of the counties of the country.

More than half of the people of Norway are already living in twelve such city regions having more than 50,000 inhabitants, while eighteen medium-sized urban areas, having between 20,000 and 50,000 inhabitants, have upwards of 13% of the population (See Table 3.2).

The remaining third of the population, living in smaller conglomerations and distributed throughout the country, are to a large extent dependent on these urban areas for their economic activity. Socially and culturally, they too belong to urbanized Norway within their respective regions. This sparsely settled but still urbanized Norway, however, has its rural characteristics, too, which is practically nonexistent in other European countries where urbanization has more pervasive traditions.

But even these rural characteristics are constantly being influenced by urban culture and technology. The sparsely-settled populations in the smaller agglomerations are seldom far from major centers. They are exposed to the same urban and international sources of information from the mass media as the rest of the population. As a result of the even distribution of income and economic resources in Norway, the patterns of consumer goods consumption, cultural pursuits, and leisure time activities are practically the same throughout the country.

The smaller urban areas with populations of 10,000-50,000 have in Norway played a more important role with respect to urbanization than in other

countries in Scandinavia and in Europe. New industries were deliberately located in these smaller
urban areas in the 1960s and especially in the 1970s
(See Table 3.2).

The twelve largest urban areas, however, have
been the most important cornerstones for regional
development in the first thirty post-war years.
Four of these are discussed in Chapter Seven,
together with Tromsø, which in 1984 had more than
47,500 inhabitants. It is hoped that these five
city regions, with superior environments for
education and research, will be both centers of
innovation and motive power for Norway as it
participates in the high-technology developments
demanded by the age of oil in a post-industrial
society.

In these five major city regions, old
industry has been expanded and new industry introduced to such an extent that the regional balance
between the five main regions of the country has in
the main been preserved despite the rapid process of
urbanization during the postwar period (See Figure
3A and Table 3.1). To what extent this balance can
be maintained in the future is an open question.
Nevertheless there is much to indicate that in a
society like Norway's, as described above, there is
no reason to expect great changes in that regional
balance for the next 20 to 30 years.

Assessments of Urban and Regional Future

The trends discernable today indicate that
Oslo and East Norway are economically the strongest
part of the country, where the likelihood of stability with some expansion is the greatest. On account
of the oil in the North Sea, there are tendencies
toward stronger growth in the southwest, where
Stavanger continues as the country's most important
oil city. Thus the prospects of regional imbalance
vis a vis the southwest is diminished.

Parts of the oil activity on land will, however, be moved to Bergen, which will then also have
opportunities for new expansion. That, however,
will hardly be strong enough to disturb the regional
balance, since the rest of west Norway has a slight

286

decrease in population. The growth of the oil metropolises does not on the whole create great in-migration to these city regions. It mainly contributes to modernization and restructuring of the old industries, putting idle capacity to use in the city regions themselves as well as in their surrounding areas.

Northern Norway is the part of the country that is most exposed to the structural changes created by industrialization and urbanization. Finnmark, especially, where employment is largely concentrated in the fishing industry, has experienced disturbing problems resulting from increased efficiency in fishing methods and the related over-exploitation of the fishing resources. In Finnmark people live in sparse settlements or in small agglo-merations. Only in one place, (Alta) is a small city region developing which to a certain extent is adapted to an economy of a post-industrial society.

In 1984, however, only 77,000 people lived in Finnmark which, for political and strategic reasons, is of special importance to the country. It is therefore to be expected that the political authori-ties will continue their policy of subsidizing developments in that county. This will undoubtedly result in a modest concentration into smaller city regions and a further increase in the efficiency of the fishing industry both on the sea and on land. Public services and investments will also undoubt-edly play an important role in Finnmark's emerging economy.

In the other two counties of Northern Norway--Nordland and Troms--there are also areas that are just as exposed to structural changes as Finnmark. These areas will be more subject to changes resulting from demographic developments since these counties are of less importance stra-tegically from the vantage point of Norway's foreign policy than is Finnmark.

There are three rather large city regions in North Norway--Tromsø, Bodø, and Harstad--which are centers of the urbanization process and serve as the most important contact points for communication with the rest of Norway and have modest direct contact with foreign countries. A few other smaller city-regions also by North Norway standards, participate in the urbanization process. Since North Norway is the least urbanized part of the country, it is mainly in its city regions that one can expect continued urbanization.

Compared to the rest of the country, however, North Norway's economy is rather poorly developed. In order to maintain employment and avoid having a large part of its population move to the south for improved job opportunities, it has been necessary for the state to make substantial investments in the development of its infrastructure and in the expansion of its public services. A plausible prognosis regarding future Norwegian regional policy is that such public support will continue with the same results as before with respect to urbanization and population development on the macro-level in the area.

Test drilling for oil, however, is taking place off the coast of North Norway--especially north of Tromsø. If promising deposits of oil or gas are found there, considerable new industrial activity will be created on land, too. Tromsø will then be the city region most strongly affected by the oil activity. But concomitant effects will also be felt in the rest of the region in the form of increased commuting and increased employment in high-technology occupations which up to now have been largely non-existent outside the university in Tromsø.

All in all, Norway has already passed through the most important stages of the urbanization process on the macro-level. Future changes will be smaller than before with respect to population distribution between the city regions and the rest of the country, except for North Norway, where urbanization is still at an early stage. The developmental problems of a post-industrial society during the next twenty-thirty years will be only slightly linked to population redistribution between larger and smaller regions.

Two types of problems will be particularly important in Norway's urbanized future. One will be the problem of maintaining full employment in a post-industrial society and achieving the fairest

possible distribution of welfare services among the
various groups of people and the various regions of
the country. The other will be the new types of
social and cultural problems stemming from the fact
that people are well-off and live in a newly-
urbanized society.

Heretofore, the socio-cultural changes have,
among other things, reduced the population fertility
to less than two children per family, and substantially increased the divorce rate. Consequently,
most families are small, consisting of one to three
persons. This will have consequences for the social
networks, with less contact with and support from
kinship groups than before--with all that this will
entail so far as the use of leisure time and changing life styles, and the formation of new contacts.
In the longer term this may also change the housing
supply and the very shape of the future city--two of
the most critical aspects of urbanization.

II.   New Housing in Post-War Years

The Stock and Increase in the Number of Dwellings

The results of the outward expansion are
readily discernible in the geographic landscape in
the form of new housing construction in and around
the old urban areas. On account of the strong
equalizing policy that has been pursued, however,
many new dwellings are also found outside of urban
areas. To create the right conditions for this
nationwide housing construction has been one of the
most important tasks of social planning in the
entire postwar period. A large-scale housing construction was necessary in order to satisfy the new
demands created by the post-war socioeconomic
changes. It has also helped bring about these
changes.

The Joint Program of 1945 took note of
Norway's acute housing shortage and placed high
priority on housing in its program of post-war
construction. It put first priority for new housing
in such war-ravaged areas as Finnmark County, the
city of Bodø, and other smaller towns that had been
bombed or destroyed by the Nazis. Its second pri-

ority was given to covering the housing shortage
created by the virtual cessation of housing construction during the war. But no one in 1945 could
imagine the size of the demand that would be created
by the changing demographic structure, the increased
prosperity, and the resulting elevation of housing
standards. Thus, despite a large-scale steady
program of housing construction, it was not until
1981 that one could speak of a balance in the
housing market in all parts of the country. Oslo
was the city region where the demand for housing was
the last to be covered.

Table 9.1   Supply of Norway's dwellings and the
            number of persons per dwelling 1946-1980

	1946	1960	1970	1980
Number of Dwellings	787,448	1,075,145	1,296,760	1,523,508
Number of Persons per Dwelling	3.9	3.3	3.0	2.7

As indicated in Table 9.1, Norway in 1946 had
787,448 dwellings, with a housing density of 3.9
persons per dwelling on a national average. But
there was considerable regional variation in the
housing standard at that time. The housing density
varied from 3.1 persons per dwelling Oslo to almost
5 persons per dwelling in rural areas.
By 1980 the housing conditions had improved
substantially. The number of dwellings had
increased to 1,528,508, almost doubling the supply
of 1946. The national average in housing density
had declined from 3.9 in 1946 to 2.7 per dwelling in
1980. At the same time a regional equalization of
the housing standard had taken place.
The maintenance of a high and steady production of housing has been an important part not only
of Norway's welfare policy, but also of its economic

employment policy. To implement these policies, the state created the National Housing Bank (Husbanken) for making relatively low cost loans to the home buyers. At the same time its taxing system has permitted the deduction of interest on loans from income before tax assessments. Together with inflation this has led to great capital accumulation in private hands, with 59% of the households owning their own dwellings, and another 17% owning their dwellings through cooperative or private profit-sharing societies. Only 14% of the households are pure tenants (See Table 9.3).

During the 1950s almost 29,000 dwellings were built annually. In the 1960s approximatley 30,000 units were built each year, while in the 1970s the number of dwellings built each year approached 39,000 (See Table 9.2).

Table 9.2   Dwelling Units completed 1951-1980

	Detached houses		Semi-detached houses		Multi-dwelling houses		Total	
	Number	%	Number	%	Number	%	Number	%
1951-1960	93,302	32.2	133,317	46.0	63,229	21.8	289,848	100
1961-1970	155,393	51.2	62,414	20.5	85,991	28.3	303,798	100
1971-1980	169,907	43.4	125,507	32.0	96,574	24.6	391,988	100
Total	408,602	42.5	321,238	32.6	245,794	24.9	985,634	100

Source: Historisk statistikk and Statistisk Årbok

During the first years of the 1980s (1981-1984), housing construction declined to 35,000 units a year—and possibly down to as low as 30,000 in 1984. It is arguable whether this decline was because the housing demand had been better satisfied than before or whether it was because financing conditions had become so much worse. The answer probably depends on one's partisan perspective and one's insight into the housing demand structure. In any case, it is certain that the market for the procurement of housing is more flexible than previously.

Of the dwelling units built after 1950, 42.5% were in detached houses, while 32.6% were in semi-detached. But with a more restrictive city planning

291

policy regarding area size allowed for housing, the construction in the 1970s became more compact (See Table 9.2). The number of units built in multi-dwelling housing after 1951 made up 24.9% of the dwellings built. This compares with 70% of such housing built in Sweden.

Norway's large investment in detached housing is one of the reasons that construction in its urban communities has been spread over such large areas. In decentralized decision-making structures, small producers and land owners have collaborated with municipalities and home buyers to build in many small dwelling areas.

Ownership of the Dwellings

An important feature of Norway's social-democratic housing policy has been that people should own their own dwellings, alone or jointly with others. In the 1950s it was the social democratic partisans that championed this ideology, rather than the members of the Conservative (Høyre) Party. These ideological differences were due to the fact that the Conservative Party was supported by housing landlords with houses for rent. The Labor Party was the party of those who lived in rented houses and it championed the idea that "no one should profit from the housing needs of others." This social democratic ideology has today become generally accepted, and it is probably the Conservative Party that has best understood how to exploit it politically by acting as defender of the house-owners' interests against tax assessments. Thus, housing policy has acquired new relevance in the 1980s, but in a different manner than previously.

Table 9.3 shows the ownership status of the households with respect to the dwellings where they live. It shows that in Oslo/Akershus those who own their own dwelling outright are fewer than in the rest of the country. On the other hand, there are more cooperatively-owned households and private share owners in Oslo than in the rest of the country (34%). This is due to the fact, among others, that in Norway's largest city it has been important to organize housing construction in larger

292

units than in the rest of the country; such as was done in its satellite towns. This building policy has been best suited for multi-dwelling housing and cooperative forms of ownership.

Table 9.3   Households in groups by ownership and dwelling tenure status 1981.

	Owns the dwelling	Part owner in cooperative housing and private share owners	Ordinary tenant	Service dwelling and social insurance dwelling	Total
	Pct	Pct	Pct	Pct	Pct
All households	59	17	14	10	100
Main regions					
Oslo/Akershus	36	34	20	10	100
Rest of					
East Norway	70	9	12	9	100
Southwest Norway	71	8	13	8	100
West Norway	59	13	15	12	100
Mid Norway	61	14	14	11	100
North Norway	67	8	14	11	100

Source: Boforholdsundersøkelsen 1981

Oslo/Akershus is also the place with the most tenants (20%). This is due to the fact of its flexible labor market where many young people live temporarily as tenants until they later settle down as owners of their own dwellings either in Oslo or in other places in the country.

Table 9.3 also shows that tenancy is not very widespread in the rest of Norway. West Norway with the country's second largest city of Bergen, has the greatest number of tenants (15%). Norway's housing policy has undoubtedly contributed much to the fact that urbanization in that country has taken place in many small and medium-sized city regions.

III. The Dynamics of Internal Transformation and Readjustments within City Regions

The Twin Process of Transformation and Expansion

In the same manner as in the development of the national city system, the outward expansion in the individual city region is rooted in economic growth. This growth within the city region is, of course, also the sign of new production and increased employment, which leads to population growth by excess births and in-migration.

This outward expansion creates demands for larger areas for industry and its relocation within the city region. The increased population growth leads to demands for new construction of dwellings. The splitting up of the population into smaller households creates an additional demand for new dwellings even if there is no increase in the population. In Oslo, for example, almost 40,000 new dwellings were built during the period 1971-1980, when the population decreased by 26,000 persons. This is a reflection of the fact that while the population in Oslo decreased from 478,000 in 1970 to 452,000 in 1980, the number of households with their own dwellings increased from 196,000 in 1970 to 222,300 in 1980. (In the period 1970-1980, 14,000 older dwellings also ceased to be used.)

Implicit in this increase in the amount of housing is a thinning out of residential density, defined as the number of persons per unit of the built-up area and with fewer persons per apartment. This thinning out, together with the increased population, has had the effect that the outward expansion of the cities has spread out beyond their administrative boundaries. In order to satisfy the demand for areas for new dwellings and new industry, new areas for city development have constantly been made available also in municipalities located at remote distances from the original city, whose economic functions have always been the driving force behind the outward expansion.

This outward expansion means not only that areas which are increasingly distant are used for new city development but also that the older city

areas change their character and acquire new functions. This is what E. Kant calls "the twin process
of internal transformation and readjustment combined
with outward expansion."

This process is illustrated in the model
shown in Figure 9A. The model is a generalization
of the changes in population and building that occur
in zones around Norwegian city centers, whether
these are centers in small or large city regions and
whether these city regions consist of one administrative territory (a city municipality with a large
area, as, for example, Tromsø or Trondheim) or
whether the city region consists of a central city
municipality surrounded by several smaller municipalities (which in Norway are also independent
administrative territories). Most of the city
regions in Norway belong to this latter type.

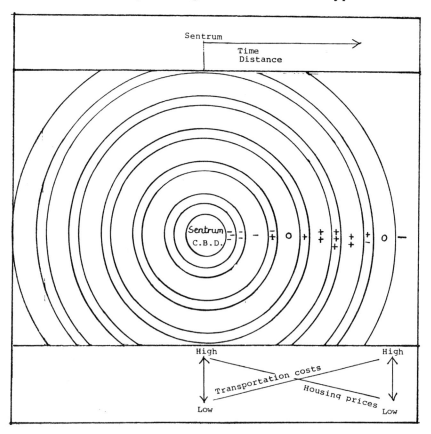

Figure 9A   Pattern of Changes in the structure of
housing and population in the Circular
Zones around the city nucleus.

295

The pattern illustrated in Figure 9A may be understood and interpreted in several different ways as an expression of changes in several of the most important variables of the city structure. The pattern should be regarded as dynamic, with the content of the individual zones of the city region changing in the course of time. At the same time the pattern is concretely geographic in that the physical distance of the zones from the center is an important variable.

A Model for Change in Zones Within City Regions

In order to understand and interpret the pattern, one may usefully start with the earlier phase of urbanization in Norway. Up until the 1950s, before motoring fundamentally altered daily mobility, Norwegian cities were, from the viewpoint of housing, quite compact with great residential density in the inner parts of the city. Oslo, Bergen, and Trondheim solved their internal passenger traffic problems by means of light rail and city buses. A few other cities also had city buses which provided passenger transportation between the center and areas near the city. The cities grew in the classical pattern, partly in concentric zones around the city nucleus where topography made this possible and partly in sectors on both sides of the major communication lines. Only around Oslo did commuting by railway play a prominent role up to 25 kilometers from the city's center.

The increased prosperity after 1950 was accompanied by a strong demand for new and better dwellings. Younger people moved from the inner zones of the city to the nearest outer zones, resulting in a declining population in the inner zones of the city. The decline was most marked nearest the center. The decline was smallest in the zones nearest the new building zone where the population increased. This is shown by the symbols "+,"

"-," and "0" in the central parts of the pattern.
(Cf. also Tables 5.1 and 5.3).

In the 1960s and 1970s the population growth
spread to building areas in municipalities increasingly distant from the center. Even around small
city regions one finds housing areas 30 kilometers
from the city's center which functionally belong the
to the city. Around Oslo one finds housing areas
that functionally belong to the city region 50-60
kilometers from the city's center. In extreme
cases, one can find smaller housing areas 80 kilometers from the city's center, where more than
20% of the employees commute to Oslo. Commuting to
places of work in the city region is then done by
private cars, and the time of travel is often more
than an hour's ride.

At a distance sufficiently far from the
city's nucleus those who move there to new housing
areas become increasingly few in number. The rural
municipalities on the outer edges of the city region
have a stagnating population, as shown by the
symbols "-" and "0" on the outermost part of the
pattern. The boundary zone of the city's surrounding commuter area is also generally located
there. That boundary zone determines the outer
limits of the city region in Norway.

Thus it is the new construction of dwellings
that causes the population to grow in the zones
increasingly distant from the city. Those moving
into these new dwellings are typically young adults
in small households generally, a couple with 1-3
children.

The dynamic of this outward migration is
explained partly by the fact that these young adults
leave their parents in the inner zones and form new
households. The dynamic is further explained by the
fact that the city region has a surplus of young
in-migrants. As a rule they are individuals who
find themselves a smaller, temporary dwelling in an
inner zone. As they later form couples and beget
children they move to the new dwellings in the outer
zones.

These dynamics also affect the age distribution in the various zones of the city. In the 1950s
and 1960s, inner zones of the city region acquired a

population increasingly made up of older people. The outer areas acquired a population of younger couples who generally had children. These dynamics may also be illustrated by means of the model in Figure 9A. The symbol "-" indicates a preponderance of old people; "0" indicates an average age distribution and "+" a preponderance of young people.

But time does not stand still. One of the few things which is certain for humans is that one becomes a year older every year unless one dies. The people who moved into Oslo's first satellite towns in the 1950s were, for the most part, 35-40 years old. The 50% of those who still live there have become 60-70 years old in the 1980s. The children have left home and moved into new satellite towns in Oslo, or into housing areas in one of the surrounding municipalities.

Nor did time stand still for the older people who remained in inner-city dwellings. Many of these are today 70-80 years old and have moved into housing especially designed for the elderly. Others have died. Hence, in many older parts of the city near the center younger people have moved in, so that these inner zones have again acquired a population whose age composition is close to that of the national average. These constant changes in settlements and age distribution of the population create large problems for municipal planning, which often fails to be flexible enough to adapt itself to the new situations that arise. This problem is discussed in Rasmussen (1981).

Some Vital Questions for Future Forms of Urbanization

In Chapter Five it is pointed out that "the population decline of inner city Oslo does not mean a decline of urbanism, but rather a spreading out of the metropolitan community." This statement is confirmed in the pattern for outward expansion, internal transformation and readjustment, as described above. This is an interpretation of postwar urbanization around larger nuclei of cities which differs from much of the international literature on the

298

subject, where catchwords such as "counter-urbanization," "decentralization," "exurbanization," "turn-around," etc. are used to characterize the trends. (Cf., e.g., Pahl (1965), Hall (1973), Berry (1973), Spence et al. (1981), Lunden (1984).

Without further elaboration of these interna-tional technical discussions, an interpretation will be given here of the Norwegian situation with respect to "suburbanization, urban sprawl and commutation," following E. Kant's conceptual nomen-clature. It is hoped in this way to help explain distinctive patterns of dwelling localization around the older Norwegian city nuclei in the last 20-30 years as described above.

One of the first questions that needs to be addressed is why built up urban areas would be allowed to sprawl as far outward over the country-side in a regulated and planned society such as Norway. While there is rarely any simple answer to such a complicated social question, it is possible to identify some important factors involved. Here seven such factors will be presented.

(1) In the first place, Norway inherited from its nineteenth century rural order an administrative structure made up of many small units of government, i.e., municipalities. These were established when horse-drawn vehicles on poor roads, pedestrian travel, or transport by rowboats and sailboats along the Coast determined the daily travel distance.

Even though there were municipal reforms in the 1950s, 1960s, and 1970s, combining two or more municipalities into one, the reforms were not thorough-going enough to bring about adequately rational municipal structures throughout the whole country. (The number of municipalities was reduced from about 1200 in 1950 to 450 in 1980). Oslo, Bergen, Trondheim, Kristiansand, and Tromsø did to be sure, obtain large territories during this period. Stavanger also received a boundary expan-sion, but not enough to make the territory a large enough unit for rational planning of physical city development. In some other places, too, there were thoroughgoing changes resulting in adequately large municipalities.

An important feature of the changes carried

out, however, is that even the cities which through mergers obtained large municipal territories, were still surrounded by smaller municipalities that have great freedom of action.

(2) Decentralized decision-making has also contributed to Norway's spread-out pattern. Even up to the present, Norway has preserved much of its decentralized structure in determining who decides what dwellings are to be built and how these dwellings are to be produced. Except for the large housing cooperatives found most extensively in Oslo, and a few major entrepreneurial firms which also build mainly in Oslo, the decision regarding housing construction are made on the customer side by individual persons and on the producer side by minor entrepreneurial firms. The financing arrangements through the Norwegian national housing bank and the tax system have favored this small-scale building process.

(3) It is also important to note that in Norwegian housing plans, it is the municipal authorities who have the task of procuring sites for housing construction by buying up areas for such sites, planning, and making investments in infrastructure. However, Norway is also a country of many small property owners. They have collaborated with the municipalities (or vice versa) in preparing sites for housing construction, which has consequently taken place on many small areas simultaneously.

(4) Furthermore, Norwegian municipal authorities in the central city have, on the one hand, lacked sites and, on the other hand, have often been too late in their physical planning and in making investments in the needed infrastructure. Consequently, the demand for sites has generally been greater than the supply, not only in the central city but also in the smaller municipalities in the nearest surroundings. This pressure of demand, or shortage of sites ready for construction, has had a spillover effect on municipalities increasingly distant from the central city.

(5) Among the highly prized ideals of Norwegian democracy is local self-government. This means that the individual municipality is responsi-

300

ble for meeting the needs of its inhabitants for public service. The tasks involved include the procurement of sites for housing construction. To solve this task, the municipalities receive national public loans and guarantees. Even without any increase in the population, some sites are prepared for construction in order to meet the local demands from new households for improvements in their housing standards. The municipal planning authorities in these smaller municipalities in collaboration with local property owners and entrepreneurs have often managed to meet such demands from both local residents and the new residents moving out from the more central urban areas.

(6) As has already been noted in this book, an important Norwegian ideology influencing community development has been the strong commitment to preventing the use of tillable land for urban expansion. This has been strictly enforced, especially after 1955. This ideology is partly rooted in a puritanical legacy from a rural past, when the lack of land for cultivation was a serious obstacle to development.

The result has been that even in small municipalities which at the outset had only one or a few smaller agglomerations, new housing areas have been built on bedrock or in the woods with 20-50 houses or more, in places that may often be located at a distance of several kilometers from the administrative service center of the municipality.

It is obvious that this is not rational from the viewpoint of transportation and economics, either for the individual municipality or for the city region as a whole. In the long run it may also be inappropriate for the individual household. However, values other than the long-term economic and rational have been preserved by this development policy.

(7) The sum of these factors has given city regions a large expanse of area in relation to the population. The built-up area appears as a densely built-up nuclear area in the central parts of the city where the old city was located. In the surrounding landscape, within a radius of 20-50 kilometers depending on the population of the city

301

region, the built-up area appears as large and small clusters of houses with large areas of woods, mountains, water, and cultivated land between the clusters of housing.

It is natural to ask whether Norwegian planning legislation might not have prevented this. The answer is yes. The building law of 1965 enjoins the municipalities around the cities to make physical regional plans for the coordination of land-utilization, location of industry,and housing construction. In practice, however, such regional planning has often functioned poorly, because it is the individual municipality that is responsible for any implementation of the regional plan. These municipalities have often given priority to the local development which they themselves have felt the need of and wished to satisfy.

Under Norwegian law and administrative practice, the state could also have directed the development of the building pattern in several ways. This was one of the main principles underlying the building law of 1965. Local plans for smaller development areas could have been also approved. Economic means could also have been used to influence the policy of the municipalities regarding built-up sites and the conditions for financing dwellings in places considered irrational from a broader perspective. However, the state has failed to do this, for reasons which are both political and ideological.

Politically it may be risky for a central government to get into conflict with local interests. Furthermore, it has not been easy ideologically either, because Norwegian central authorities have a keen awareness of the socio-cultural values found in the "rural" city-development model. For it has been an explicit goal--most forcibly expressed from social-democratic quarters as far back as the early fifties--that every Norwegian family should own a dwelling of its own. This goal has been most easily achieved through scattered urbanization with construction of small houses in municipalities around the central cities. (On this point Norwegian social democracy has chosen a housing policy different from that in Sweden, which has stronger urban

302

traditions than Norway.)

An underlying tone in this chapter has been that this scattered urbanization within the city regions has from a responsible planning standpoint been technically and economically irrational, especially with respect to transportation. It is conceivable, however, that the localization pattern has other qualities that outweigh the disadvantages of these transportation costs. The municipal authorities and the local inhabitants with high housing standards in small dwellings obviously believe this and have acted accordingly. It is not difficult, however, for a detached social analyst to point to a number of socioeconomic disadvantages that may in the long run make themselves felt.

Another question, closely related to the concern about Norway's scattered urbanization, is how far outward Norway's city regions will develop and how long this outward thrust will continue. This question is simpler than the first question, but not necessarily easier to answer correctly. A few factors in the answer may be noted. In the first place, changing transportation technologies and changing social conditions have greatly altered the possibilities of commuting between work and places of residence. In the 1970s the private automobile became the common property among occupationally active people. Futhermore, the public bus routes subsidized by the state are now so well developed that in many places one may use them for work trips even if one lives 30-40 kilometers from the center, without taking more than an hour for such a trip. For people living in the border zone far from the main highways, however, the private car is a necessity for work trips.

Many Norwegians are financially able and willing to accept long commuting distances. When the searchlight was first directed to the increased commuting around the larger central cities of Norway (Rasmussen, 1966) in the earliest phase of motoring, data regarding commuting in 1960 were used to define the term "city region" in a Norwegian context. It was found that on the outer edge of the city regions there was a gray zone where a sharp line could not be drawn as the boundary of the city regions' surrounding commuting area. The boundaries of the city regions were therefore determined from practical administrative and statistical considerations.

Observations on commuting in 1970 and 1980, however, showed that people's willingness to accept long commuting distances (with the accompanying long travel time) was underestimated in 1966 in the case of Oslo. Nevertheless, it may safely be said that only a marginal part of the labor force lives in the border zone outside of what was defined in 1966 as the Oslo city region. For statistical and most practical purposes, it is therefore quite immaterial whether one says that the boundary northeast and southeast of Oslo--where the boundary is most diffuse and the border zone broadest--is 40, 60, or more kilometers east of the city's nucleus.

Toward the south and west of Oslo, the boundary is sharper because there are in that area two large cities with their own surrounding areas of commuting. These cities (Moss, Drammen and Hønefoss) are situated 40-60 kilometers from Oslo. Even if clear boundaries can be drawn around them for their own commuting areas, these cities are also in a situation where they have rapid, direct rail connections with Oslo. Consequently commuting occurs directly between the centers of the city regions, just as there is an overlapping gray zone in the boundary areas between them. Corresponding gray zones and boundary lines are found around the other city regions.

Another aspect of Norwegian urbanization that influences the spreading-out limits for city regions was discovered in 1960. That was that Norway has many weekly commuters and others who commute at long intervals. Many of them work in building construction, road construction, oil operations, etc. Many choose to live in smaller municipalities where they have family and social ties. Studies indicate that, for a large number of Norwegians, their preference for a high-standard, single-family house of their own at a price they can afford, outweighs the disadvantage of being long-interval commuters. The mobility of Norwegian society with respect to work trips has thus increased greatly during the last 20-30 years.

Nevertheless one may probably assume today that the most important part of Norwegian urbanized settlements is taking place within a surrounding area 40-60 kilometers from Oslo and 20-30 kilometers from the core area in the other city regions.

It is not easy to predict how long this spreading process will continue. Still, there is much to indicate that it is coming to a close in the case of persons who settle in the marginal zone for daily commuting to places of work in the city's nucleus or other places within the city region. This is related to the fact that the housing market is being saturated.

Oslo has vacant apartments and the more central municipalities in the city region have enough sites for the construction of new small houses. The prices of dwellings in central areas have been declining since 1981 on account of the financial policy of the conservative government. This has led to a comparatively greater drop in the price of small houses in several outer municipalities in the zones adjoining the city regions. It has become considerably less expensive to buy a house 10-20 years old in outer zones of the city regions than it is to build a new house oneself. This is a new situation. Since, in the 1970s the demand was greater than the supply, buyers had to pay about the same price for old houses as for those newly built. This was an important cause of the comparatively extensive new construction of dwellings in the outer areas, where the sites were less expensive and easier to buy than in central areas.

Even if the spreading out of Norway's city regions may have reached its likely limits, there remains another vital question concerning the structure of Norway's urban future. That question is, how long will the population of the inner city areas continue to decline, and what changes will take place in the population and age distribution in the more distant built-up areas? In the answer to this question, one will find important cues to likely form and content of Norway's future urban structure.

The two decisive factors that will determine this structural outcome will be the demographic changes and population movements within the city regions. The latter factor is closely linked to the cost and number of dwellings built in the various parts of the city regions. The following comments relative to these factors provide helpful clues to likely future developments:

(1) In the commentary on the pattern illustrated in Figure 9A, it is pointed out that many of the dynamics of population development of the individual zones within the city region are determined by the age distribution and the large increase in the number of new households, together with the desires for a better housing standard with respect to the area of the dwelling. The same conditions will determine the development in the next decade.

It is possible to calculate, zone by zone in the city region, the age distribution in future years on the basis of the existing age distribution and assumptions regarding migration. After Norwegians have established themselves with their children in a good dwelling, there will be little migration. It is reasonable to assume that the housing area dominated by younger families with small children today will be occupied by older couples in 20-30 years or less. Even today it is possible in many places in Norwegian city regions to talk about housing areas in the more centrally located municipalities from the 1960s with people in the age of silver weddings. Parallel with the calculation of the age distribution one can also calculate the likely development of the population. This will gradually decline as children grow up and move away from home.

In the inner city it is pointed out with respect to Oslo that large parts of the population have already become so old that new people, often young, have taken over the apartments. The population is being renewed. This aspect is also found in all the other city regions.

In the case of Oslo one must take into account that the decline in the population of the inner city has come to a standstill. The population has dropped to 146,000 in 1982 (Table 5.3). However, the inner city had 92,000 dwellings in 1980. This means a residential density of 1.6 persons per apartment. The residential density will possibly deline to 1.5 persons per apartment. If it does, the population of the inner city will drop to 138,000.

It is consequently the number of apartments that will determine the population in the inner city. If this declines, the population will decrease; if the number of apartments increases, the population will increase. The question of population development in the inner city, whether it be in Oslo or in other city regions, is therefore dependent on what city-planning policy the authorities will follow regarding new construction or demolition of housing in the inner city. This subject might require further analysis. Here it will merely be stated that there are strong tendencies toward improving the existing housing and increasing new housing construction in certain parts of the inner city in many city regions in Norway. There seems to be a good market for these dwellings, even if they are comparatively expensive.

(2) These tendencies are naturally related to the market demand and the prices people are able to pay for their dwelling. In 1983 the price paid per square meter for newly-constructed dwellings in Oslo's best section in the inner zone was 10,000 or more kroner per square meter of floor space (as of 1983 an American dollar was worth approximately 7.0 Norwegian "kroner"). For dwellings 50-60 years old in the same area which are modernized, the price per square meter runs from 5,000 to 7,000 "kroner.)

In less attractive sections of the city the price per square meter of floor space drops to 4,000-5,000 kroner for older apartments, while it may go up to 6,000 kroner per square meter for new apartments.

In areas of small houses in the municipalities around the city, the price per dwelling varies greatly, depending on the standard and location of the dwelling. Both expensive and moderately-priced dwellings are found there. For an understanding of the dynamics in the internal readjustment, the least expensive dwellings are of the greatest interest here. They are often of a good standard, of at least 100 square meters net, divided into 4-5 rooms.

However, it is mainly the location which determines the price of these dwellings.

If such dwellings are built today, one must expect production costs of 5,500 to 6,000 kroner per square meter. Dwellings which are 5-10 years old in these areas may, however, be purchased today for 3,000-4,000 kroner per square meter.

The market mechanism for determining the price of dwellings has asserted itself more strongly since 1981 than it did before. This will surely contribute to increased segregation between socio-economic groups in various parts of the city region. It is also a fact, however, (Bysveen 1984) that Norwegian households have a strong tendency to improve their housing standard by moving from a good dwelling to one that is even better. Such upward mobility in housing naturally depends on the presence of buyers for the dwellings from which people move. Many of those who move into centrally-located, attractive dwellings leave behind them a housing experience in less expensive dwellings in other places in the city region. It is in this way, and with aid of tax regulations, that Norwegians accumulate capital for acquiring better and better dwellings.

(3) If one were to risk a careful prognosis as to how the population and age distribution will change in zones within Norwegian city regions in future years, it is reasonable to assume, against the background of the market situation described above, that the construction of inexpensive dwellings on the outer edges the city regions, generally for younger families, is coming to an end. Those who are looking for a high housing standard in inexpensive dwellings have this need satisfied today by the purchase of dwellings 10-20 years old. One can, if the occasion arises, modernize and improve these oneself. Only people with a special attachment to these areas will continue to build new dwellings there. Others will move closer to the center from these outer areas if they are able to sell their old dwellings.

The age distribution will then to a high degree be affected by these moves, in that it will be the older people who will live in the most central dwellings, while younger people with high mobility and good physical resources will be living most peripherally.

In Norway, however, there is a strong tendency for people to remain faithful all their lives to the dwelling they themselves have built and moved into. If this tendency becomes the decisive factor for most of those who built themselves single-family houses in the outer areas of the city region, this will inevitably mean that one will first have silver wedding couples and later golden-wedding couples living in these outer areas. With a reduced capacity for mobility at an advanced age, this may create new economic problems for the municipal authorities because they have the responsibility of providing good public services for their inhabitants. This can become costly when the housing areas are small and the distance between them great. People who moved into these housing areas as young people when their mobility was great may experience unforeseen social problems when they become older and their mobility is reduced.

(4) The dynamics in the relationship between age, prices on the housing market, and changes in population developments described above presuppose that the city regions will show a stagnation or only a slight increase in population. As appears from section 9.1, this is the accepted prognosis for most of the Norwegian city regions. This prognosis stems partly from the fact that the excess of births has become negative (fertility is under 2) and partly from the fact that urbanization has proceeded so far that the city regions no longer have population reserves to draw on from rural areas. In a state of mutual competition between the city regions it is conceivable, however, that some will grow while others decline slightly.

There are a few city regions, however, which show signs in population more than others in the next decades. This is especially true of Stavanger and Tromsø, but probably also Kristiansand. Especially in Stavanger and Tromsø it is reasonable to expect continued growth also in the outer areas. On the other hand, in these city regions, too, there are clear tendencies for those seeking new dwellings to prefer the more centrally-located housing.

IV.   Some Concluding Comments

It is, of course, impossible to predict what the future will bring. Nevertheless, in the fields of community planning and policy making it becomes necessary to take as a point of departure certain perceptions of likely future developments. Such perceptions will never embrace an adequately holistic view of the entire human situation. In practical planning and policy making, judgments of the future are typically sectoral and within such sectors also partial. Even within these limitations, one's judgments about the future can miss the mark.

Whatever judgments one makes must necessarily be based on assumed premises which themselves may be uncertain. Hence it becomes necessary to make known these premises in order that the reader can be aware of the parameters of uncertainty within which the writer's futuristic judgments are made. Insofar as this book addresses urbanization and community building in Norway's future, it is assumed that Armageddon will not strike. It is assumed that the power balance in the world will not be significantly altered and that neither large nor small wars will upset the bases for a somewhat peaceful coexistence among the nations. Along with the continuation of these hopeful assumptions, it is assumed that economic developments will, as in the past, proceed with moderate waves of change and that the future long-term trend will likely reflect a nongrowth or possibly a slowly growing economy. Apart from such assumptions, all other judgments about the future become meaningless. Positive community developments presuppose peace. This is the foundation upon which Nordic community planning and policy-building rest.

Against this background and based on the socioeconomic developments of post-war Norway as described in this book, it can be expected that Norway, as well as the other Nordic nations, have reached a mature stage so far as economic growth and urbanization are concerned. Only minor changes can be anticipated in these aspects of society. With a somewhat trendy terminology, it can be said that Norway in 1984 finds itself in the beginnings of a post-industrial period.

In this post-industrial situation, the problems of the future will be somewhat different from those of the past. The material problems will in the main have been solved and the production surpluses will be divided among the nation's groups on a basis which will not create any unacceptable inequalities. There is a national consensus about this. Only marginal changes can be anticipated in the future.

Construction in the future will, more than in the past, take on the character of maintaining the existing structures and increasing the efficiency and effectiveness of the nation's infrastructure. Such new structures as will be built in the future will be marginal in comparison with those that are already built. They will mainly contribute to increased capacity and improve the qualitative standards of the existing built-up environment.

Most of the types of problems in the coming years will have already been experienced in today's society. Some of them, however, will become more central than in the past. They will, therefore, require greater effort than before in order to work them out and solve them.

The problems of urbanization in the post-industrial society will shift from concerns about the outer physical and material plans to concerns regarding the organization of work and of society itself. Who shall have the possibility of influencing outcomes within the democratic decision-making bodies, and how? How shall work and income be divided among individuals and groups of individuals? What is a just distribution of obligations, goods, and responsibilities?

These new issues are hardly any simpler than the old ones. For the older generation they will often appear as problems associated with affluence. But the older generation also knows that "it takes a strong back to carry good days," in the words of an old Norwegian folk expression. For the new generation, the problems will be experienced as altogether real.

The future is uncertain. That has always been the case. Even more uncertain are prognoses

311

concerning the future when they involve societal developments as a whole or even as limited parts of it. It has, however, been a fundamental premise of this book that Norway and the other Nordic countries have long traditions for developing societies in growth and harmony, with tolerance and a will to resolve conflicts peacefully. Hence it is reasonable for the writers of this book to expect that the same spirit and the same fundamental law-ways will continue to guide Norway's future societal developments.